S uccess in business demands the effective James C. Morgan, who for nearly three decades led the high-tech powerhouse Applied Materials Inc. to both financial success and to the designation as one of America's most admired companies and best places to work, provides a simple, straightforward set of principles and tips that he says can help anyone be a better manager. Applied Materials is one of Silicon Valley's great success stories and it helped propel the digital revolution. But Jim Morgan's management techniques are not reserved for high-tech: *Applied Wisdom* shows how the same approaches, tools, and values work at any scale, from start-ups to middle management in a global corporation — and even to non-profits. Rich in stories and practical examples, it's a must-read for those seeking a timeless and proven management manual.

Advance praise for *Applied Wisdom*

"Jim has had great success managing in large and small, for profit and non profit, domestic and global organizations. I have been a beneficiary of Jim's wisdom as we worked together to get things done and this book makes that wisdom come alive for new and experienced leaders alike."

— Henry M. Paulson, Chairman, The Paulson Institute; former Chief Executive, Goldman Sachs; former U.S. Treasury Secretary

"Jim Morgan used the ideas he brings to life in this book when he built Applied Materials from a tiny, struggling, near-bankrupt company into an innovative global leader. Managers of any size business or non-profit group will find solid advice for building agile and effective organizations in this book."

— Meg Whitman, CEO, Hewlett Packard Enterprise, former CEO of eBay

"Jim is one of the icons of Silicon Valley and I can tell you 30 years running a high-tech company in a cyclical industry is not easy. I have seen Jim use the advice in *Applied Wisdom* with great success, most notably: looking for trouble out into the future as conditions change, and always showing respect for people. In partnerships, Jim notes that both parties have to be successful — that is why he was so successful, especially as the company expanded in Japan and Asia. A lot of young businesses have a very selfish attitude, but success often takes compromise. *Applied Wisdom* reinforces the importance of going beyond slogans and lip service and committing to basic, but very important values."

— Willem P. Roelandts, Chairman of the Board of Directors
of Applied Materials, Inc.; former CEO of Xilinx;
30-year veteran of Hewlett-Packard Co.

"*Applied Wisdom* is a treasure trove of useful insights from a true master of leadership in the business of technology about how to build the best, scalable decision-making process in a high-tech company.... Rare is the leader who can successfully grow with a company from start-up to multi-billion dollar enterprise. Rarer still is one who openly discloses the secrets he learned along the way. Jim Morgan pioneered many of the business axioms that we take for granted today, such as the value of finding solutions over the simple offering of products and the importance of globalization into tough regions like Japan and China."

— G. Dan Hutcheson, CEO and Chairman of VLSI Research, Author
of *Maxims of Hi-Tech: Rules of Engagement for a Fast Changing
Environment or How to Thrive in What Is the Extreme Sport of Business*

"Jim's wise managerial advice has been enormously valuable to me — and many others — at the Nature Conservancy over the years. It's great to see him sharing his simple, practical 'Morganisms' in this excellent book. *Applied Wisdom* is a must-read for anyone who wants to have a more productive, focused and motivated team."

— Mark R. Tercek, President and CEO, The Nature Conservancy

"I often tell young entrepreneurs that your homework is never done. There are many brilliant people with great ideas, yet very few who can successfully lead and scale up a high-impact company. It's inspiring when an executive of Jim's caliber says that he believes the vast majority of great managers are not born, they create that capacity by learning and changing. If you want to be a better manager follow his straightforward prescription and tips."

— Heidi Roizen, Operating Partner, DFJ; Fenwick and West Entrepreneurship Educator, Dept. of Engineering, Stanford University

James C. Morgan

I am pleased to share with you a copy of my recently released book *"Applied Wisdom — Bad News Is Good News and Other Insights That Can Help Anyone Be a Better Manager"*.

In the process of writing this book, I reflected on how many individuals have made a positive contribution to my life. No one is successful alone, and I am grateful for the support of so many over the years.

The goal of the book is to help women and men who are managers accelerate their development as leaders of any size or type organization — profit or nonprofit, startup or turnaround, small or large — and benefit from the tried and true management tips that I learned and collected through my varied experiences in farming, military, aerospace, venture capital, Applied Materials, and The Nature Conservancy. I truly believe that the role of a leader is to help others realize their full potential and I placed these management tips in the context of my own memoir to offer an example of how they were helpful to my experience.

Our complex world is in need of leadership, now more than ever, and perhaps the sharing of this story will inspire others to step up and demonstrate the courage to lead and lead well.

I wish you all the best for a great 2017.

Jim

This book is available on Amazon and other e-book retailers.
All profits will be donated to philanthropic causes.

Applied Wisdom

Stee,

Thanks for all you
do for our community

Jim

Applied Wisdom

Bad News Is Good News
And Other Insights That Can Help
Anyone Be a Better Manager

JAMES C. MORGAN
with Joan O'C. Hamilton

Chandler Jordan Publishing

Applied Wisdom: Bad News Is Good News and Other Insights That Can Help Anyone
Be a Better Manager
By James C. Morgan with Joan O'C. Hamilton

Published by Chandler Jordan Publishing
Los Altos, California

www.appliedwisdombook.com

First edition: November 2016

ISBN (paperback): 978-0-9983292-3-9
ISBN (ebook): 978-0-9983292-1-5

Cover and interior page design by Geoff Ahmann, AKA – Ahmann Kadlec Associates
Publication consultant: Thad McIlroy, The Future of Publishing

Printed in the United States of America by IngramSpark

All profits from this book will be donated to philanthropic causes.

TABLE OF CONTENTS

To my wife, Becky, and to the Applied Materials family who made this story possible. To my son, Jeff; my daughter, Mary; and for my grandchildren Sean, Morgan, Julien, Lucie, and Sophie who inspired me to pass along important lessons as my dad and granddad did for me.

A note to my readers

This book is designed to help anyone who wants to learn to make better decisions, manage more effectively, and more successfully lead organizations. I talk about my personal journey, embedding in my stories a set of tips and insights that have worked for me over a long career that began in the low-tech world of farming and vegetable canning but eventually led me to manage high-tech innovation on a global scale. As my involvement in non-profit organizations increased, I realized those same tips work in the non-profit sector as well. I was motivated to share them in a way that I hope is useful to a wide audience of managers working their way up the ladder or running small organizations.

Excellent managers are not born. They develop by learning: to identify critical driving forces in their environments; to build momentum by timely decision-making; to collaborate in a transparent and ethical manner; and to implement basic structures and processes in an overall climate of respect.

The best managers help people maximize their potential. Every person, regardless of education, training, or current position, is capable of improving his or her management skills, whether in a start-up, a global company, or a non-profit rich in passion but limited in resources.

In the Appendix, you will find a set of worksheets designed to help you assess your management skills and identify which areas may need development.

To your success...
Jim Morgan 2016

Introduction

I grew up in Cayuga, Indiana, a small town of about 800 people near the confluence of the Wabash and Vermillion rivers, not far from the Illinois border. My grandfather James Morgan and my father, Russell, owned and ran a farm and vegetable canning business called Morgan & Sons Canning. Our lives revolved around the cannery operations, which in turn revolved around the seasons of agriculture: spring planting, summer growth and harvest, summer and fall canning, and the winter period of rest, repair, and preparation before it all began again.

Morgan & Sons was a small, intense family business that employed between 25 and 200 people over the course of each year. I was born in August of 1938, and I began working there at an early age. Eventually, I learned how to do practically every single job in the cannery, from farming to driving a forklift to negotiating contracts and paying the bills. When I was growing up, Morgan & Sons was Cayuga's biggest employer. There is nothing that better reinforces the importance of integrity and treating others with respect like managing and working alongside neighbors you know you also will see at the grocery store, at a ball game, and in all the other aspects of life in a small town.

Eventually I ran a company, Applied Materials Inc., which when I retired employed over 15,000 people in 18 countries. In between those jobs, I had a lot of valuable experiences: an excellent education in engineering and an MBA from Cornell University; a very meaningful two years in the U.S. Army as an officer in the Army Materiel Command Board; and several years in high-tech business and investing. Often throughout my career, I realized how my experiences in the cannery connected to other challenges and opportunities in business; many of those experiences became the basis of homilies and ideas I would talk about on the job. At some point, members of my Applied Materials team started calling them "Morganisms."

For example, one thing I learned at the cannery is that when you're running a business with a lot of complex machinery, it's not unusual to hear a problem developing before you see it or experience it. When a motor doesn't sound quite right or there is an unusual grinding or clicking in a line, that's the time to stop, investigate, and fix it — before a small problem becomes a disaster.

Canning sweet corn and green beans might not seem like it has anything to do with a high-tech semiconductor equipment business. Applied makes some of the most sophisticated equipment used in the production of every semiconductor chip made in the world. Chips, in turn, power the global digital revolution. But the management principle of being alert to signs and sounds of trouble still applies.

Throughout my career I have seen business leaders give in to a common failing of human nature. They hear an unpleasant "noise" which might be customer complaints, or employee concerns, or innovations from competitors. Instead of recognizing it as a threat and addressing it, they try to mimic the three monkeys over a shrine I once saw in Nikko, Japan, and "See no evil, hear no evil, speak no evil." They rationalize the situation and hope it will go away.

We had a saying at Applied Materials: "Good news is no news. No news is bad news. Bad news is good news — if you do something about it." I'd like to think that attitude is one reason we turned a company that was on the verge of bankruptcy into one of the most successful global technology businesses ever. We trained ourselves to listen for signs of trouble — and either fix the problem or treat it as an opportunity for innovation or a strategic shift.

Leading a company where people consistently recognize, confront, and fix problems early is not at all inevitable or easy. In fact, it's not even common. I was reminded of that one evening recently, driving just a few miles between my home and San Jose. Sign after sign mentioned companies that started here in Silicon Valley — Intel, Apple,

Google, HP, Netflix, Cisco, Facebook, YouTube, and others. As I looked at those names, some decades-old, others relatively new, I realized that there is never a lack of exciting new ideas around Silicon Valley. All those companies — and hundreds more that didn't make the cut — began with game-changing new technologies and passionate founders who convinced early investors to fund a dream.

Yet those qualities are not enough for success. At some point, almost every organization faces challenges or even a crisis that has to do with the fundamentals of managing human systems. Communication breaks down. Employees focus on blame instead of solutions. A new product is developing more slowly than forecast. A once-promising partnership frays. A competitor appears from the blind side. Key employees threaten to leave. The bad news grows, but the organization's founders paper it over.

In some cases, the company may simply lose its way and disappear. Or it may become what I call the "living dead" and exist, but not thrive. In the case of the companies whose names I read on those signs, when these issues arose, the founders rose to the challenge, educated themselves, and grew into their jobs. Or, the company recovered only after experienced managers were brought in.

I think many more companies could survive. I have never believed that the skills required to successfully manage a technology company, or *any* other kind of organization for that matter, are reserved for a special or chosen few. What has often been lacking in founders or leaders is a deep appreciation of management, as well as simple, straightforward insights and tips that can help most people improve their management skills.

The night before my drive through the Valley, a former Applied Materials executive I spoke with at a philanthropic event mentioned that he often used the collection of my Morganism management tips. In fact, he had used several in a meeting at a new start-up that very day. They are ideas for motivating and empowering employees. They are practical recommendations for managers trying to improve their management skills.

On my drive, I realized that I could help fill the management void not only in the Valley but for any person hoping to become a better manager by passing along those same tips that were useful on my journey. I believe they work for anyone trying to develop a superior organization of any size. In fact, if you are interested in growing your start-up to be a large organization, it's important to begin discussing management and leadership concepts with your team when you are very small.

What follows is my attempt to share these tips within the personal stories where I learned them. It's not always easy to appreciate the value of management ideas in the abstract. I hope this makes the ideas easier to remember and implement, and also reinforces how these ideas apply in different settings. I also have used them in philanthropic projects that occupy a large share of my time these days, and they seem to inspire effectiveness in the non-profit setting as well.

I have always encouraged people to develop their own sets of guiding principles; perhaps mine can help shape yours. For many years I collected articles, lists, notes, and ideas I picked up reading, listening to speakers, or just talking with people. I urge everyone to do that as a habit that serves as a constant reminder that we evolve over our lifetime as managers, and there are always new ideas that can be helpful — or old ideas that suddenly apply to a situation in which we find ourselves. There are many ideas within the chapters but at the end of Part II, I've compiled my Morganisms into a "Top Ten" list. In the Appendix, meanwhile, action-oriented readers will find a self-assessment and a checklist for the ten most important tips to help with evaluating what you are doing well versus what you need to work on.

Our society has promoted the idea that the great leader is special, perhaps born to lead, or requires the highest levels of academic training. Business books and magazines often focus on dramatic examples of heroic acts or moments of truth; of the against-the-odds gamble; or of the diving catch that saves the day. This makes for dramatic writing, but I don't buy it. I believe it's well within most of our grasps to learn how to lead and manage better. My management approach is to avoid the need for the diving catch or other heroics. In basketball, every coach would rather a team plays good, fundamental basketball and is ahead by ten points with three seconds on the clock, rather than have the game's outcome hinge on a buzzer-beating three-pointer.

I've had a long career, one of the longest running of a CEO at a major Silicon Valley high-tech company. I've managed through recessions, industry cycles, trade wars, talent shortages, you name it. I've advised three U.S. Presidents on matters of technology and trade policy and I've sat on the boards of some of the most innovative and successful companies in the world, including Cisco, Genentech, and Komatsu. Applied Materials was a leader in globalization before that became a buzzword. We were among the first high-tech companies to offer customers solutions, not just products. We had a diverse workforce before that became fashionable. We invested in understanding and then cracking the technology markets in Japan and later in China when others had failed. Through it all, we established a reputation as innovators and technology leaders.

None of those good things happened by relying on diving saves and make-or-break-moments. They happened because we created an excellent culture of accountability where highly trained, skilled employees were supported and encouraged to speak up when they saw or heard a problem developing. Insulated leaders sometimes kid themselves that the "average employee" doesn't know what's going on or doesn't get the "big picture." In my experience, that is not the case. The key is to listen respectfully so employees feel comfortable telling you what's going on. Then, you can form an effective partnership and build something you're all proud of.

Working on my 'court sense'

CHAPTER 1

Early years

I'll begin with my family history as far back as I know it: The Morgans originally came from England and Wales and, at least along my father's family tree, many seemed to have had an adventurous and entrepreneurial streak. My great-great-grandfather, William Amsey Morgan, was born in Brisconshire, England in 1804. (That same year, Napoleon assumed control of France. Thomas Jefferson was President of the United States and he dispatched Lewis & Clark to explore what is now the Western U.S.). Within a few years, William left England for Pratts Hollow, New York, where he met my great-great-grandmother, Mary Moses. They had two daughters and a son named Lewis, who was born in 1836. According to a family history compiled by my late cousin Armour Morgan, when Lewis was about eight, William took him across Lake Erie and down the Erie Canal. They eventually landed in western Indiana and the town of Perrysville on the Wabash River. There, William bought and ran a tavern.

From his research, Armour reported that there were "Mills, Stores, Packing Houses... and Shops" and soon, Perrysville's version of technological progress: "In 1850 a plank road was built west to Georgetown and wagons and carts brought lines of grain and hogs to be prossed [sic] and sent down the River to New Orleans."

Apparently William moved on west within a few years, but Lewis Morgan stayed in Perrysville; there, he married his first wife Anna Chenoeth, in 1859. During this period, the U.S. was expanding. The original 49ers had been streaming to California for a decade, and in 1859 the Pike's Peak Gold Rush began in Colorado. Opposition to slavery was building, and within two years, the Civil War would begin after the Confederate States of America fired on Fort Sumter in South Carolina. Lewis was not involved in the war, but he "engaged in many businesses," according to Armour, including "store, lumberyard, pork packing, beef slaughtering, and farming." Eventually, he opened his own bank and owned 1000 acres of farmland in the area. Lewis had ten children with three wives and lived to age 90 (outliving all his wives). The family historian Armour was Lewis and Anna's grandson. My grandfather James, born in 1886, was the son of Lewis and his second wife, Rachel.

James moved about nine miles downriver from Perrysville to Cayuga, Indiana. He originally had a lumber business — being near the Wabash River, he could transport lumber by barge. But James bought a local canning business with three partners in 1911, and then he bought the partners out a few years later. Early on, there wasn't much equipment or capital involved. Morgan Adams Canning Co. (later Morgan & Sons Canning) consisted of a big brick warehouse and canning room and wooden processing sheds with holding bins and tables. James also owned horses to work his 500 acres of fields, and he hired workers who did the canning by hand during the annual "pack."

My grandmother Mary, James' wife, also was from Perrysville. She was treasurer of the company, and she taught piano to the children of Cayuga. James and Mary had two sons, John and Russell. Russell, my father, was born in 1911, and his younger brother John was born in 1916.

James started Russell and John early working at the cannery. My dad never stopped working at the cannery until we closed it down in 1965, except for four years when he attended Indiana University in Bloomington to study business. At IU he met my mother, Frances Jordan, who was from Mishawaka, Indiana, just east of South Bend. They married in 1932, and moved outside of Cayuga to a property called Knollcrest that was part of several parcels of land that Grandfather James had purchased through the years. Knollcrest was a fancy name in a town whose defining physical feature was its flatness. Many years later my wife, Becky, who is from Vermont, could not imagine that the slight rise we called the Knoll merited that description. I once asked if she wanted to go to "the hill" to see the cattle. We got there and Becky said, "I see the cattle; where's the hill?"

From everything anyone who ever met her told me, my mother, Frances, was a wonderful person—kind and well-liked. I have a picture of her in which she looks happy and has a very pretty, warm smile. Unfortunately, I have few memories of her, as she died from a cerebral hemorrhage when I was two years old. Her family also came from England. A relative on my mother's side constructed a family tree reaching back several generations to a woman named Esther Brownell. Esther descended from two different Pilgrim voyagers on the Mayflower, Francis Cooke and Richard Warren.

After my mother's death, for a few years my grandmother Mary took over most of the duties of raising me. My father would drop me off at James and Mary's home in the morning and pick me up after work (it was not unusual for him to work from 5 a.m. until 10 p.m. during the summer packs, so I spent a lot of time with Grandmother Mary). When I finally started school, I would walk a mile down a dirt road and stand by the edge of the two-lane State Route 63 for the school bus in the morning. After school I would either go to the cannery or to my grandmother's house in town, where my father would pick me up.

Just a year after I was born, Hitler's planes began bombing Poland and World War II broke out. The U.S. entered the war three years later, after the Japanese bombed Pearl Harbor. Food production was critical to the war effort, and my father stayed to run the cannery, but my Uncle John joined the U.S. Army and served with General Patton's Third Army as a captain in the Quartermaster Corps. I remember as a young boy we followed the war over the radio and in the pages of *Life* magazine and *The Saturday Evening Post*. We'd occasionally get letters from Uncle John, who served in France and later in Germany. John came back to the factory in the 1950s, but then he moved to Florida.

My best childhood friend was the son of James and Mary's next-door neighbors, Doc and Daisy Beardsley. Joe Beardsley was my first business partner. We picked sweet corn in the summer and piled it in a little wagon and sold it door to door. We also shot basketball at a hoop and backboard Joe's dad nailed up to a light pole. Our "court" was a sloping dirt patch and was messy in the winter, but we were happy to have it. Joe and I also started in scouting early and Joe's mother was our Cub Scout Den Mother. Later, his father was our Scoutmaster. Fortunately, they kept us engaged learning many practical skills and experiences and eventually we both became Eagle Scouts.

I liked school, and I especially enjoyed playing basketball on the school team. In fact, the Indiana small town of about 800 people where the basketball movie *Hoosiers* starring Gene Hackman takes place reminded me very much of growing up in Cayuga. In fifth grade, I remember I played 23 regulation team games. That was an impressive schedule if you consider that our league was made up of small town school teams scattered over many miles. Parents took turns piling the team into the back of a truck or station wagon and off we'd go.

Playing basketball helped give me court sense, or the ability to pay attention to more than one thing going on, predict where the opening or opportunity might be, and adjust to fast-changing variables. I have always liked basketball because it is an intense and fluid game: there is no standing around waiting for a pitch or lining up waiting for a snap. You have a game plan, but you have to adjust on the fly. You study your opponents' tendencies and focus on exploiting the opportunities as they arise.

"Court sense" is the alert, action-oriented posture that sports like basketball demand for success. In business, it means not only paying attention to your own agenda and actions, but realizing that a manager must learn to simultaneously track the movements and momentum of the entire team, the entire company, the competition, and driving forces beyond the present position of an organization on any given day. It's critical to adopt an alert, ready posture, constantly reminding yourself to look up, look forward, and look around. A closely-related concept is that of "driving forces" and those sources of change that every organization must align with or risk being run over by. The better your court sense, the sooner you will see and adjust to driving forces.

MORGANISM

Between my own curiosity, my friends, school, and the factory, Cayuga was a great place to grow up. In the winter, for example, when a prolonged cold spell was expected, the local fire department would open its hoses on a stretch of four blocks on one of those famous "hills" (again, everything is relative). That would create a frozen track for local kids to sled down. As I recall, there was only one family in Cayuga that protested this, but they were overruled. Although the slope of the hill was tame, it's hard to imagine a town getting behind something like that today!

Another fact of life in Cayuga was that every summer, Midwestern summer thunderstorms swelled the Wabash and Vermillion rivers. They often flooded and, depending on the timing and whether and where various levees and dikes gave way, it could have disastrous impacts on crops and also do damage to homes and businesses. A few times, the situation was so serious that the Military Reserves would use actual landing craft to rescue people who had been isolated by a flood.

The silver lining of the floods was that there was a big gravel pit near where I lived. The flooding of the Wabash would often fill those swimming holes with more water — as well as fish! During particularly heavy flood years, the waters would reach flat, lowland areas and create shallow bayous. My friends and I would go out with pitchforks and stab hickory shad, bass, buffalo, and sometimes catfish that the floods had stranded in ditches and fast-drying puddles.

Like a lot of agricultural communities in the U.S., our town had not experienced the Great Depression the way cities had. However, the bad economy overall had hurt the cannery's business, and the can companies and banks foreclosed on my grandfather's cannery twice during the Depression. But both times, he was able to get it back. More broadly, everyone had enough to eat. Everyone I knew had a garden. There was plenty of good fishing in the local rivers, and people routinely shot squirrel, rabbits, or birds. I don't recall folks in town losing their homes.

When the U.S. finally entered World War II, it triggered demand for canned goods to help supply the war effort. That was the beginning of a prosperous period for our family business that lasted throughout the early 1950s. There was rationing during the war, but because of the cannery, our family always had access to salt, sugar, and gasoline. I remember we did have to carefully lock it up, because those were basics many people couldn't get their hands on legally.

Russell remarried in 1946 when I was eight. I liked his new wife, Madeleine, who had grown up on a farm in Illinois. We shared the same birthday. At one point, my father was managing both our farm and factory, plus Madeleine's family's farm, which grew field corn, soybeans, and oats.

I think my stepmother hoped she and I would become close, but that did not happen. By the time they married, I was relatively independent. I did a lot of things Madeleine thought were too dangerous for my age, like swimming in the gravel pit or running my pony, Tony, around the farm. In fact, I was rarely home. I was closely bonded with my grandmother who lived in town, and since my best friend lived next door to James and Mary, I often went to their house after school to play with Joe and other friends. My half-brother, Edward, was born to Russell and Madeleine when I was around 10. That was a big age difference and I would soon go away to high school, so we were never close. Eventually, Edward joined the Air Force as a pilot. Russell and Madeleine divorced when I was in college. Edward moved away, and I lost track of him.

Madeleine did her best to make me into a proper young man. I resisted. We got along fine, but she almost didn't forgive me for a stunt I pulled one Christmas Eve. I was riding around with a buddy in his Model A pick-up truck and we drove near the gravel pit, which was frozen solid. We scraped off the top level of snow to slide on the ice and there, beneath the ice, we could see a huge bass. I don't think I'm using exaggerated fisherman's math when I say it was at least 17 or 18 inches long. In winter, pond fish would become starved for oxygen in the deeper water, so they would swim to just below the ice where there was a small cushion of air; they just hovered there, almost dormant. But they usually weren't this big! We cut a hole in the ice and reached down and grabbed that fish, and eventually pulled another ten from the pond. I was so excited that I went straight to the kitchen and cleaned my fish in the sink and made a terrible mess. For literally months afterward, poor Madeleine was still finding big fish scales dropping from the ceiling and walls in her kitchen.

CHAPTER 2

Morgan & Sons Canning

As I later learned in business school, Morgan & Sons was a vertically integrated operation. We owned 500 acres of cropland and bought the harvest contracts on up to 1000 more acres. We canned two annual harvests of green beans and a late summer harvest of corn. After preparing the corn for canning, we took the cobs and shucks and chopped them up to make silage to feed the cattle during the winter. The cows, in turn, fertilized the soil. And then in spring we started all over, moving the cows to pasture and planting beans and corn.

I started working in the canning plant as a boy. Over time, I learned to do every single job we had to do, from working cattle from the saddle of a horse to overseeing the picking operation, to running and fixing equipment, to managing the complexity of a workforce that would accordion from 25 full-time, year-round employees to 200 people added to the payroll during canning season. My favorite job was running the field operation and harvesting the green beans and the corn. I'd be outside all day, sometimes 5 a.m. to 7 p.m., responsible for the field crew. My office was a green Ford pick-up truck and I had to understand the equipment and the people to do my job properly. Other years, I enjoyed learning all the key jobs inside the factory as well.

Canning vegetables might sound simple. To young people today, it might even sound boring. But keeping a canning factory humming demanded focus and good judgment. For one thing, as the equipment became increasingly complex and powerful, it also became more dangerous. Training the workers and making sure they followed safety procedures was important. A shirt-tail or a sleeve caught in the canning line could lead to a serious injury; I saw men lose fingers or even a hand by being careless near gears and motors. It tended to make me cautious and further developed my court sense. To this day I see things from the corner of my eye and project the probability of an accident.

I once almost caused a serious accident myself. I was driving a brand of forklift called a Hyster to lift and move a stack of boxes filled with cans. I made the mistake of allowing one of the workers to ride on top of the stack I was moving. As I raised the stack, I tilted the front of the lift too far forward of its center of gravity and the stack and Hyster tipped forward. Fortunately, the stack caught on some of the canned goods already stacked, otherwise the worker might have been crushed underneath the load and the Hyster.

Also, field operations could be dangerous. On the farm during the corn harvest, green stalks and leaves would get wrapped around the corn picker rollers that separated the stalks from the ears of corn, which would then go back into a wagon pulled behind the picker. You'd hear a change in the sound of the roller as the stalks slowed down its RPMs. The rollers had to be freed up, and it was important to follow certain procedures. A constant risk was making sure someone didn't come along and turn the motor on, not realizing a worker was crouched by the rollers with his or her hands pulling the stalks out. Since I was responsible for my team, training and regular reminders of safe procedures were an important part of my job.

MORGANISM

In a factory, on a farm, in a meeting, at a conference, you often will "hear" a problem before it becomes obvious. It might be an odd click on a conveyor belt, or it might be silence in a work team that is usually upbeat and confident. It's human nature to want to rationalize and deny signs of concern, but that is the time to stop, assess, and do something about it. Emphasize finding a solution over assigning blame. Bad news is good news — if you do something about it.

Another critical lesson I learned at the cannery was to pay attention to small factors that could affect quality, and to motivate employees to be alert for these potential issues as well. Quality is important when you manufacture any product. But in the food business, it takes on added importance because people are going to be eating what you make. A small misalignment in the physical canning process can allow air to infiltrate cans, ruin the contents and make customers sick. What's more, canning a product like green beans meant undergoing inspection, and the grading affected the price we would get. Cans would be sampled randomly for quality; perfectly edible food would be downgraded if it had a lot of blemishes or if it was edible but not considered to have the ideal taste. There were grades of product, such as "Fancy" for Grade A; "Extra standard" for Grade B; and "Standard" for the lowest grade. We usually sold the middle-grade "Extra standard."

From a young age, I realized that Morgan & Sons Canning was important not only to our family's income but to Cayuga's. We had one school in town that went from kindergarten to grade 12, and I attended school with the children of cannery workers. Everyone knew each other and I learned to be respectful of all employees, regardless of their position in the company or in town. Our 25 year-round employees labeled and shipped canned goods, maintained the factory equipment, handled the cattle, and planted each season's crops. I spent a lot of time with these key employees, who took on other duties running and maintaining various aspects of the cannery during the more intense packing seasons. They were patient teaching me the operation, which I appreciated.

MORGANISM

As a manager you are constantly being evaluated by your team on whether you treat people with respect and whether you walk your talk. These are crucial behaviors to become a successful and trusted leader. If you are disrespectful of your employees' intelligence or you disregard their humanity or dignity, they will not trust you, and you will limit your potential for success.

I learned in the cannery to be a good observer and a good listener. I didn't want to screw up! Packing was a linear process, so an issue anywhere along the line would impact everything happening down-stream. I learned that when something unplanned happens, you must address the immediate situation, but also think beyond it. For example, we often had to make a best guess about the impact of weather on our operation, from when to begin the harvest to whether we could fit some repair or other chore in before rain or snow would make it impossible. During the pack, a delay in the delivery of boxes or cans might mean we should shift workers' attention to loading inventory until it made sense to start up the line again. Similarly, keeping alert, listening to employees' off-handed remarks, or seeing unusual body language might head off distractions or even accidents. Regardless of training and reminders, some employees were not cut out to work with dangerous equipment; they might be competent doing something else, so you were constantly making sure employees were in a position to utilize their strengths and not let their weaknesses hurt them. I also learned that women were great employees, especially when the workplace had a feeling of family. Some jobs, like running the corn cutters, were mostly done by women. It was very important to show an interest by checking in periodically. Things seemed to go smoothly if I did.

Listening to and interacting with people at every level of the cannery also helped me throughout my life in having rapport with people, whether they were ranked well above me or they performed more entry-level jobs. At Applied Materials I had no tolerance for anyone who lorded their position or power over others. Nothing would land an executive on my bad side faster than me overhearing a "Don't you know who I am?" speech to an employee.

The meaning of good service

In the abstract, nobody ever argues with the idea that it's good to fix problems while they're still small. But it's also true that shutting down a production line in the cannery was never a decision we made lightly. Since we had to borrow money at the beginning of every packing season to pay the workforce, we could not afford to have workers standing around with nothing to do for hours while we tinkered with the machinery. Add to that concern the pressure that you are working with a fresh food product with a short shelf life — it will start to degrade if you don't process it according to a certain timetable.

Facing that pressure taught me the business value of offering the best possible service to your customers. In this case, my teacher for the lesson was the Continental Can Company technician Mike Travaglio, who serviced our equipment. During the pack, the pressure was "on" and typically, our factory would run two shifts a day, the first beginning at 7 a.m., and the second ending at 11 p.m. If you started to hear a funny sound in a motor, or if some misalignment in the canning or the movement of the line developed, we would have to make a decision to stop the line and call in the service team to fix it. It was crucial that when the employees showed up at 7 a.m. the next morning, they could immediately go to work.

Even as a teenager I was aware of Mike's devotion to doing a good, fast job for us. In all the years I worked around the factory, I do not remember ever missing a 7 a.m. factory start. Mike's dedication was crucial. He realized how important his immediate response was to our success, and he came through on every service call, every time. He wouldn't think twice about working on the problem all night. He wasn't just a service provider, he was a partner in our success. My dad would place half the orders we gave to Continental Can directly with Mike, even though he was a technician and not a salesman. I do not know if he received the commission as my dad intended. But we were loyal to Mike, and he gave us critical help at critical times as a result.

Many years later at Applied Materials, we made equipment that was crucial to other businesses being able to produce their products. Our global service commitment became one of the most important factors in our success. The equipment needed to produce semiconductor chips is incredibly complicated; the slightest misalignments or malfunctions will ruin an entire run. During the 1980s, for example, a common figure cited was that only 80 percent of the equipment made by the entire industry worked properly. Part of the challenge was that our customers were so anxious to get new equipment and take advantage of any competitive advantage in a new product that they begged us to ship the equipment before it had been thoroughly tested and fine-tuned. This was a constant source of tension for every company in the semiconductor equipment industry, because after making these demands, the customer would then make even more service demands if the equipment did not perform perfectly when it was installed.

We battled those pressures better than many competitors because we were committed to making sure our customers were as confident in our desire to help them succeed as my dad was in Mike Travaglio to get our canning line back online. I felt like it was useful for me to be able to talk to our service people about my experience at the cannery with Mike. It built trust. I realized the effort it took to satisfy customers. But our service teams knew that if they got a call about a problem, they were authorized to do whatever it took to help our customer immediately. It was not unusual for us, if there was not the critical technical specialist nearby, to have somebody on a plane to a customer's location anywhere in the world within a few hours of hearing that the customer needed help from us to get back on track. We realized that our customers relied on us as a vital link in a chain. When you take the customer's issues and pressures as seriously as you take your own, you will have a long and productive relationship. We built a culture at Applied Materials where everyone understood this.

MORGANISM

If you approach all your business relationships and collaborations with the attitude that your partner needs to be successful for you to be successful... you will be successful.

When I began taking on more responsibility at the cannery, I was fortunate that my father would take the time to explain to me the big picture of topics like customer service. My father and I got along very well. He conveyed that he had confidence in me, and that allowed me to have confidence in myself. He and my grandfather also set a good example of treating everyone with respect. This is not a value you realize you're learning at the time it's taking root. You just act a certain way and you're corrected if you act any other way. We did not treat people differently based on their educational level or social status. The cannery employee who first taught me how to drive was a man who was on parole from prison. Working at the cannery was the only job he could get, but he was very capable. We never talked about his past or what he had done to be incarcerated; he was judged on his job performance, which was good.

Respect for competence was a key element of the culture we created at Applied Materials. We built an exceptionally diverse workforce with top engineers and other functional skills that represented many ethnicities: Indian, Chinese, Vietnamese, Mexican, Japanese, Israeli, Iranian, Russian, various European, and others — and including both men and women. In Japan, our willingness to hire capable women was a competitive advantage in a labor market in which it could be difficult for foreign companies to compete with Japanese companies for top university graduates. As I will explain, I would occasionally "porpoise" in on meetings and sit in the back of the room. I noticed these brilliant employees leaning in and listening very carefully to what was being said. Our meetings were in English (although they might be conducted by someone with an accent), but it was clear to me the employees did not let that faze them. They concentrated on the essence of the ideas. That reinforced what I think of as a "listening culture" that was not necessarily common on Wall Street or in more sales-oriented companies that valued aggressiveness.

Because of the high level of competence we insisted on in hiring, our employees knew it was worth making the effort to pay close attention to each other; we all had something to learn from one another. Not all companies successfully managed global diversity at the time we were building Applied Materials, but it became a real advantage for us.

MORGANISM

At Applied, our "listening culture" developed organically because of all the languages our employees spoke, but a listening culture is always a valuable asset. You can have clashes between disciplines (marketing and engineering, for example) or you can have misunderstandings of agendas or motivations that prompt people to dig in and talk louder instead of struggling to be clear. As a manager, model and support calm, well-reasoned discourse — not bravado and yelling. That creates a respectful workplace.

CHAPTER 3

Headed east

For all the benefits I received from working in the factory, the experience also impressed upon me the value of an education. Canning, farming, or menial jobs were the only option for many of our workers who had not even completed high school. My family and I figured I might end up running the cannery, but my father also made sure I had options.

I went to school locally in Cayuga through eighth grade. That summer my dad came to me and said he had been talking with his friend Ralph Cover, who ran a corn canning equipment company called The United Co. or TUC. My father had a lot of respect for Ralph, who had sent his son to a college prep boarding school called Mercersberg in Pennsylvania. His son had had a good experience there and eventually went on to Dartmouth. My father thought Mercersburg might be better preparation for a good university than our local high school. I agreed to go and that September, at age 14, Dad took me to Terre Haute, Indiana, about 40 miles from Cayuga. I boarded the Pennsylvania Rail for Pittsburgh. There I was picked up, and a few hours later I arrived at my new school.

Mercersburg Academy was founded in 1893. It's about 90 minutes from Washington, DC, and was an all-boys boarding school when I attended. The best-known alumnus at the time I was there was the actor Jimmy Stewart, but other alums have made their mark in politics and other fields, including the Nobel Prize-winning physicist Burton Richter.

I enjoyed my time at Mercersburg, and I remember that the school's history teachers were particularly good. I played basketball, football, and learned to play tennis. We had structured exercise every day in high school and it established a pattern for me that I have maintained throughout my life. I transitioned from team sports to more tennis and skiing as the years went on, but at minimum I do some kind of work-out or walk at least four or five days a week. I also played the clarinet in a dance band on campus and my senior year, 1956, I was editor of the yearbook: Volume 63 of *The Karux* (in Greek the name means "herald").

I remember working hard in my classes and having study hall every weeknight, but if you read the yearbook it seems like our main interest was pulling pranks. Names were not mentioned, of course; it was as if all the pranks pulled themselves. According to the *Karux*, during one winter rally, "Several icy missiles found their way into the musical instruments of the Band, and a few narrowly missed one very prominent member of the faculty." In an account of the annual Field Day, the reader learns, "The morning ended peacefully, with a pile of socks smouldering in some trash cans."

In terms of escapades that didn't make the yearbook, there were many. My roommate Dick Preininger one night put a small snake in my pajamas; it encircled my ankle. I also recall that by running the laundry distribution, Preininger and I managed to find a secret place to store an occasional beer. But few pranks matched the satisfying revenge Preininger and I exacted on one of my classmates who had a habit of stealing candy from our room. We left a small, unmarked box of what appeared to be chewable chocolate candies on the dresser. It was actually "Ex-Lax" laxative. Much of the next day, we would see the aforementioned thief suddenly stand up in the dining hall or even in class and race to the closest bathroom.

After graduation, I took a terrific road trip with one of my best friends — Gerald McCulloh from West Chester, Pennsylvania — and a friend of his. They flew to Indianapolis where I picked them up, and we drove north through Wisconsin and Minnesota. We then continued into Canada and west to Vancouver. The transcontinental highway was under construction at the time and as we drove through the Rockies we sometimes had to avoid large Euclid earth movers that would suddenly appear from behind a boulder or a bend in the road. At the time, we had to go 300 miles by gravel road up and around the Big Bend of the Columbia River on our way to Vancouver. We crossed back into the U.S. and visited Seattle, then turned east again to Boise, Salt Lake City, Denver, and back to Indiana. By sharing $5 rooms and occasionally staying with relatives and friends, we did the entire trip for $125 each.

Our last stop before Indianapolis was St. Louis, where McCulloh's uncle was the County Coroner. He treated us to a steak meal, quite a treat for three hungry teenagers. An unusual memory from that evening was that as the uncle was paying the bill, I noticed the people at the table next to us had about the same meal but paid less than half what we did. The uncle said that local people who went there were charged what they could afford and no one complained.

McCulloh was our class valedictorian and we all thought he would be very successful after college at MIT — very likely a U.S. Senator. Very sadly, he was killed in a car accident when he was a cadet at the Naval Flight School Pensacola. He was my first close friend to die.

By the time I was a senior, I had decided that even though I wanted to run a business, in college I would major in mechanical engineering. I was interested in the machinery of the cannery and felt I could read to learn about liberal arts. Many of my classmates at the time went to Princeton, but when I looked at my different school options, I saw that Cornell not only had an engineering program, it had an agricultural school and offered food technology. It also offered a chance through a five-year engineering degree for a more liberal education, which interested me. Having been with all boys for four years, I knew I wanted a co-ed school (although I didn't realize how few co-eds there actually were at Cornell — the ratio was about three males for every female). I applied early and I was accepted. I was also accepted at the University of Wisconsin, but I took a trip up to Cornell and visited the campus. Even though I took a hard fall on the ice outside Library Slope, I knew right away I wanted to attend Cornell.

Ironically, Cornell is located "far above Cayuga's waters," as Cornell's alma mater goes. It turned out people from Ovid, New York near Lake Cayuga settled my hometown in Indiana, and named it for their prior home. Cornell also turned out to be the choice of 11 of my 88 Mercersburg classmates, and my first year I roomed with one of them, Bob Grieves. Two more were on the same floor in my dorm (including Jeff Dando, who years later would be best man at my wedding).

By the time I went to Cornell I was used to being on my own, so I don't recall any homesickness or culture shock. An important decision I made my first year at Cornell was to enter an election to serve on the Freshman Class Council. It was there I met one of those rare co-eds, Rebecca Quinn, who went by Becky.

The odds so favored the girls at the time that the only way I could get a date scheduled with Becky was to go to Sage Chapel with her Sunday morning two weekends in the future (she had dates both Friday and Saturday night both weeks). When you're a freshman with a crew cut, no car, no fraternity yet, and that much competition, you have to maintain your focus and determination. Looking back I think I knew on the walk back from Sage Chapel that Becky was the "right one." After freshman year Becky continued with student government, but I did not. I was quite sure politics was not my calling (although it turned out to be hers!). I refocused on my mechanical engineering schoolwork, on ROTC, on my fraternity activities, and on Becky.

Cornell's lessons

At Cornell, we were introduced to computers that ran off punch cards. We didn't even have calculators. We used slide rules — what I call the engineer's six-shooter — for our calculations. But in those days engineering was a five-year program, and that gave me room in my schedule to take some courses outside my mechanical engineering curriculum. I took an electrical engineering course and I got a look at a brand new technology — transistors, which eventually evolved into the semiconductors we have today. While it was interesting to me at the time, little did I realize I would someday run a company that would play a role in creating practically every semiconductor used in millions of computers, cameras, airplanes, cars, and other equipment all around the world.

At one point I seriously considered changing my major to food technology, and over time I realized that I was more interested in the business side of engineering than in actually building or running the equipment. One reason for that was that someone had given me a book called *Ideas that Became Big Business*. I can't actually recall who gave it to me, but I still have it. It is a series of short, punchy accounts about companies including: Hershey Chocolate Corp., Ford Motor Company, and Gillette Safety Razor Co.. The book inspired me to think about new ideas and what they could become in a holistic sense. I found the idea of running a business appealing. I didn't necessarily want to start a business, but I was drawn to the idea of running all the different aspects of a business. Size or product did not seem important.

One of the most important single lessons I learned at Cornell that influenced my personal management style was in a basic statistics class taught by Professor Berman. It had the usual topics such as determining probability and the margin of error in a given analysis. But the critical lesson I learned was what I call the "cost of perfect information."

You always want good information. You want *extremely* good information when you are calculating a moon shot or planning a brain surgery. But the cost of *perfect* information is too high for most business decisions — and many other important parts of life. Others may express this as "paralysis by analysis," or they paraphrase Voltaire's observation "the perfect is the enemy of the good." I have always believed the critical thing is to make a decision and then manage the consequences. Too many people agonize too long making a decision, but then they don't pay enough attention to managing the consequences. They neglect to establish contingency plans and milestones and then do an honest assessment of whether the plan is working as the company reaches (or doesn't reach) those milestones. Once in motion, they sometimes neglect the course corrections necessary for success.

In basketball, if you have an open shot, you don't stand there for ten seconds analyzing the physics; you take the shot. But you don't assume it will always go in; you optimize the outcome by immediately moving into a position to get your own rebound in case you miss. At Applied, we developed some ways of talking about this that empowered our people to keep moving forward at all times, even when it was difficult to predict what the competition would do, or where the economy might go, or whether we could meet an ambitious goal. Given the choice between waiting for complete information and riding momentum, I will take momentum every time.

MORGANISM

The cost of perfect information is too high. Most people over-analyze decisions and under-manage the consequences. Do basic analysis, make a decision, and then pay attention to managing the consequences. Success is 10% strategy and 90% implementation.

My first management opportunity beyond the cannery emerged my senior year at Cornell. Cornell's motto is "Freedom with Responsibility," which has always appealed to me. It's at the heart of my first management insight that respect and trust for your people is the foundation of all good management. You hire the best people you can and then you trust them to use their judgment to do the right thing. Micro-managing or nagging is insulting and usually counter-productive. However, if people fail and do not learn from their mistake, you must move on and make changes.

So, the management "opportunity" came after bad behavior and irresponsibility on the part of some of my Psi Upsilon fraternity brothers landed us in hot water and in danger of being kicked off campus. My friend Bruce Waterfall and I agreed to split the duties of getting our house to shape up. A few of us agreed I would be president during the Fall Semester and Bruce would be president during the Spring Semester. We got the elected officers for that year to establish a set of rules for behavior to be a member of Psi Upsilon. A few brothers resigned, but the remainder followed the rules. Afterward we laughed that it was my first turnaround (but not my last!). Bruce, who eventually started a hedge fund in New York, would stay a lifelong friend. Many years later when he learned I was going to become president of Applied Materials, he was one of the first investors.

Wedding bells and other plans
Becky and I dated all four years of college. Before arriving at Cornell, I

had somehow decided I would be at least 29 before I got married. Our first date kind of set the tone and I realized that plan needed some modification. I gave her my fraternity pin our sophomore year and I asked her to marry me the spring of our junior year. We picked out an engagement ring together.

Confident and excited about our future, we came up with a detailed plan: We would get married in Woodstock, Vermont, her hometown, right after she finished her degree in home economics and graduated in June. After a car trip for our honeymoon, we would return to Ithaca. Then, we would work the rest of the summer to save money, which we'd use to pay for me to finish my engineering degree (mine was a five-year program) and for Becky to get a master's degree in home economics. I planned to double register in the Cornell Business School during my fifth year of engineering, and then I'd be able to get an MBA in just one more year. As an ROTC Officer, I owed the U.S. military two years of service, which would have to follow my MBA. The Army usually gave deferments to finish advanced degrees.

Initially, everything was on track. In June 1960, we headed to Woodstock for the wedding. I have fond memories of our wedding weekend, including some funny ones. There was a rehearsal dinner the Friday night before the wedding, and after dinner we went with some friends to the Woodstock Inn to have a drink in the bar. The problem was, Becky was not carrying her drivers' license and they wouldn't serve her. You might have thought in a town this small where Becky had grown up and her parents still lived, somebody could have convinced the bartender that the local bride being celebrated was 21 (which she was), but no dice. So, I drove her back to her parents' farm, she went in and collected the license and we went back for our drink. Her parents, being teetotalers, were confused as to why we were going to all this trouble.

The next morning was a beautiful day and our wedding was a fun ceremony at the Woodstock Universalist Church presided over by a close family friend of the Quinns', a Universalist minister named Rev. Mounir Sa'adah. It wasn't a traditional wedding in certain ways; for example, Becky and I went swimming in a lake the morning of the wedding, which bothered people who thought it was bad luck for the groom to see the bride on the day of the wedding. We're approaching 56 years of marriage as I write this, so I think we dodged that bullet.

Becky sewed her own wedding dress and the people in the wedding picked the flowers we put around the church. Right after the ceremony there was a "dry" reception in the community center. Some of our college friends were a bit distressed that there wasn't any alcohol, but we had a wonderful outdoor lobster feast for lunch. Becky's father brought out sawhorses and planks and we covered them in newspaper and everyone enjoyed the food. I remember that on wedding night, there was a huge full moon.

For our honeymoon, we drove in our Ford Fairlane to the Poconos, a popular honeymoon destination in the Pennsylvania mountains. It rained nonstop. Then, we drove to Indiana, where my dad had a small reception for us. I was proud and excited to bring my new wife home to Cayuga. It was early in the canning season and things appeared to be going well. Unfortunately, that would soon change.

We returned to Ithaca by way of Woodstock so we could pick up our wedding presents. While out on a hike, we were climbing around a rock wall when Becky slipped and banged her left hand. She looked down at the wound and then realized the diamond had popped out of her wedding ring set. I told her to stay where she was and I started doing the engineering thing — trying to recreate possible trajectories and velocities to figure out how far the stone might have flown. Sure enough, after a short time of searching, there inside my search grid was the diamond, stuck on a green leaf. It was incredible that we found the small gem among all the rocks and plants and dirt, but I took it as a good sign, and it saved us money since we did not have to replace it!

We returned to Ithaca and our first apartment. Our first significant domestic project as husband and wife was to replace the head gasket on the Fairlane. Becky got grease all over her hands, and she had trouble getting it off. Between having taken her engagement and wedding rings off to be repaired and fingernails that wouldn't come clean, she was a little self-conscious her first day on the job at Cornell's Mann Library. I had a job at Morse Chain Co. where grease under your fingernails was a badge of honor.

Everything was going along just fine for a couple of months, and then came a call from Cayuga: I learned that my father had worked himself into a psychological breakdown. Starting around August every year, my father started to suffer terribly from hay fever and asthma, which was made much worse by the corn silk in the air during harvest. He had to wear a mask and was miserable. The crop was unusually big that year and the pack was underway, but my father was exhausted and had been sicker than folks realized. He'd become erratic and actually fled to Mexico. And he had let some critical things at the cannery go.

One issue was that he had not secured the loan we took out early in every canning season to pay our workers until the proceeds from the pack came in. We had to have enough inventory canned to secure the loan, but we couldn't go too long drawing on our reserves. With that year's bumper crop, we'd made big commitments to our partners, such as the growers and box companies. As of this call, we didn't have the money in the bank to pay our people and pay our bills through more than a couple of weeks,

My grandfather spelled it out to me: I needed to come home immediately, and then go find my dad and get him medical care. But I also needed to step in and run the cannery, and one of the first orders of business would be to convince the banks that we were still solid for the financing. If I didn't do that, we could lose the cannery.

At age 22, it was a lot of responsibility handed to me very suddenly. Fortunately, because of my work experience in summers and after school, I understood what had to be done. I knew most of the employees and I had good relationships with them. My grandfather was retired and was partially blind at the time, but he was around to provide some advice (as you might imagine, that could be both helpful at times, but also challenging). I was worried about my dad and unclear what kind of medical help he needed. I had to go to Mexico to find him and get him treatment. The other obvious challenge was that I had a brand new wife in Ithaca and plans we would have to turn upside down, and I would have to get her out to Indiana somehow.

Becky has always risen to our challenges. I had flown back to Indiana, so she took on packing up our things into a U-Haul trailer.

It was a huge favor when our friend Bruce Waterfall volunteered to drive with her all the way from Ithaca to Cayuga, which took a couple of days. It was reassuring to me to know someone I could trust was helping and looking out for Becky on this trip. Becky drove straight to the airport and dropped off Bruce to fly back to Ithaca, and suddenly, there we were — newlyweds in Cayuga.

CHAPTER 4

Rebooting the plan

I'll never forget the day I kissed Becky goodbye and headed to Indianapolis with our small town banker to renegotiate the loan for the cannery. As we drove in silence, the pressure was on: If the banks did not go along, we could not make payroll the next week and would have to shut down the cannery. That would not just be a disaster for my family's business, it would hurt dozens of people in our town who depended on their jobs at Morgan & Sons to put food on the table.

I succeeded in getting funding to meet payroll and get the operation back on track. Instead of finishing my engineering degree, I worked long hours in the cannery throughout the next year. Becky picked up some part-time work substitute teaching. My father's health improved, and eventually he came back to work. I had commitments for about 35 percent of the orders by the end of packing season. In the fall we received a large government order which was enough to cover our loans and keep the business going, and we were on track to sell out the pack.

It was hard work, but it wasn't all work. Becky and I found time for an occasional movie or picnic, and we once took a weekend trip to Chicago. She obtained access to a saddle horse which made her very happy and one day she raised eyebrows when she rode it inside the open cannery doors! Also, the year at home let me finish something important to me. I'd been active in scouting most of my life and wanted to get my Eagle designation, but there were two badges I had not earned before I went off to college: lifesaving and my community service badge. There had been no place in Cayuga to take lifesaving when I had the free time to take it, but I was able to take care of that at Cornell. However, when I went back to work at the cannery, I signed up to help lead a Boy Scout troop. That fulfilled my service badge requirement and I finally became an Eagle Scout at 22. (Many years later Becky framed all my badges and my Eagle Award to hang in my home office. I enjoy having them and it reminds me of a lot of great times outdoors and a lot of practical learning. The whole Scouting experience probably influenced my commitment later in life to work to encourage conservation and a sustainable planet.)

It was satisfying to me to get the cannery back on its feet. However, in the spring of 1961, something happened that rang a giant alarm bell for me that my family needed to get out of the canning business.

My father was a good businessman. As more automated equipment was invented over the years, he had upgraded our operation. He even invested in Ralph Cover's company, TUC, which made canning equipment. As an investment aside, I learned it was not a good idea to make your investments all in just one industry or in all illiquid investments. He chose TUC over IBM at the time.

Those improvements made us more efficient, but they also changed our fixed cost structure. With a highly manual operation like my grandfather originally ran, most costs were variable. If a crop came in light, it was easy to adjust. You hired fewer people. You made less money, but you had lower expenses too. During my dad's tenure, the interest on the money borrowed to buy equipment and the principal had to be paid back on schedule, no matter how big the harvests were or whether we signed profitable contracts to sell the goods. With a debt that had to be serviced, the risks of losing money increased.

At the same time we added debt, consolidation was starting to roll through the food industry. Large companies like Green Giant, Stokely-Van Camp, Del Monte, and Libby were building huge facilities with significant economies of scale that canneries our size could not hope to match. They had plants in various geographies, for example, while we relied on our limited, nearby farm acreage. A local weather issue like late rain or a drought that cut yields in a given year could be catastrophic for us. Big canners buying in different areas were insulated from setbacks on any one farm.

The big canners were landing huge orders that several smaller canneries would have combined to fill in the past. The way I first learned that small and medium-sized canneries were starting to fail was that money became tighter for me away at school. Dividends from my dad's investment in TUC initially helped pay my Cornell tuition. Back in 1959, I had to add an extra job working in a nearby fraternity house kitchen to my schedule because TUC stopped paying those dividends. Profits were dropping for TUC because the canning equipment market was flooded with second-hand equipment as smaller canning companies failed.

I went to Indiana in the summer of 1960 realizing the business was getting tougher, but it wasn't until the next spring when I realized just what a predicament we were in. The year I ran the cannery, I figured our costs were around $1.15-$1.18 per dozen, for #303-sized cans of sweet corn. The wholesale price for that grade was $1.35. By spring, we'd placed about 75% of our inventory. Then, Libby announced it was dropping its price to $.90 per dozen. We still managed to sell out the rest of our pack at a small profit, but it was clear to me going forward, there was no way we could compete with prices that low from competitors. Also, large grocery stores increasingly wanted fewer but bigger deliveries of different kinds of canned goods, instead of many single variety lots coming in from independent canners.

I shared my concerns with my dad and grandfather. I thought we should try to sell the cannery while we still could. My grandfather and father didn't agree. They figured people always needed food, and there would be plenty of business for everybody going forward. My grandfather pointed out that he had lost the cannery to the banks a couple of times during the Depression, but he had always been able to rebound and buy it back. I understood their commitment to the business and to the town, but times had changed. The size and scale of the emerging competition and the fixed costs to pay the debt on the improvements was poised to wipe them out.

This situation was another example of the lesson I learned on the cannery floor: in business you "hear" problems beginning before you actually see them materialize. TUC's struggles should have been a warning bell to my dad, but he liked Ralph and hoped it was just a temporary setback. After I returned to Cornell in 1961, I took a business course called "Analysis of American Industry." There were 16 of us in the course and each of us took an industry to analyze; I took the vegetable canning business. I studied companies like Del Monte, Libby, Green Giant, and Stokely, and I visited some canners in New York state. I knew some small vegetable canning operations were starting to convert to new product categories, such as juices and sweetened juice drinks like "Hawaiian Punch." But it seemed only a matter of time before the large conglomerates took that business, too.

I couldn't convince my family to sell, but I realized that I would not have a future running Morgan & Sons. My grandfather and dad had prospered for a long time because when they heard a glitch in the canning line, they stopped the line and fixed it, preventing a bigger mechanical break-down. But what our family business was facing was a business model breakdown.

This experience reinforced several lessons that have been valuable to me over the course of my career, especially the importance of what I call "driving forces." In every market opportunity and in every business decision, there are driving forces you need to consider. Change creates opportunities and new driving forces. Once the automobile was invented, for example, people also needed gasoline and mechanics. The rapid market acceptance of cars was a driving force suggesting an ambitious entrepreneur should open a gasoline service station rather than a feed store for horses.

But it's easy to mix up a dynamic with a driving force. Sometimes there is a lot going on and you don't clearly see which driving force will prevail. For example, the idea that people will always need to eat food is a dynamic of the food business. You do not have to convince people they need to eat the same way you need to convince them they want the latest music headphones or sneakers. For a long time, that was a driving force in my family's success as an independent cannery. My grandfather and father saw their business survive the Great Depression because basic food staples were a priority for everyone and the competition was small and medium size canners.

However, competition and consolidation arrive. New technology allows for large-scale production; preferences change; larger economic factors influence even basic demands. Unfortunately, it's natural to hold on to old ideas about the driving forces. Consolidation among the big canneries was the new dominant driving force; our family cannery offered a commodity product in a market sector where large players had lowered their costs and reduced their risks so much that we would be the very last option for any buyer. That's not sustainable.

The point is there are variables you can't control, but you can control how alert and quickly you move to exploit opportunities. There were times later in my career at Applied Materials when we would strike out in a new direction early. Wall Street might be skeptical. Competitors would go on with business as usual, and they would not invest in new technology and ideas. In a business that evolves as fast as high-tech, you have to stay alert and adjust your strategy constantly. Just like in the cannery, if you rely on your past accomplishments and another guy figures out how to sell green beans cheaper, you'll find yourself out of business.[1]

MORGANISM

It's been said the one constant is change. A good manager is constantly looking at the driving forces that are likely to impact the future of an organization. They may be macro or micro, everything from labor costs to interest rates to customer trends to competitive innovation. Get used to looking for them early in your career, and your ability to perceive and incorporate them into your strategy will improve over time. Every significant decision should include an assessment of the relevant driving forces.

As soon as my dad was able to take over the cannery again, Becky and I returned to Ithaca in the fall of 1961. I went back to school and Becky

---

[1] The cannery stayed in business only a few more years. It closed in 1965. After Grandfather James died the following year, my father sold all the assets he could and moved to Indianapolis, where he bought a hardware store that he ran for ten years before he died.

started working as an assistant 4-H agent. We didn't have enough money for both of us to return to school (she would eventually get an MBA, but that comes much later), so she not only worked but helped me by typing my papers. We were happy to be back together and pursue our plans. Naturally, they would change again very soon.

Uncle Sam is on the line

By the end of the 1962 spring semester, we had some decisions to make. The Reserve Officers Training Corps had commissioned me as a Second Lieutenant to serve two years active duty and granted me a deferment to finish my MBA. But as the end of the school year got closer, a new list went up and I learned I was part of a group considered to be "critical duty." They had cancelled my deferment and I was supposed to report that summer!

We quickly settled on a new plan: As an officer, I would have an income and we'd have free officer's housing for two years. We figured that it would be a good time to start a family. After serving my two-year hitch, we'd go back to Ithaca and I could finish my MBA at Cornell.

Phase one of Plan B went smoothly. Then, shortly after Becky realized she was pregnant, the government changed its mind and regranted me the deferment.

All of a sudden, I had some new pressures. My dad admitted the cannery was struggling. Prices were down and my dad was not in top shape. I knew they really needed my help. The other issue was now Becky was pregnant, and I was scheduled to be a full-time student in the fall instead of having free housing, healthcare, and an Army paycheck. In Ithaca, Becky had a full-time job that paid fairly well, plus use of a car; prospects for summer work for me in Ithaca were not very good. I could live cheaply and save money in Cayuga working at the cannery, but it was unlikely Becky would find a job there that paid close to what she was making in Ithaca. The baby was due around Thanksgiving. We figured the best way to balance all these factors was for Becky to stay in Ithaca in our apartment and keep working and for me to work the summer pack at the cannery in Cayuga. So, we had to live apart for the summer.

It was a tough three months. Becky had to manage the early part of her pregnancy on her own. Both of us were lonesome. I was working long hours in a business I could see was not going to survive. Compared to the year we were in Cayuga together, running the summer pack under increasingly difficult financial conditions left little time for anything but work. I called Becky when I could. There were no cell phones, no texting, and no email. Becky worked during the day and I sometimes worked late into the night, so we mainly caught up by phone on the weekends.

Finally, I finished the cannery pack and came home with the grubstake to start my final year and finish my MBA. Life brightened up quite a bit. Becky was doing well and we moved into an apartment building and became good friends with five other young couples. We were all enthusiastic about school and our young families. The apartment was old, but fairly spacious and close to campus. But as Thanksgiving came and went, Becky was overdue and getting more and more uncomfortable. We tried to keep our mind off the waiting by going to hockey games and other campus activities.

Another couple in our building had a baby (frustrating for us, because ours was due first!) and there was going to be a little party to celebrate on December 13. But that afternoon, Becky realized her time had finally come. I let them know we wouldn't be at the party. I drove Becky to the hospital and took up what was then the father's assigned spot in a waiting area outside the delivery room.

I remember waiting out Becky's labor and delivery in a drafty hallway. Becky's labor went all night and I ended up catching cold after sitting shivering for many hours. I remember discussing all sorts of subjects with a man whose wife was also having a baby; he worked on a garbage truck and he had a badly mangled hand.

The funniest memory I have is of two friends who lived in our building coming over after the party to wait with me around 2 a.m. One of them was the center on the Cornell football team and a big guy. He wanted a large family of boys, but his wife had given birth to a girl first (they would have three more girls before they were done). I remember he came over and picked me up and (no doubt inspired by a few rounds of drinks and toasts at the party) said to me, "Jim, don't worry if it's a girl. You're going to love her just the same."

The baby was a boy. The labor nurse who helped Becky with the delivery also lived in our building, so after Jeff was born, she made a special trip to bring him out to me. My first memory of him was Jeff flailing his arms around like a little prizefighter, like he'd been held back and now he was full of action and ready to go. He's still like that.

CHAPTER 5

General leadership

We were young and very busy parents. I was hustling to finish school, and Becky only took a few weeks' maternity leave. The living arrangement in the apartment helped because all the moms helped watch each other's babies. We were able to pay one of the other new moms to take care of Jeff on the days when Becky worked.

I managed to finish Cornell about three weeks earlier than originally planned, and I was approved to start officer's training in May instead of July or September. I pushed to start early because then I'd be earning money. For a few months we lived outside Aberdeen Proving Ground in Maryland in private housing, then we were able to move onto the base.

I've always said the first thing I learned in the U.S. Army was that it pays to wash your underwear.

Before Becky and Jeff arrived in Maryland, I was in officer's training at Aberdeen for six weeks and I was in the laundry waiting for my clothes to dry. I struck up a conversation with another officer in training who had come from Cornell. He mentioned that his roommate worked for the Army Materiel Command Board (AMCB). I was immediately interested. I felt like I had had good platoon-style management experience at the cannery, but the AMCB helped develop strategy for all Army, R&D, Procurement, and Logistics. Based on what I had already learned getting my MBA, that sounded like valuable experience that would have a lot of benefits in the private sector.

The roommate ended up introducing me to Colonel "Cotton" Lollis, who worked directly for General Frank Besson, the Commander of the entire AMCB. Col. Lollis interviewed me and requested that I be assigned to that group. As my officer's training came to a close, the usual drill was for the Army to send someone to try to get you to increase your commitment beyond two years. The carrot they held out was that they would guarantee you the assignment you wanted.

I was fairly sure I did not want to be in the military longer than my two-year hitch, and I knew General Besson had a lot of clout. He was a four-star general and the youngest head of the logistics command in U.S. Army history. I took a chance and told the officer trying to upsell me that I appreciated the opportunity, but that my uncle who had been an Army officer had suggested I wait and see if I liked being in the military before I made any longer term commitments. Thanks to General Besson's high standing, I got the command I wanted anyway.

The Materiel Command Board usually had six or seven strategic studies going on simultaneously. They focused on challenges relevant to military research, management, procurement, testing, and global logistics operations. The personnel in the command were colonels, majors, high-level civilians, and a few lieutenants (I joined as a Second Lieutenant). The studies would take a significant amount of work and analysis, and then twice a year we'd present three big projects to the 21-member board made up of all the headquarters staff and the commanders of the Huntsville Missile Command in Alabama; the Test and Evaluation Command at Aberdeen Proving Ground, Maryland; the Mobility Command in Detroit; the Aircraft Command in St. Louis; and many others.

General Besson would convene the meeting and we'd tee up our findings and make conclusions and recommendations. In fact, he did something I've copied all my life: he required us to begin every presentation by starting the first slide with conclusions and recommendations. Particularly with technical or complicated subject matter, a long presentation where listeners don't know where you're going often becomes tedious and confusing. Instead, General Besson made sure the group around the table was focused on the key issues and had the opportunity to question and make suggestions. Most impressive, he made sure the headquarters staff and the leaders of the various commands did not leave the meeting without making decisions on every recommendation. If there was concern or confusion, he'd schedule an early morning golf game and hash over the problem until relevant commanders felt sufficiently clear on the issue to vote. He did not always get the decision he favored, but he did not allow the project to get swamped in dithering or internal politics. He insisted on a yes or no. General Besson was an impressive manager, and I was lucky to be there. From a purely logistical point of view, the Vietnam War was a successful model in terms of materiel and troop support, and people widely credited General Besson's contributions to those operations.

When you're trying to communicate something important to a group, begin by stating your conclusions and recommendations. Then get into the why's and the supporting data. People will focus better if you help them connect your ideas and data to your conclusion from the very beginning.

As engineers, we were still mostly using slide rules, but the original ENIAC, which stands for Electronic Numerical Integrator And Computer, was near us in the Ballistics Research Lab. ENIAC was considered the first actual "computer" and took up most of a big building. It was originally developed to calculate artillery firing tables and also used to study the hydrogen bomb. Eventually, the computing power in that entire building was dwarfed in capabilities by small devices like an iPhone. I had studied transistors and seen some later punch card computer systems at Cornell. It's interesting how primitive the early computers were and how quickly that technology developed.

During my two-year hitch in the military, Mary was born, and we were very happy to have a boy and a girl. Our family joke was that the Army charged us $7.42 for Mary's delivery and that she was worth every penny of it.

The assignment to the Army Materiel Command turned out to be a fortunate one for me. One study I worked on involved decentralized management at some of the military's major suppliers such as GE, Digital Equipment Corporation, Chrysler, and a company called Textron[2]. I got an inside look at how these very successful companies operated. Textron particularly interested me because it was a highly diversified company. It actually began as a textile business in the 1920s, with the founder, Royal Little, selling silk thread as he traveled around New England in his own airplane. By the time I learned about Textron it had bought up an incredible variety of companies one at a time, everything from Speidel Watch Bands, Scheaffer Pens, the Homelite Chainsaw Company, and a chicken farm, to Bell Helicopter, Hovercraft, and missile warhead delivery systems. Textron had acquired companies in consumer goods, aerospace, automotive, defense, machine tools, and other technologies.

As my time in the Army came to a close, I went prospecting for my next job. The Jewel Tea Company in Chicago was a big food and house-hold products company run by a Harvard MBA; it had a manufacturing division. I interviewed with Jewel Tea and they offered me a job. Consulting was a common first job for MBAs, and McKinsey & Company's Washington office also offered me a job. But I was most interested in Textron, which was based in Providence, Rhode Island. I had a connection from Cornell on the board of directors. As I saw it, the opportunity was that as a collection of many different kinds of companies, they didn't necessarily have many technical guys like me with general business experience, too. They tended to acquire companies with their existing management intact, and there wasn't much of a corporate executive team. I saw it as an opportunity to get broad exposure to technology and to management situations. I also figured that after two years of that kind of experience, if Textron didn't work out I could go back to McKinsey or Jewel Tea and join them at the same level as if I'd taken an entry-level job and worked my way up for two years.

In the meantime, I was talking with my Colonel, and I learned that he knew a senior Textron executive named Harvey Gaylord. Harvey had built the Bell Helicopter in Texas for Larry Bell, the founder of Bell Aerospace. Eventually, Textron bought Bell Aerospace. By the time I met him, Harvey was a Textron Executive Vice President and a director. He

---

[2] I was at Aberdeen Proving Grounds working on the report about decentralization in November of 1963 on the day we got word that President John F. Kennedy had been fatally shot. The cliché is true: When you hear news that shocking, the scene where you are when you first learn the news is permanently burned into your memory.

kept an office in Washingtons rather than Providence. Harvey agreed to meet with me and go to lunch. I later learned that the general in charge of all U.S. Army personnel was a friend of Harvey's and had provided him with my entire file to review over the weekend before our meeting. After our meeting and then lunch, Harvey basically hired me on the spot and asked "Would $10,000 be all right?" Anything would have been all right.

The irony of that day was that when I arrived home, literally that afternoon, there was a letter from Textron human resources rejecting my application. They said they just didn't have a good position for me. I ended up working for Textron for the next seven years. Those were great years. I worked for excellent executives who taught me a lot, and Textron was involved in pioneering important and interesting technology.

CHAPTER 6

Work for the best managers you can

One of the most valuable experiences a young, ambitious person can have is to work for excellent managers. Both my grandfather and father had very good business minds. They were managers who paid attention to every aspect of their business, worked extremely hard, and treated their employees, partners, and other stakeholders in an ethical and fair manner.

The next break was my military assignment: Based on conversations with others who joined the military to serve ROTC duty, the odds of being assigned to a highly efficient, high-caliber management team in the military are far from guaranteed. However, General Besson's Materiel Command was a top-notch operation in every way. Not only did I learn management and analysis tools that I've used ever since, that experience connected me to Harvey Gaylord, who was a significant role model and mentor.

After I joined Textron, I worked in Harvey's Washington, DC, office at Connecticut and K Streets. The office consisted of Harvey, a retired major general, two support staff, and me. There were five divisions with sales offices on our floor that reported to their division presidents, and the presidents reported to Harvey. They all sold technical products, mostly to the government. Harvey was smart, capable, and a natural executive. He was a great guy who talked to everybody; he always wanted input on what was going wrong, and it didn't matter where the information came from.

Harvey and his team had built a culture at Bell Helicopter that was impressive. Within the company, one of Bell Helicopter's notable accomplishments was how consistently it met its schedule targets. Often government contracts come with penalties for missing milestones or deliverables, but Bell always delivered. I remember visiting Bell Helicopter in Hurst, Texas, outside Fort Worth, one time when an executive named Edwin Ducayet was running it. Ed was president when Bell designed its Model 206 helicopter and named it the Jet Ranger. That became a very successful aircraft, as was the Cobra Attack helicopter. I was speaking with a machinist, and I asked him, "How is it you guys have such a good record in meeting the government's schedules?" He smiled and said, "Well, I don't know anything about the government's schedule, but I wouldn't want to be the guy who had to tell Ducayet I wasn't going to meet his schedule." His respect for the boss was clear. When I heard that, I could see that a strong and productive corporate culture permeated the whole organization.

MORGANISM

> **Nothing beats working for excellent, principled managers. The key is to turn your court-sense on fully, and ask yourself: What are the structural and management driving forces creating success here? If you convey a sincere desire to learn and improve your skills, a good manager will be glad to help you do that.**

Textron was one of the first and most successful conglomerates. It grew by acquisition, but it didn't go shopping for struggling turnarounds. It bought companies that were really good in their niche and it usually let the existing management run it after the acquisition. Textron was a true conglomerate with 35 divisions. The parent company provided financial support and discipline and a willingness to make other acquisitions to make a given division even stronger. Top management paid close attention to the bottom line of every division, every company.

I met some interesting people during those days. I remember so clearly a day when Bell Helicopter's chief test pilot, Joe Mashman, came into the Washington office because he had brought a manufacturing prototype of the Jet Ranger helicopter to Washington from

Texas so he could demonstrate its capabilities for some generals. He invited me to take a ride with him, and I jumped at the chance.

Joe was a legend in the helicopter world, and there are many stories about his bravery and accomplishments, including being the first pilot to actually cross the Andes Mountains in a helicopter. He was in Peru and flew to 13,000 feet elevation (very dangerous and technically difficult) in bad weather to rescue an injured girl who could not get to a hospital any other way. I have been in a lot of helicopters in my life, both for my job and for fun things like heli-skiing, and I can confirm that Joe was an extraordinary and capable pilot. I never had any fear at all. He went underneath bridges and down ravines and even lightly clipped the leaves of trees. It seemed like the machine talked to him the whole way. At that time he had flown every helicopter type in the world; even during the Cold War, the Russians would ask him to fly their helicopters at air shows to see what he thought of them.

Another unique person was Walter Dorenberger. He was the number two reporting to Wernher von Braun, the legendary head of the German V-2 Rocket program and later head of the U.S. missile effort. Dorenberger was one of the scientists brought to the U.S. after WWII. He headed Bell Aerosystems' R&D efforts. A brilliant scientist with a thick German accent, it was always interesting to hear him discuss future technical strategies for Bell.

Bell Aerosystems had more different technologies being developed than any company its size — there was the "Bell Rocket Belt," displayed in the first Super Bowl by two "air men" in space suits, the Ducted Fan Airplane, guidance for Minuteman Missile warheads, night vision goggles, air-cushioned vehicles, and many more.

When I joined Textron, we discussed that after two years I should move to one of the divisions. After two years, I was ready. My take on Washington was that it was a good place to start if you had an entry-level job, because there were lots of interesting opportunities. It also was a good place to work if you were at the top and running something. But in the middle, there was a lot of bureaucracy. Becky also was ready to move on. Although we had a nice house in Vienna, Virginia, the atmosphere wasn't very stimulating for Becky. She did dressmaking to earn some extra money for us, but that was a solitary activity. She found she didn't have much in common with many of our neighbors.

Bell Aerosystems was interested in bringing me in to work, but that division was located in Buffalo, New York. They had great people and exciting products, but I was not excited about Buffalo. I stalled, hoping some other division might want me to join it. One day Marty Martenson, who ran one of the smaller divisions called Hydraulic Research in Burbank, California, came in and said, "Hey Jim, how'd you like to come out to Burbank and work for us?" I just said: "Sure!" I didn't ask how much money, or what job I'd have. In those days you weren't so particular about opportunities, we were just glad we didn't have to go to Buffalo.

Becky and I flew out to Burbank to look for a house in April of 1967; it had just rained and the entire area was beautiful and green. We found a place to rent, and then in the summer, we packed up our house in Virginia in a U-Haul and the four of us set off cross-country to our new home. By now we had a yellow Dodge station wagon, and in order to see family and friends, we took a meandering route — first to Indiana, then to Denver, then south to Albuquerque to see an army buddy, then the Grand Canyon, then to Las Vegas, and finally to Burbank. Poor little Mary got the mumps, and I can still see the image of her sitting in the back of the wagon wearing an Indian headdress and beating a toy drum we bought in Santa Fe. She had a big swollen neck.

It turned out that summer in Southern California wasn't quite so beautiful as spring. What had seemed so green and fresh in April was now brown and dry. Plus, in those days, July in Burbank at the east end of San Fernando Valley meant day after day of nearly suffocating smog. You literally choked driving under some underpasses.

I worked in Burbank for about a year. Hydraulic Research was another well-managed Textron division and Marty Martenson, the president, was an excellent executive. Its specialty was servo valves and actuators for aerospace and industrial control systems. In the early days of flying, the pilots provided the physical control energy, moving everything through cables. As planes got bigger, the aerospace designers combined fluid mechanics, electrical, and mechanical engineering and other

Great moments in technology — and with Mr. Lincoln

Working at Textron in the 1960s, I had a ringside seat to some important milestones in technology. It was the "space age," and several of our divisions developed important enabling technologies for aviation and space exploration. For example, Bell Aerosystems in Buffalo, New York developed night vision equipment and also a large "ducted fan" vertical airplane that looked very much like the small drones coming on the market now. A vertical airplane, sometimes called a VTOL (for vertical takeoff and landing) combined the flexibility of a helicopter with the longer range capacity and stability of an airplane. Propellers inside ducts or round enclosures could be rotated vertically for takeoffs and landing, then switched to a horizontal orientation to power forward flight. Textron's Spectrolab, meanwhile, was a pioneer in solar cells for spacecraft, which were a critical enabling technology to generate energy without having to carry fuel.

My division, Hydraulic Research and Manufacturing Co., made the actuators that steered the Saturn V rocket into outer space. Astronauts would come by the company to discuss the various controls and technology; addressing some of the challenges of space exploration through innovation was a constant topic. Later at Dalmo Victor up in Belmont, California, we made the antennae for the Lunar Excursion Module and Apollo that broadcasted the first live video of Neil Armstrong walking on the surface of the moon in 1969.

One of the most unique contracts Hydraulic Research ever had involved cutting-edge technology that helped people go back in time. We worked with Walt Disney to create a lifelike "audio-animatronic" version of Abraham Lincoln. Disney was a big admirer of Abraham Lincoln, and the State of Illinois asked him to help with the state's pavilion for the 1964 World's Fair in New York. The Disney team designed a robotic version of Lincoln who stood up on a stage and delivered a speech to the audience. His mouth, head, and arms moved as he spoke. The gestures were subtle, and the effect was lifelike. Hydraulic Research made the small servo-motors that created these gestures.

Later, "Great Moments with Mr. Lincoln" became a popular attraction at Disneyland itself, and we continued to work with the Disney people on the attraction and other prototypes. For kids who have grown up with Hollywood special effects and computer animation, animatronics might seem primitive, but at the time, visitors were amazed. You can search on YouTube for clips of Walt Disney talking about how his team put the robot together, working off an actual "life mask" that was made of Lincoln's face in 1860.

I wasn't involved with Disney when I was in Burbank because I was working on the Boeing project. But I remember that when we had employee meetings, the fact that we hadn't done so well financially with Disney would come up. Someone at the meeting would suggest "Why don't we just get out of that project?" Then, somebody else always wisecracked: "What — and quit show business?" We stayed in.

systems to power flaps, ailerons, and rudders. It was the early days of what was known as "fly by wire." For example, you sent an electrical signal via a switch in the cockpit to the servo-motors, which had hydraulics to cause flaps or ailerons to go up or down.

Hydraulic Research made the actuators for the 737 and DC-9 airplanes, and I worked on a project for the Central Lateral Control System for the 747. That was a well-managed program at Boeing, and it produced a successful plane. The 747 has always been my favorite plane, and I have flown 747s many times all over the world. Textron made two complicated hydraulic control systems located in the hull underneath the wings that have been in place on every plane manufactured since.

The Margarita factor

On the Boeing project, I used another management technique I learned from General Besson — namely, that it pays to get work teams offsite to meet and socialize a little bit so that they form good relationships. When I was at Hydraulic Research, I worked in the program office. That meant that I had responsibilities for the Boeing Control Project, but the management style was indirect. I had to get the planning done and get the team to meet schedules and technical specs. I had to provide oversight and follow-up, but not come across as meddling too much in the day-to-day functional management. This gave me early exposure to the necessity and complexity of managing what has become normal in modern global corporations: a "multi-boss" project or business unit. More on this later.

We had a routine where every two weeks all the key executives either at my level or above would stop at a Mexican restaurant near Griffith Park. We'd go dutch: we'd have one margarita and Mexican food, and we'd hash over tough problems informally. We talked as colleagues receptive to giving and taking advice about how to keep things on track. We agreed on approaches and made decisions. I never had a project that didn't run on time.

I've talked about my belief that as an executive and a leader you must be willing to make decisions on less than perfect information. That does not mean you agree to pursue long shots or ignore troubling data just to make sure you do *something*. For example, while I was at Hydraulic Research we were involved in bidding on a contract with Lockheed to help build the L-1011. Later called the "Whisperliner" it was a big, exciting new passenger jet with a lot of advanced electronic features. Unfortunately, it was a very difficult technology challenge to integrate all the different suppliers' components. Lockheed was not in terrific financial shape, and asked contractors to finance the cost of the work until Lockheed itself was paid upon delivery.

We were excited to work on the L-1011, but we did not like the caveat about financing the work. We submitted a bid that added extra payments to address the cost of that money. We did that knowing there was a good chance we wouldn't get the bid, and we were willing to walk away if Lockheed would not agree to it. As I knew very well from the cannery, adding a fixed interest cost to your expenses when there were a lot of variables you couldn't control was a risky proposition. Sure enough, Lockheed ran into a lot of delays and setbacks with that project. If we had agreed to the original financing proposal, the interest costs to us to wait out the delays would have been significant. It was a function of a good management team with the strength of their convictions that we stuck to our guns and ended up not damaging our company.

CHAPTER 7

North to Silicon Valley

Textron had a division in Northern California called Dalmo Victor (DV). It was the company's first acquisition in aerospace. DV was a sophisticated defense contractor based in the San Francisco peninsula town of Belmont. But DV got itself in financial trouble, and the president at Hydraulic Research Marty Martenson was made acting president. DV had won a government contract for a project known as APS109; it was a passive airborne radar system for the F-111 fighter jet that was supposed to alert a pilot to the status of any radar signals pinging from an aircraft, surface-to-air missile (or SAM), or anti-aircraft weapon. It was designed so that a fighter pilot, for example, would be alerted that other aircraft with the potential to lock on to the plane's coordinates were in the area. The pilot could then execute defensive flying maneuvers or release "chaff," or pieces of metal, that would fly in erratic patterns designed to confound enemy radar.

When they called in Marty, it was clear there were two big problems: First, the engineers were having trouble making the technology work. Secondly, the contract had not been well-negotiated and Dalmo Victor's internal team and outside auditors predicted that by project's end they would be $7 million in the red. That was the largest loss any Textron division had ever experienced.

One day, Marty came by my office and said he'd like me to go to Belmont with him for a couple of weeks and help him dig into the project so he could figure out how to stop the red ink. I agreed, and spent two weeks talking with people at every level of the company. Things were much worse than reported. The management team had been used to much simpler technologies like antennae and they hadn't run a big organization. William Miller, who would later become Secretary of the Treasury, was the CEO of Textron at the time. He flew out for a meeting that turned out to be just Bill, Marty and me. I thought I was just there to answer questions, but Marty turned to me and asked me to summarize the situation for Bill. I explained that a better prediction for our losses on the deal was probably in the $15-$18 million range. I literally watched the blood leave Bill's face, and then his neck turned white as well. He was a lawyer, not an operating executive and suddenly a technology challenge he had no idea how to fix threatened to significantly hurt Textron's bottom line.

Bill told Marty to do what needed to be done. I spent six months traveling back and forth to Burbank trying to understand what was going on at a deep level. Marty finally asked me to move to Belmont and run the project. Personally, it was one of the best career opportunities I ever had. First, I gained experience thinking through and solving a very complicated business problem. Secondly, although commuting for six months was tough, Becky and I moved to Palo Alto, and we realized it was exactly where we wanted to live and raise our family.

Valley of Heart's Delight

We moved to the heart of what is now Silicon Valley, but you never heard that term in those days. The northern corridor from San Francisco to San Jose was mostly called "the peninsula." At its southern end, the huge number of orchards and agricultural land had actually been given the nickname "The Valley of Heart's Delight." Becky and I lived near Middlefield Road in Palo Alto; still the peninsula, but in 1968, the whole region had an open, rural feel to it. There was even a horse pasture not far from us at the corner of Page Mill Road and El Camino Real. The air was clean, the weather was mild and warm, and the people we met were friendly and optimistic "can-do" types.

Every day I would drive the few miles north to Belmont and DV. Priority one was to make sure we got a grip on our internal management. I started a new internal value that everyone's work had to be "on time, within budget, and demonstrate technical excellence." I sought and found technical help with a high level of competence from within DV and other Textron Divisions like Bell Aerosystems. An outstanding engineer at DV who eventually ran Loral, Frank Lanza, took over running the APS 109 technical development.

I also initiated morning stand-up meetings to get the program on schedule. These were action-oriented meetings to resolve issues and share information. This worked so well at DV that it became routine throughout my career. At Applied we called the rooms where we met "War Rooms." We would gather in person, by phone, or videoconference regularly to be sure decisions and plans were prepared and agreed to globally.

MORGANISM

Always reserve 5-10 percent of your time for planning. This is another simple business tool that managers neglect when they get busy. If you just bull forward without stopping to assess where you are and what is changing or might change, you can go off track. Making time to plan and confer creates a useful rhythm and a routine.

Another critical thing we did was hire an outstanding lawyer named Walter Pettit to help us renegotiate the contract that was bleeding us. General Dynamics (GD) was the prime contractor for the Air Force on the project, and we were the subcontractor. There was no question we had made some mistakes ourselves in underestimating the scientific challenge and in the way we originally designed the contract. But both GD and the government knew that we could not move forward productively with the threat of a huge loss. There was room to renegotiate, but it had to be done fairly.

Walter steered us through the contract negotiations with a lot of skill. He was an old-school counselor who did his homework and who realized the importance of give and take in negotiations. We moved forward and agreed on a new contract with General Dynamics that we felt was fair, and we were ready to go and settle the deal with the government. Then, as can happen when egos and rival motives get involved, progress suddenly veered off track. Textron hired a new controller who came out to help us close the deal. He had come from General Dynamics and

I think he saw an opening to renegotiate the contract to squeeze more money out of us. The new controller wanted to both make his mark with Textron and accommodate his former friends, so he advocated renegotiating. The then-President of DV John Pamperin, Walter, and I huddled and decided that no, we had a contract ready to go and we would not open it up again. Our controller was angry and went back to headquarters. We braced for possible negative reactions from Miller, but Bill backed us and we settled with the government and eventually delivered the technology and the profit which continued to grow as the contract expanded over the years.

Building a quality culture

Dalmo Victor taught me about another crucial element of running a high-tech business. I had about 1600 people working on that contract. We had 100 different projects, including the various test equipment and support programs. One reason the situation had escalated out of control was that the company's leadership had not run a large, complex process before. They did not understand the importance of creating processes and formal ways of organizing technical, operational, quality, and service elements.

Quality is never an automatic in business, but it is easier to monitor and enforce in small businesses with a simple product. In a small organization, everyone is close enough to the products and to each other that quality and accountability is a value and mindset. At small scale, managers don't address quality as a function. As you grow, however, you get gaps. In technology companies that tend to grow fairly quickly, you have to plan to measure and monitor quality.

I've come to believe that almost all start-ups resemble a wheel with a hub (founders and top management) and spokes (functional departments). Information comes in from the spokes, and then decisions go out the spokes. But as the company grows the people on the spokes get more and more distant from the hub and isolated from the other spokes. They don't talk as much to each other and they may send in recommendations or plans that don't take into account issues occurring on the other spokes. Conflicts develop that delay decisions. There are reversals of decisions employees that thought were settled. If you don't create processes to handle how you make decisions, your people will stop making them, or the employees who don't like a decision will ignore it, hoping it will be overturned.

Management must recognize this change is occurring and develop the structure and processes to successfully make a transition. This demands a transition to a more hierarchical structure; one or two top leaders cannot successfully manage a hub-and-spoke structure past a fairly small size. Employees usually don't like these changes and they resist or even sabotage new reporting requirements or communication steps. Many companies outgrow their CEO because a technical or sales-oriented entrepreneur does not know how to lead the company through this kind of transition.

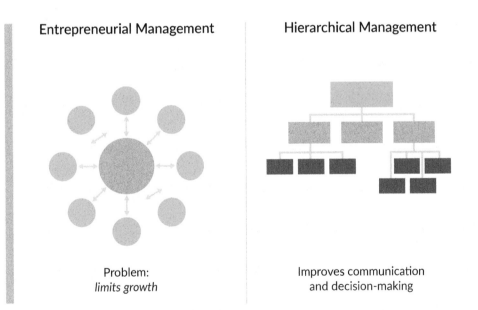

Entrepreneurial Management	Hierarchical Management
Problem: *limits growth*	Improves communication and decision-making

MORGANISM

As an organization grows and takes on more discrete functions, such as manufacturing, marketing, and finance, information will not flow efficiently and confusion will develop over decision-making if the early "hub and spokes" structure (above left) **does not transition into a hierarchy where lines of authority and decision-making are clear** (above right).

In my experience a vital element of making that transition is getting employees focused on building what I call a quality culture, like what we had at the cannery. As a company grows, you need a process to make sure every employee knows exactly what the key quality issues are related to his or her job. When the company is small, everybody worries about everything; every employee must flag any issue or impediment to getting a product developed and out the door. As the company grows, people may not realize the new dimensions of quality beyond whether a product works or not; there are quality responses to customers, for example, and degrees of quality in managing raw material or inventory. You have a quality process and then you have to have quality inspection, you need a quality strategy, a quality plan, and test equipment. It might sound bureaucratic, but without these processes, complex operations can get dysfunctional very quickly. Without clear processes, companies can take on a "victim" culture rather than an accountability culture. When everyone is circling a hub that may or may not be communicating effectively to all the spokes, it's easy to always blame quality issues on the other guy that didn't do his job. Those are the frictions and misfires that can tear a company apart.

CHAPTER 8

New ventures

After three intense years at Dalmo Victor, it appeared we might have to move to the East Coast again. That was not a happy prospect for Becky and me; we'd moved eight times in nine years. After all our different situations and climates, we could see that we wanted to put down roots in Palo Alto. Jeff and Mary were entering school, Becky had made friends and was involved in community service, skiing was four hours away, and the high-tech business world was full of opportunities. The more time I spent working and talking to local engineers and entrepreneurs, the more I could see the area was about to explode with business activity.

I looked at my options, and one industry that intrigued me and addressed a business where I had not had much experience was venture capital. The idea of venture capital of course was not new. There have always been individuals and funds interested in investing in the ground floor of new business ideas. But in high technology, the enabling technologies were complicated, and you needed some familiarity if not training in engineering to appreciate innovations streaming out of university and government research.

I had two friends from Cornell who knew Steve Weiss at the investment firm Weiss, Peck & Greer and they arranged a meeting. Steve's partner Phil Greer had worked out a deal with Bank of America's holding company to do an institutional venture fund called "WestVen" funded with $21 million. Today, firms will put that much or more into a single deal, but at the time, $21 million was a lot of money and in fact it represented the largest institutional venture fund. I thought it sounded like a great opportunity.

When I told Textron I was turning down the offer to move because I wanted to stay in the West and pursue venture capital, they made a tempting counteroffer. Textron was in talks to buy a company called American Research and Development Corporation (ARDC), the first publicly traded venture capital and private equity company. ARDC was started by the former Harvard Business School Professor Georges Doriot, and its claim to fame was turning a relatively small investment in Digital Equipment Corporation into a huge return. Textron offered to bring me in to ARDC; unfortunately we would have had to move to Boston. I thanked Textron, but I joined WestVen.

This was an exciting time. The main "high-tech" companies of the day were working in aerospace and defense. I remember going to the Western Electronics Association meeting one evening at the Palo Alto Hills Country Club to hear Roy Ash, founder of Litton Industries. Roy had become the very first director of the Office of Management and Budget working for President Nixon. The Varian leaders were there, as was Dave Bossen of Measurex and Dave Packard. There were executives from Fairchild, Intel, and American Micro Devices (AMD). There were about 45 of us, but most of the attendees were the leading players in Silicon Valley, and already they had created a business culture where they got together and talked and shared ideas. They were mostly engineers by training who were much more excited by the idea of building great new products and building good companies than by the financial rewards.

I learned a lot from talking with and listening to these pioneers and I made lifelong friendships, not only among the entrepreneurs but among the other venture capitalists investing in new ideas as well. There also were monthly meetings of the Western Venture Capital Association and all the key VCs attended, including Sandy Robertson, George Quist, Bill Hambrecht, Art Rock, Dick Kramlich, Bill Draper, Pitch Johnson, Steve Merrill and Reid Dennis.

Phil Greer had extensive investing experience; what I brought was high-tech operating experience with an appreciation of financial management. My combination of interests and experience was not very common. Companies tended to be dominated by technical founders and/or by salespeople who were good at promoting and selling a product. But in between the innovation and success were a lot of steps I had spent considerable time at Textron working on — selecting people, meeting schedules, process management, manufacturing issues, quality control, negotiating contracts. Brilliant ideas do not translate to brilliant companies unless you manage all these less flashy elements to make all these functions work.

Bought right — half sold

As a venture capitalist, I learned about a broad array of industries and sometimes happened upon insights from unexpected places. One of them involved the steel service industry. We provided some investment capital for an entrepreneur putting together a network of steel service companies he called Unimet. Stainless steel was an industrial product in great demand across many industries; it's used in industrial applications like cabinets and tables, and increasingly it was becoming a component of high-tech systems as the shell for various kinds of equipment. These service companies would buy huge rolls of stainless steel in bulk, then they would cut it to the specifications of customers.

I didn't know much about the business, so I decided on a trip to New York that I would stop in Philadelphia and visit one of the companies that Unimet was considering investing in. I drove deep into one of Philadelphia's grittier areas and entered a gated yard. I remember wondering if my rental car would be there when my meeting was over. I entered the building and there were several flights of stairs. The fabrication floor was on the ground floor of the building, the executive offices on the top. I remember that the carpet of the bottom stairs was black with grease; the higher you climbed, the more of the red of the carpet shown through until the top floor had a pretty clean carpet in front of the President's office. The President was about 35; his uncle had started the business.

We talked about the industry and his experiences in the business. I then asked him, "What would you say is the essence of this business?"

He got right to the point. He smiled slightly and said: "Bought right, half sold."

I've never forgotten that comment and I've repeated it many times. It applies to every kind of business. If you buy your raw materials for a low enough price, if you buy real estate at a low enough price, if you buy stocks low enough, you've done half the work of making a profit. I take it as a reminder to be careful getting entranced with some fancy, clever aspect of a stock or a deal or creating a proposition where your costs are high and your success hangs on a complex set of future conditions. This man's business was about making a decision day in and day out about whether he was paying a low-enough price for steel so that he could reasonably resell it for a profit. It was a good reminder to keep things simple.

MORGANISM

The essence of all successful business is selling a product or service for a profit. Many otherwise smart people have failed by focusing on "mindshare" or investing fads. As a smart and successful businessman once told me, "Bought right — half sold."

In the early 1970s, a lot of high technology stocks were in a slump. There was a broader recession and new equipment purchases had sagged off. In October 1975, I think you could have bought all of the public high-tech Silicon Valley stocks (except for Hewlett-Packard and Varian) for a few hundred million dollars,. I remember taking a trip to the East Coast to go to a regular Unimet board meeting. I would plan to have dinner with another board member and friend in New York. He worked in a huge office building that was almost empty because of all the lay-offs. On the way home I stopped in my Indiana hometown. It was the same as when I left years ago. I knew the industrial world was not going to end. I knew that the potential that technology was creating was enormous and there was bound to be an economic rebound.

When I returned to California, the opportunity to profit from these undervalued stocks seemed so obvious that I recommended that WestVen start buying technology company stocks in the open market. Our investors didn't like the idea. They felt they had other resources to buy public stocks. They wanted us to focus on funding the early stage technologies and entrepreneurs that would be the public stocks of the future. I looked at the price of so many stocks and thought "bought right, half sold" and I made my own personal investments. Although I had very little capital, I eventually managed to get venture capital returns on those investments, which is pretty rare. If our institutional clients had gone along, they would have made as much or more than they made investing in early stage deals. To me, this was not rocket science, it was court sense.

Porpoising at Paradyne

The most dramatic situation I was involved with as a venture capitalist involved a company called Paradyne, which was based in Largo, Florida. Paradyne was an early player in telecommunications and it pioneered some of the first modems and other technology that allowed for remote terminals. WestVen had been a seed round investor in the company and I coached the two founders, the president and the head of marketing, as well as the next layer of management.

Paradyne quickly developed several challenges common among start-up companies. The two most significant were an inadequate understanding of the time, effort, and expense it would take to develop the technology; the second involved communication issues between the founders that created conflicting messages to employees. Once again, the hub and spoke problem was sabotaging progress. As a company develops, you have to manage communication and decision-making between management, engineering, manufacturing, marketing, and finance. Paradyne's leadership was not doing that.

For a year or so I mostly helped Paradyne from a distance. I visited maybe half a dozen times, stopping in Florida going to or returning from the Northeast. I could see the management was struggling and behind in meeting targets, but the key development was a call to my home one Sunday afternoon: it was from an executive a level down from the CEO who said, "Jim, this is a disaster." The two founders were not communicating at all. Each had a different plan for what needed to be done. The CEO would issue a set of marching orders in the morning, and the marketing guy would change those orders by the afternoon. My contact explained that the company needed someone to take charge and make decisions.

I caught a red-eye to Florida that night and met with the two executives Monday morning. It was clear neither was up to running the company, but the good news seemed to be that they could see that. The first major mistake that the CEO had made involved the recent round of venture funding. They went out to raise $3 million at $3.50/ share; the technology was very appealing and a young venture capitalist from Heizer in Chicago stepped forward to give them $5/share to get in on the deal. The rest of the venture funds stepped up at the higher price; the trouble was, the CEO didn't take more money, he just gave up less stock for the same amount he'd gone out to raise. He underestimated what the product development would cost and in six months, they were out of money.

The founders agreed to let me take over as interim CEO; my WestVen partner Paul Ferri started a search for a permanent full-time CEO. But we had to do another financing round. Some of the leading VCs from the first round would not commit new money, but WestVen, CitiCorp, and Sprout Ventures did a financing valued at $2 million and we shamed Heizer into participating since they had helped create the problem. The previous financing valuation was $50 million.

I camped in Florida for six months. I hired a chief operating executive before we even hired the CEO he'd be working for, but it was essential that we get products developed fast. At first, it was touch and go. But with the new financing and a good CEO my partner found, we got Paradyne back on track. Eventually they sold the company to AT&T for $255 million, which was a home run return for us. Paradyne was the deal that gave me a reputation among venture capitalists as a turnaround specialist. Because I was part of a group of venture capitalists who'd invested, my partners understood the challenge and what we had managed to achieve.

There were elements of the Paradyne turnaround that I think apply to most turnaround situations. One of the most important is that while you often have to change the top leadership when it lacks the skills to manage a transition, I believe it's not helpful to replace a lot of employees lower in the organization. Some turnaround executives always replace existing management and technical staffs with a team of their buddies they've worked with in other situations. I don't believe in doing that.

When an organization has significant strategic challenges or competitive threats, you have to consult experts who understand the market sector and changing industry conditions. But when it comes to operations and executing a strategy in place, most employees are just as savvy as any management consultant in seeing what the problem is. Sometimes they are better at identifying the people problems and steps in a process that are slowing things down or creating friction. In most cases, they just haven't been in a position to make changes. They need direction and leadership, but they have useful knowledge that takes new people a long time to learn. It may pay to salt a few key people into the existing organization, but I feel a minimal number is best.

The next obvious question is how do you unlock that useful knowledge? At Paradyne and later at Applied, I made a deliberate effort to seek that knowledge by what I call "porpoising." This also applies to the ongoing management of any organization but is particularly useful when you have to come up to speed quickly. Bill Hewlett and Dave Packard used to call it "management by walking around," but I always did it with an agenda. The idea is to personally visit work teams at every level of concern to you and ask straightforward questions about how things are going. Sometimes I would take a sack lunch and eat with employees; sometimes I would just drop in, or sit in the back row of a meeting. You can also do some of this with strategic phone calls to managers, investors, customers, suppliers, and community leaders.

The point is not to show up with your guns drawn and announce, "There's a new sheriff in town, folks," like a scene out of an old Western movie. Porpoising also is not a detective mission to find perpetrators of mistakes or a way to play "gotcha." Porpoising is a management technique that is designed to collect information valuable for the long haul, and the longer you do it and do it with discretion and a low-key, sincere desire to understand what is going on and what may be getting in the team's way, the more the team will trust you and give you actionable information. From my earliest days at Applied, I would talk to people at every level in a group, including clerical staff and other non-technical, non-management employees. I asked simple questions: What is going on here? How do people here feel about what we're trying to do? Is the organization getting in your way? Why are schedules slipping? What would you do to fix that?

You have to handle the information you unearth very carefully. The ability to successfully porpoise disappears if you betray or "out" the people who share their insights and opinions with you. The most important goal actually is to assess the decision processes deep in the organization, not second-guess the decision-makers.

For example, suppose you have learned there are disconnects between the marketing materials produced to support sales and what the sales team says customers want to know. Who's at fault? Probably no one person or group. It's very likely a decision process issue. Functional managers need to improve their communication and planning, perhaps through regular meetings, perhaps by assigning a specific manager to coordinate these activities and be accountable for the successful alignment of these interests. In a situation like this, I would encourage the various division heads to designate someone either part time or full time to work with the sister division like an outside customer, understanding needs and helping their organization.

Accountability vs. victims

When things aren't going well, which tends to be the case in every turnaround situation, there is a tendency for employees to personalize their anxiety and frustration and create "villains" and "victims." In fact, I eventually created a slide addressing this culture issue that I would show in management presentations at Applied Materials.

The slide shows the difference between a corporate culture characterized by accountability, versus one characterized by a victim mentality. This is an extremely important distinction and in my experience, it's not simply dictated by the personalities of the people involved. As you'll read in the next section, the transition from hub and spoke management to a more scalable, effective organization demands that employees focus on solutions, not blame, and on raising a red flag and helping reengineer processes that aren't working. It goes back to stopping the canning line at the sound of trouble; if employees feel empowered to make decisions and supported when they report issues and try to solve the problem, you get an accountability culture.

Accountability vs. Victims

	8	Get On with It
	7	Find Improvements, Solutions
ACCOUNTABLE	6	Own It — Take Responsiblility
	5	Acknowledge Reality — Get the Data
	4	Wait and Hope Things Get Better
	3	Make Personal Excuses
VICTIM	2	Blame Others
	1	Unaware There's a Problem

Process management can sound abstract and theoretical. Managers can create elaborate flow chart presentations designed to deflect blame. But Suzie in accounting, Joe on the manufacturing line, or Zen in engineering has to deal with the consequences. They see the quiet, competent heroes as well as back-stabbing between rival managers; they know who delivers consistently versus a group where they have to adjust their work for reports that haven't been filed or parts that don't get ordered when they're supposed to; they know who can and who can't make a decision under pressure; they live daily with the consequences of a process created too quickly or with faulty assumptions; they know the limitless ways that clever people can sabotage a decision they just don't like.

I enjoyed the exposure to different situations I encountered in venture capital and I learned a lot, but after a few of years in that field, I wanted to get back to running something. When you are on the board of a company as an investor, the only time the CEO really listens to you is when the company is struggling or needs new money. I missed being involved with all the aspects of running and growing a business.

> **As a manager, "porpoise" periodically to make sure you understand important issues, changes, and challenges in your organization. Be careful to approach this exercise as a seeker of knowledge, not as a detective trying to ferret out guilty parties. Your real goal is to make sure the systems and processes in place support the company's strategy. This should extend to checking in on a regular basis with customers, suppliers, and community sources.**

Opportunity knocked at just the right time. Sandy Robertson, the respected head of Robertson Coleman, Siebel & Weisel knew what I had accomplished at Paradyne. He had his partner Tom Cable call and say he wanted me to meet the CEO of a company with a lot of potential that was struggling and losing money. It happened to be just a few miles from where I lived. That last part sounded particularly good to me at the time. Little did I realize the meeting would change my life.

See inset of Jim (right)

Clockwise from top: Morgan & Sons Cannery in the 1940s. Those are corn wagons in lower right corner and the structures where we husked, cut, stored, canned, packed and shipped our harvests of corn and green beans; That's me standing on the rock near the office, around age 5 (inset); Our cannery workers put in long hours of physical labor; My best friend Joe Beardsley and I rode Tony the pony, with my dog Mac; My father, mother, and me in front of our house.

Clockwise from top left: Three generations of Morgans—my grandfather, James, my father, Russell, and me; Grandmother Mary and my Uncle John Morgan during World War II; Cornell University 'high above Cayuga's water'; Becky's and my wedding in Vermont; my graduation photo from Mercersberg Academy, Becky and I in front of her family's barn in Vermont.

Clockwise from top left: Becky and Colonel Reis help me pin on my 1st Lieutenant bar in 1964; At Textron, I helped support such products as the Bell Helicopter Jet Ranger and the flight system for the Boeing 747, a workhorse aircraft still providing reliable service today; At Dalmo Victor, a Textron Company, I was program manager for the F-111 APS 109 Radar Homing and Warning System.

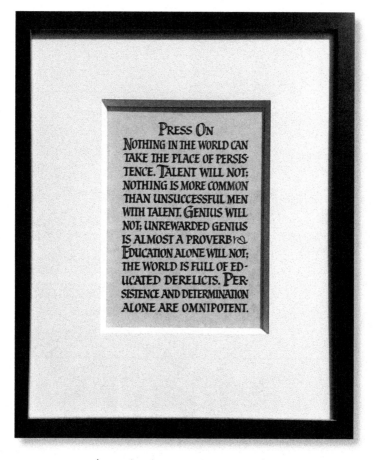

PRESS ON
NOTHING IN THE WORLD CAN
TAKE THE PLACE OF PERSIS-
TENCE. TALENT WILL NOT;
NOTHING IS MORE COMMON
THAN UNSUCCESSFUL MEN
WITH TALENT. GENIUS WILL
NOT; UNREWARDED GENIUS
IS ALMOST A PROVERB.
EDUCATION ALONE WILL NOT;
THE WORLD IS FULL OF ED-
UCATED DERELICTS. PER-
SISTENCE AND DETERMINATION
ALONE ARE OMNIPOTENT.

*I kept this reminder on
my office wall.*

Applied Materials

In Silicon Valley, companies often end up working on products that the founders hadn't even imagined when the company was started. When Dave Packard and Bill Hewlett were tinkering in their first garage, they worked on all sorts of one-off projects, including a bowling alley foot fault indicator. I doubt that Steve Jobs had the iPhone in mind when he and Steve Wozniak were soldering the first clunky Apple motherboard in their garage. This would also be the case for the struggling, nearly bankrupt company the noted San Francisco investment banker Sandy Robertson asked me to check out in the summer of 1975: Applied Materials Inc.

Sandy's introduction set in motion opportunities that not only changed the prospects for the company, they changed the course of my life, and I don't think it's exaggerating to say that they played a role in changing the world forever. Applied Materials would eventually propel a worldwide revolution that continues today; components of every single one of more than one billion semiconductor chip-based electronic devices sold annually continue to be touched by our tools. We also would pioneer a way to do business in Japan that became a model of global business practices. We delivered solid returns compounding at 29 percent from 1976 to 2003 for our shareholders and we became famous for providing our customers with very good service. It was exciting and challenging and often fun, but it was never easy. We had to be fast on our feet and constantly adapting and changing. More than three decades later, I have to agree with my friend the analyst and author Dan Hutcheson who calls running a high-tech company the "extreme sport of business."

There are several reasons why tech companies must so often shift their emphasis or reinvent themselves entirely. One is a phenomenon that has been in the news quite a bit recently because 2015 was the 50th anniversary of what is called "Moore's Law." Moore's Law is not a proven scientific principle; it began as an observation about the past that became a prediction about the future. In 1965, my friend Gordon Moore was director of R&D at Fairchild Semiconductor when *Electronics* magazine published his prediction that the number of components on a single silicon chip would double every year from about 60 at the time, to 65,000 by 1975. Gordon was not a futurist banging the table trying to get attention; he was a low-key, analytical technologist basing his forecast on data, always humble about whether the prediction would hold up.

It did. It held true for that decade, and then came the amazing update: In 1975, he predicted the doubling would continue every two years. Since then, the pace has continued roughly every 24 months.

Three years after this famous initial prediction and the year I moved to Silicon Valley, Gordon co-founded Intel, a company whose intense focus on innovation and boosting chip performance helped drive Moore's Law. Nobody actually called it Moore's Law until the mid-1970s, when it took on a larger connotation. Subsequently, the power of innovation it predicted has been called "the heartbeat of the modern world" and "creative destruction on steroids," as Michael Malone wrote in *The Wall Street Journal*. In fact, one analysis of the consequences of Moore's Law is that today the price-per-transistor is nearly 2 billion times lower than it was in 1960. It has ushered in a world of social media and instantaneous search; of powerful and affordable smart watches and home climate systems; of hundreds of millions of tiny sensors measuring everything from the water content of snow packs to the movement of endangered species in remote locations; of 3-D printing capability. Naturally, this pace of innovation has opened up opportunities once reserved for science fiction.

That pace of change is hard on companies. When you sell instruments or tools or devices, at some point, you have to stop adapting and upgrading. Ultimately, you must actually finish and ship a product.

In a fast-growing sector every new innovation hits the market with a target on its own back. The attributes you use to sell it become the performance measure your competitor will focus on beating. What you produce today will almost certainly become obsolete; if not tomorrow, then next year, or in five years. And so you not only have to invest in making and shipping a quality product. To survive, you have to invest in making your own product obsolete. If you don't, your competitor will.

This level of intensity is not for everybody, but I think most successful technology company leaders enjoy that challenge. As you'll read later, my team came up with a model for innovation in our industry that involved continually improving products (or *kaizen,* as the Japanese called it) while at the same time investing in developing "leapfrog" products that would make obsolete our own and others' entire categories. The risk is high and so are the rewards. But the most rewarding aspect of it all is building something that makes the world work better and that empowers more people to do more useful and interesting things.

Applied Materials became a successful, innovative company we were incredibly proud of and that blazed some new trails. Dan Hutcheson reminded me recently that Applied was one of the first high-tech companies to use the word "solution" in marketing, and later we rolled out the "Total Solutions" program. At the time, hardware companies sold products, and it was up to customers to figure out how to use them. It was revolutionary for us to frame our products as a solution to customer problems and needs. We had to not only understand what we were doing, but what our customers were trying to do, and that changed the way we thought about innovation and product development. Meanwhile, we adopted as our vision statement the slogan "Information for Everyone" to convey that our products fit into a larger system made up of the many applications in computers, phones, satellites, and medical products. At first some of our customers and their customers bristled that we were invading their marketing turf, but over time they realized that by using a systems lens on solving customer needs, we served them better.

In this section, I'll point out the management and leadership techniques and themes that we used that were most important to our success. Needless to say, there is a lot more to innovation than locking researchers up in a room, giving them a budget, and waiting for them to do their thing. Perhaps not so obvious is that tried and true, basic values of leadership and management that I learned in simpler arenas turned out to be key to our success in this one as well.

CHAPTER 9

Luck is when preparation meets opportunity

In retrospect, my next move was a lucky one, although I tend to agree with the statement that "Luck is when preparation meets opportunity." By 1975, I had experience working in organizations ranging from a vegetable cannery to the U.S. Army to an aerospace innovator. During my time at WestVen, our firm had invested in a variety of technology deals, but we also invested in start-ups outside of tech, such as the steel service business. We'd looked beyond Northern California for deals, including one of our fund's home runs, Federal Express, which started in 1971 in Little Rock, Arkansas. I'd worked for excellent managers in government and at Textron, but I'd also rolled up my sleeves in turnaround efforts where existing management had hit the limits of its capacity. Unlike many engineers, I had a first-hand appreciation for the value of not only technical success but also both financial and process management. I'd seen some up and down economies and experienced a couple of recessions — including one that was just starting to abate.

There was a feeling around this time in Northern California that technology companies as a group were poised to take off. Today, Wall Street and others often refer to "tech companies," but in the early years they were identified by the sectors the companies supplied: defense contractors, aerospace companies, and medical or scientific instrument makers. The list of pioneers included Lockheed Aviation (it began in San Francisco in 1912), my first local employer Dalmo Victor, Hewlett-Packard, Ampex, Varian, and Litton Industries. Watkins-Johnson launched in Palo Alto in 1957, as did Fairchild Semiconductor. Over the span of those decades, the U.S. military had expanded to fight World

War II, the Korean War, and our involvement in Vietnam as it ramped up throughout the 1960s and early 1970s. The new weapons, transportation, and logistics demands of modern warfare created significant demand for the electronic instruments and aviation control systems these companies were inventing and producing. There was a mutually beneficial environment that developed between these companies and Stanford University and UC-Berkeley's engineering and computer science schools. There were service professionals in finance, law, recruiting, real estate, and other supporting roles for technology companies that steadily gained experience, all in a fairly compact geographic area. These factors created a fertile ecosystem that spawned more and more spin-offs. As technology emerged from the military to be used in civilian and industrial uses, instrument markets began to grow.

Many of the early companies had created important new technologies, but they tended to be self-contained — an instrument in a metal box with buttons and dials. They built most of their own components. In some cases they created a capability that had never existed before, then they had to go out and find an application for it. Hewlett-Packard gave its engineers lots of freedom to be creative and come up with new ideas, and eventually this posture became known inside the company as the "next bench" syndrome. An engineer would hear about another engineer's project stalling or become focused on fixing some limiting problem of his or her own. Employees, alone or in teams, would invent an instrument to solve their own problems, and then HP would end up selling that instrument to other companies. It was an era of great creativity, not unlike today's explosion in software and "app" creativity, but it was in hardware and devices.

By the mid-1970s, I knew I did not want to make venture capital my life's work. I wanted to return to operations. The good news was that this occurred just as a second and an even more vigorous wave of innovation in electronics was emerging. Gordon Moore's prediction for semiconductor capacity had been proven true and semiconductor chips were appearing in many different kinds of instruments and systems. I realized my business experience combined with my engineering training gave me a unique set of skills to run an electronics technology business.

Unfortunately, the previous few years had been chaotic on the larger scene in the U.S. and the economy was unstable. It was mostly events outside of Northern California that consumed conversation and newspaper headlines. The Vietnam War and the Civil Rights movement had been divisive and at times violent. There were widespread student protests, including at Stanford and UC-Berkeley. Martin Luther King Jr. and Robert Kennedy were assassinated. Nixon was elected, but then fatally scarred by Watergate and he resigned and Vice President Gerald Ford became President. By the end of Vietnam, the Department of Defense was scaling back from its war spending, and that was impacting the defense and electronics companies. Oil prices shot up in 1973, inflation was very high, and interest rates were in double digits. As I mentioned earlier, most electronics companies were struggling in the early 1970s, and in the fall of 1975, you could have bought the entire Silicon Valley high-tech industry except for HP and Varian, for under $600 million.

The business climate was mixed. Some companies were emerging from the hard times, others were still struggling. There were a number of opportunities for me to join companies, but most were outside Northern California and Becky and I just did not want to move again. I kept looking.

Big machines that make little chips

Back to that fateful meeting: It was the summer of 1975 when Sandy Robertson asked me to meet with the CEO of a struggling company called Applied Materials. The CEO's name was Mike McNeilly, and he was a former basketball player at Gonzaga and a charismatic, sales-oriented executive. Mike was trained as a chemist and armed with $55,000 in start-up capital. In 1967, he had brought some engineers together in a small industrial unit garage on Middlefield Road in Mountain View. What was then called Applied Materials Technology Inc., later changed to Applied Materials Inc., made products to enable technical processes that were of use to (and frankly only understood by) a relatively small number of semiconductor companies.

To appreciate what Applied was doing, first you have to understand some basics about semiconductor chips, one of the 20th century's most significant technologies. It is challenging to explain semiconductors in simple terms; the details involve materials science, physics, chemistry, optics, software, and circuit design. To complicate it all further, there have been improvements and changes in semiconductor design and new technologies to build them over the years that are as much or more complicated to explain than the original innovations. What is indisputable, however, is that semiconductors have fundamentally changed how we live, work, learn, travel, communicate, and play.

(For those who are interested, in the Appendix I've put together a basic summary of semiconductor technology and how chips are fabricated. In the meantime, I think you can appreciate the basic business of Applied Materials if you understand that Applied made "the big machines that make the little chips," that are used in devices like computers, phones, and cameras to process information quickly and at nanoscale. Unlike companies such as Intel or Texas Instruments, which are "semiconductor companies" that actually design the circuits and figure out how the semiconductor chips will function, semiconductor *equipment* companies such as Applied Materials focus on large automated machines with wafer-processing chambers that reliably produce huge numbers of chips efficiently. One way to think of it is the food business: Applied Materials and other semiconductor equipment companies are like the companies that make the ovens and grills, while semiconductor companies such as Intel are like companies that develop the recipes and cook and sell actual food.)

The fundamental reason why semiconductors are a huge advance over previous technology is that they have so dramatically increased processing power of computers, which allows electronics companies to reduce the size of their products. (Before chips, there were just transistors, and before that tubes. All the integration was done on boards.) By the time I joined Applied Materials, the industry was packing thousands of transistors on a chip the size of your fingernail.

Applied Materials Technology Inc. got its name because its original intention was to supply chemical gases, particularly silane gas, to semiconductor manufacturers. Silane was one of the gases that when "applied" created a useful film on the chip surface. The company saw this as following the Gillette model of building as good or better a business selling disposable razor blades as the razors. Mike McNeilly originally thought he could build a business selling consumable ingredients for making chips.

However, the industry was still small and sales were slow. Before long, Mike could see that the gas business alone wasn't going to support the company, so he started adding other product lines, too. What's more, he needed to raise more money and Applied's investment bankers felt that the markets would be much more receptive to a diversified company than one dependent on one or two technologies. Mike had attracted some very skilled people to Applied, including a Merck scientist named Walt Benzing, who brought with him a patented process called epitaxy, or the depositing of a crystalline layer over another crystalline substrate. Mike diversified into other businesses and instruments for the semi-conductor industry and other industries.

Unfortunately, Mike didn't have a solid strategy. The chip companies were coming up with new designs and the equipment companies were scrambling to accommodate these innovations with equipment and tools that could manufacture them. Early in any new technology company's development, it's not unusual for companies to get in this same pre-dicament Mike was in. Competing approaches are battling for customer attention and investment; smaller companies are trying to differentiate what they offer to seem more attractive.

As early as 1968, an Applied Materials executive named Herb Henderson described Applied's product philosophy as "Anything we could get an order for." That's a red flag. When a small company's major asset is engineering talent, you have to focus your people and limited financial resources on a core strategy. Generally, you can either stake out a major technology area and lead by innovation (like Apple did in the personal computer business), or else produce and keep developing a product or service that is so vital to fast-growing customers that you grow right along with them (like Network Appliance or other data storage companies). Once you've chosen your path, you have to consider what General Electric's long-time CEO Jack Welch used to say, which is if you can't realistically hope to be number one or two in an industry segment — or for a more local business, in your region — you should reconsider being in that business. Below that level is a difficult place to sit strategically, and I call companies who end up there "the living dead."

Applied had had some successes and managed to become profitable in 1972, when Robertson, Coleman, Stephens & Weisel, one of the early West Coast investment banking houses, was able to take Applied Materials Technology public. Technology did not have a good reputation on Wall Street at that time. Sandy advised dropping technology from the name, which they did, although my first years at Applied, customers and others in the industry continued referring to "AMT" as the company's shorthand name. Sales grew to $29 million by 1974, but by the time I met Mike, some poor acquisitions and challenging product efforts were dragging the company into the land of the dead. The semiconductor industry went into a slump in the mid-1970s. Revenues were nearly halved to $16 million, and Applied Materials accumulated about $9 million in debt.

I was not an expert in semiconductor technology, however I could see its potential. WestVen had not invested in Applied Materials, but we had invested in a company called Four-Phase Systems, which was launched in 1969 by a former Fairchild executive. Four-Phase was one of the first companies to actually assemble a computer from what were called MOS semiconductors. I was WestVen's representative to the board at Four-Phase, and it was obvious that semiconductor chips had the potential to drive huge markets for all kinds of instruments and equipment.

As the market for chips expanded, clearly the market for the sophisticated equipment and supplies required to build chips would expand as well. Unfortunately, it was pretty clear to me (and to its investors) that Applied had hit a familiar hurdle for start-ups. There needed to be a management change.

Technical people and marketing visionaries are critical to a start-up. Mike McNeilly was a dynamic and smart marketing visionary. He led the company for about ten years and established a small but solid product base in Chemical Vapor Deposition (CVD) reactors including the difficult epitaxial processes. He had tried to improve the business methods and had hired a Motorola executive named Ted Benedict.

Unfortunately, Ted died, and Mike was originally looking for me to replace Ted as a number two.

As I studied Applied in 1975, the problems were strategic as well as operational. Mike's board included three people closely associated with Wall Street, and the belief in the financial community was semiconductor equipment was too cyclical to build an entire company around. They urged Mike to diversify outside semiconductors, but that was a bad strategy. When you read that Applied sold "anything we could get an order for," on one hand it shows they were motivated, working very hard to try to make it. However, a strategy of selling "anything" means you're probably not going to sell *enough of* anything to be successful.

One of Applied's biggest mistakes had been buying a company called Galamar, which made the basic wafers on which chips were created. By the time I met Mike, Galamar loomed like a black hole on Applied's balance sheet. Galamar was competing with some huge chemical companies. As a small player, Galamar did not have the leverage to get the best price on raw materials. Unlike the adage of my friend from the steel service business, "bought right, half sold," Galamar was an example of "bought wrong, unlikely to profit."

I liked Mike, but I did not think Mike and I would be effective together in this turnaround. In my experience, when a founder and his team have invested in certain acquisitions or strategic decisions that aren't working, it is very difficult for them to unwind all the thinking that went into the purchases. The situation at Applied was growing more serious by the month, however. Within the year, Mike called me back and said he would be willing to move to the chairman's role if I would come in as president and chief operating officer.

This seemed more interesting to me. I talked about the opportunity with some friends and colleagues. Looking back, I have to admit I can't remember anybody who thought my joining Applied was a good idea. One of the daunting things about the business was semiconductor companies battled dramatic business cycles; fall-offs in demand for new equipment would stop chip orders dead. Sometimes that occurred because of larger economic pressures on corporate spending on new equipment; or, semiconductor companies would make big bets on a new product introduction that might miss the target or flop entirely.

To use the food business analogy again, Applied's business was like a restaurant equipment maker linked to larger cycles and fads in the food business. All restaurants need basic ovens and grills, but new restaurants might order specialty equipment to roast lots of chickens or an oven that allows a team to churn out thousands of cupcakes a day. Equipment companies make bets on the tools restaurants say they will need. Sometimes they guess right on the relevant driving forces (high-volume soda dispensers), sometimes wrong (given today's healthy eating trends, do you risk investing in developing more efficient deep-fryers?).

We could all see that innovation was going to be driving semiconductors for the foreseeable future. But the risk when you're trying to design equipment for people operating at the edge of what's possible is that by the time you're finished creating a new piece of equipment, somebody else may have invented a different process that will make your product obsolete. Or, your customer's competitors may have come out with a better product, hurting the customer's sales and resulting in lower orders from your customer for new equipment. Or "what's possible" may be far from universally accepted. At the time I was considering joining Applied, several industry experts were predicting that Moore's Law would end in the early 1980s (it didn't). The upshot was: My friends couldn't imagine why I would join a nearly-bankrupt semiconductor equipment company in a cyclical industry.

It just goes to show that you can have a lot of technical expertise and business success, but still miss an opportunity. My friend, the late Bob Noyce at Intel, for example, did not think there was going to be much demand for the personal computers Steve Jobs and Steve Wozniak were inventing at Apple. Mini-computers were the current thing, and few business people saw a need or use for personal computers in the home, or even on every corporate desk. So-called "terminals" for central computing systems should be perfectly adequate, he thought. So he never invested. (His wife Ann Bowers, on the other hand, did.)

'Now that we are partners...'

I wish I could say that I immediately saw value and opportunity at Applied and knew this was the job I would have for the rest of my career. The truth is, my ambitions were short-term and, I think, realistic. I thought the company had deep strategic and financial problems, but it seemed to have good technology and some good technical people. I wasn't afraid of running a cyclical business, and I figured if I could get the company out of its imminent financial troubles and get it turned around and profitable, I could sell it and then move on to running something else.

I agreed to join Applied, and I arrived in October of 1976. I knew it was a turnaround, but I admit I came home my first day of work and told Becky, "Things are worse than I thought." Existing management wasn't trying to hide or cover up their financial troubles; Mike just did not have a strong financial team, and he honestly didn't realize how bad the situation was. The most immediate problem was the company was steadily losing money and was on thin ice with creditors. We had a $3.5 million credit line with Bank of America that had grown to $4.5 million; we also had a long-term loan with the College Retirement Equities Fund (CREF) for teachers, and accounts payable, so our debt totaled about $9 million. If BofA called in the revolving credit note, that act could violate covenants in the loan.

Fortunately, I had been in enough intense financial negotiations in my career that I realized that business as usual was not going to reassure the creditors going forward. I had to talk about a turnaround plan that made sense to them as a continuing investment. I invited our bankers in for an update. I began my presentation by saying, "Now that we are partners . . ." The bankers smiled because they knew what that meant — if they wanted to profit from our relationship, they were going to have to work with me to get Applied back on track.

In terms of convincing them to trust me, I saw two positive factors. First, there was a promising line of business inside the company that was profitable, growing, and had good margins. Secondly, we were going to cleave off the money-losers, but because of our losses we had

$5 million in tax loss carry-forwards. That meant we were going to have significant tax breaks to apply to our profits going forward, which would free up some cash to help us pay off debt. After a full review of our short-term strategy, plans, and some commitments of performance, I asked the bankers to raise our line from $3.5 to $5.2 million. I did that because a loan over $5 million had to be approved by the National Loan Committee. I wanted the backing of that more powerful group in case the situation got even worse.

The following week, our contact called to say the bank had approved the increase. He told me later that when the local bankers went to the National Loan Committee meeting prepared to make a detailed presentation the chairman, a seasoned banker, said, "Jim will pay it back. Let's move on to the next item." It turned out the banker had been on the WestVen Investment Committee a few years before, and he knew about my work at Paradyne. CREF was also supportive. We had dodged, or at least deferred, an immediate crisis.

CHAPTER 10

The power of deciding, the challenge of change

The bankers' endorsement bought me confidence from the board and the employees of Applied Materials. But we still had a mountain to climb to get back in the black. That journey began with me having to make some decisions.

At the time Applied had six product divisions and activities. From what I could see, five of them were not viable. Either they had poor margins and were losing money, or they did not support a good strategic direction. However, as I told the bankers, there was one division that seemed to have real promise: The Equipment Division, which provided equipment for semiconductor companies to perform Chemical Vapor Deposition (CVD) including epitaxy, or the deposition of thin films on the surface of a wafer. Epitaxy (or "epi" for short) was essential for what are called "bi-polar" transistors, but it was a very difficult process of coating wafers with a thin layer of single crystal silicon. I had learned that nobody else was providing this step as effectively as us, and it was protected by patents that Applied had acquired when Mike recruited Walt Benzing. I also saw that our customers were invested in this process and wanted to make the relationship work.

The Equipment Division's profits and potential had been obscured by all the bad businesses Applied had. The company was too small and too capital-constrained to have six strategically-unrelated businesses with only one making money. All our resources, including the CEO's attention, were diluted as each division was struggling with unrelated challenges. On less than perfect information and a few intense weeks of briefing, I decided we would sell or close five of the six businesses and focus on semiconductor equipment, particularly the epitaxy business and general CVD.

I suppose this may have been the most significant business decision I ever made, but I have never focused on the decision as being the critical factor. Strategically, I bet on epitaxy and CVD because I could see it aligned to Moore's Law, which was a driving force that was highly motivating to the industry. CVD was something customers believed would be critical to their success for the foreseeable future.

As usual, *making* the decision to adopt this strategy was far easier than making the strategy work. A decision accomplishes nothing except creating momentum in a particular direction. Deciding to get married, for example, does not create a long and happy marriage — it just sets the possibility in motion. What decisions do is break gridlock; they focus employee energy and build momentum *to do the work*.

From a management point of view, however, eliminating five of six divisions involved a dramatic overhaul. The previous management had put those other pieces together and I was going to have to rip them apart. People were going to have to trust my vision but then accept responsibility for making decisions about how to use their time and resources to make that vision a reality. Among the dilemmas we faced: How do you cut your losses and move forward without scaring off the best people on the teams in the division you want to keep? How do you motivate employees who are worried about the company's future?

Even amid disruption, stress goals and values

To restore confidence and create momentum, one of the first things we had to do at Applied was to improve communication. One step to doing that was to get employees physically together. As the company had grown and added divisions and activities, it had spread out over several buildings. The top executives had their own headquarters building miles away from the labs and manufacturing groups. Ironically, that building was on Page Mill Road only about five minutes from my house, but that was the first outlying office we closed. Locating top-level managers together is convenient for them, but it becomes a daunting prospect for reports to come see their bosses, especially with bad news.

Occasionally you hear management experts remind executives that "It's a much longer walk from their office to yours, than from your office to them." I got rid of the corporate headquarters and tried to make sure my executives were stationed in various buildings near the teams they were managing, not on an "Executives' Row."

Also in the category of communication, to successfully lead an organization through dramatic change, you must paint a vision of who you are and what you expect. When I first arrived at Applied Materials I could see that there was sloppiness in some parts of the company: There was clutter and peeling paint — employees were smoking on the production floor. Some were dressed in a less-than-professional way. Even though I am more comfortable in hiking shorts and boots, I wore a suit and tie every day. I had the place painted and cleaned up. I started right away having all-hands stand-up meetings on our loading dock at Building 1, so people could hear the top-level thinking directly from me. Stand-up meetings are very effective at cutting to the chase. People can't hunker down in their seat or their positions, and it's not conducive to long, windy speeches.

Next, we needed to articulate a simple, easy-to-understand mission statement to our employees to give them direction and hope. I created flip charts and walked them through my thinking, stressing two sets of companywide goals. My first chart read: "Run a well-managed, low-cost business; lead from strength; concentrate our resources; have timely reporting." The second chart reinforced a goal I must have repeated 10,000 times in my years at Applied: We must be "on time, within budget, demonstrating technical excellence, including quality."

The employees' energy and commitment were vital. As we moved forward, I stressed the importance of acknowledging these goals in everything we did. Over time, we became the opposite of sloppy. We developed a common attitude of "leave nothing to chance." If it's worth doing, it's worth double-checking and imagining variables that could get in the way early, before they hurt you. I would always try to lead by example; I would double-check the slides in my presentations myself, for example, to prevent mix-ups. It became very rare that anyone I worked with made careless mistakes. We all took responsibility for doing what our board member George Farnsworth would later call "the whole job."

MORGANISM

> **Remember that human beings tend to respond to significant change in predictable ways. It's similar to a grief process. At first they deny reality ("Oh, we've heard big talk before — this probably won't happen") and then they move through shock and anger, confusion and stress. Finally, they realize change has to come, but they are uncomfortable letting go of the past. Organizational consultant William Bridges has a model of change (see Appendix) that I use, suggesting that a good leader can anticipate these stages and, by painting a path that acknowledges the stress but provides optimism and confidence, inspire employees to attack the new reality with enthusiasm.**

As at Paradyne, I didn't feel the need to "clean house." I believe companies more often struggle because of poor battle plans and insufficient leadership, not because the soldiers are weak. As a turnaround executive, I believe that if you don't see enough good people to keep in a turnaround opportunity, move on to the next opportunity. Repopulating a company with new people with no sense of the company's history and capabilities takes too much time and wastes a lot of knowledge gathered at great cost. I saw a lot of technical talent in Applied, and I saw executives in many functions who were ready, willing, and able to work hard to make the company successful. That doesn't mean you give everybody a free pass; for those functions where you need to upgrade talent, you have to be direct and make your changes quickly so people aren't drifting around in a limbo state.

Salting in talent

As you become more familiar with an organization, you get a better sense of what needs shoring up. At Applied there was one glaring gap: We were desperately in need of tighter financial controls. That situation had to be fixed fast. I let the controller go and recruited an experienced Stanford MBA-trained controller, Steve Pursell, as my first CFO. Over the years he and other excellent financial executives were crucial to our ability to handle business cycles. It was always very important to me that our CFOs, like the long-serving Jerry Taylor, had worked as controllers with a close understanding and connection to the business' expenses and cash flow. Especially in venture-backed businesses, there often is pressure from the VCs to get to market quickly so you can go public. Wall Street-oriented CFOs can get so focused on managing growth expectations and stock price that they fail to safeguard the shareholders' cash. I have a saying that most start-ups meet their spending targets, but few meet their revenue targets. It is then that entrepreneurs learn that sometimes VCs have deep pockets and short arms or banks have plenty of money only when you do not need it.

With the strategy determined and a key role filled, we moved on. Over time we salted in good people to fill other gaps in our talent pool. At stand-up meetings and in porpoising with small teams, I had to communicate to employees that we knew what we were doing, we had a plan, and I had confidence in them to deliver on the plan. Sometimes people roll their eyes at mission statements and strategic rollout events with slogans and banners. It's possible to overdo it, but it's also important to reinforce and repeat fundamental corporate values, such as treating shareholder cash like your own, or the importance of communication between teams. Many unproductive attitudes can infect a company that does not pay close attention to its culture and values. You can get brilliant inventors who resist schedules and delivery deadlines, insisting they'll release the product "only when it's ready," or production engineers who make their budget by cutting corners needed for quality.

Over time, we made a point of challenging our employees to connect their daily activities to basic values and goals. If they encountered a conflict they could not resolve, they were encouraged and expected to communicate it to a manager who could make a decision. If an obstacle appeared that might delay a shipment or service to a customer, we wanted to be early in warning that customer. We eventually made it part of a concept we called getting the "dailies," or the routine elements of the business, right every time so they didn't create crises. We stated directly to our employees: "In making commitments, engage seriously and be certain you have an in-depth understanding of the expected results. Collaborate with your customer to define success. If other priorities impact your ability to meet all or part of your commitment, communicate early to your customer."

These values depend on the attitude of the people modeling them. At the senior level, managers must make it clear that if an employee sees something interfering with his or her ability to deliver on any element of this mission, they wanted to hear about it, and sooner rather than later. This has to become part of the general culture or the penalty to admit you are stuck can be too high. One critical element is to listen to problems or challenges someone is bringing you in an objective way. Don't make your response personal, and don't attack the motivation of the people involved. Assess the problem and figure out if the existing system failed and needs to be changed, or whether people failed the system; and then figure out why. Is the wrong person in the job? Was the system not adequately communicated or reinforced? Whose responsibility is it to solve the problem?

MORGANISM

Insist that the employee closest to a problem, for example, a sales representative who has an unhappy customer, or a warehouse manager with a flawed parts control system, has the personal responsibility to solve the problem. The individual can seek assistance from above, but cannot transfer the responsibility up the chain. If you make a habit of escalating issues to the top, it will discourage employees from making good decisions at the lower levels. I would always ask, "Who owns the monkey?"

Organizations need discipline and as you begin to instill it, the process itself reveals areas where you can create efficiencies or business advantages. One dramatic example of this occurred not long after my arrival at Applied. I was porpoising at our service facility in East Fishkill, New York, where the team supported a very important customer: IBM.

Thanks to my canning days, I always felt I had a good connection to our service teams and empathy for their challenging, critical role. I learned from the team that an Applied Materials epi reactor installed at an IBM semiconductor plant was offline because it needed a part. The team was frustrated that the Applied headquarters had not been responsive. There was a shortage of that part, and the company had prioritized new equipment assemblies over repairs to installed equipment.

I directed that a part from a new reactor scheduled to ship that month instead be sent to IBM so IBM could get its epitaxy reactor back online. Due to the timing, this decision meant that we would not be able to book the revenues from the new reactor in the current quarter. This sent a dramatic message throughout the organization that our existing customers' needs came first.

Making IBM happy was the first important consequence. But the decision also helped us reconsider our entire warehouse management process. It turned out our component inventories had not been carefully managed. If there was a problem on the assembly line, employees would go grab components from the warehouse without reporting or logging what they were doing. Sometimes we were not aware we were running low until our own line shut down, or a situation developed like the one at IBM. The information and then re-ordering gap created delays for existing customers that directly hurt their bottom lines. After the incident with IBM, we made a decision that we needed an accurate spare parts inventory management process. We also landed on a new policy that if the warehouse inventory ran low, service teams in general had priority for parts in order to get our existing customers back on line as soon as possible.

Customers appreciated that dedication, but more importantly, everybody inside Applied got the message and shaped up. When I went to East Fishkill, the team was unhappy it couldn't solve IBM's problem, but nobody had the authority to make the decision to do that at the expense of a new system scheduled to ship. My decision set a tone that allowed many other decisions like it to be made deeper in the organization without me being involved at all. This is the value of hierarchy and decentralized decision-making. You set the priorities at the top, then push the individual implementation deep into the organization where it becomes a competitive advantage.

The character of your organization will never exceed your own. Job one is to model the behavior and attitudes you expect.

As time went on, we didn't need to make difficult choices between existing and new customers. Our inventory management became more professional; we kept a closer eye on how and where parts are stored and when they should be reordered. Manufacturing managers with a large run looming checked in sooner to make sure there were plenty of parts. Everyone became more attuned to what could happen if the process broke down, including sales reps anxious to get the new machines to their customers. There is nothing glamorous or fancy about these processes — just like there was nothing fancy about Mike Travaglio always coming through for us at the cannery. What's key here is that the priority issue is the customer's success — not the convenience of the manufacturing manager or the warehouse supervisor. Over time, we built a reputation for service and responsiveness to customer issues that created extraordinary loyalty and helped us win orders time and time again.

There were other stories like this one, where setting priorities speeded up decisions and accelerated our momentum. Within a year, Applied started firing more consistently on key cylinders. We had transitioned to becoming more predictable. When I asked for a recommendation, I got one, rather than feedback pointing out all the reasons why the decision was hard to make. Toward the end of 1978, I looked beyond our own company and industry and realized there were great opportunities waiting for us if we could extend our horizon to global markets, specifically Japan.

We now had the breathing space to have a strategic discussion as to what our long-term mission should be. We decided that our goal was to be the "Leading Semiconductor Equipment and Services Company Worldwide." That was a very ambitious statement, but when I looked around, I felt we could achieve that. It was true we were competing against some very large companies, but they were not focused exclusively on semiconductor equipment. I didn't see anyone else who had the right to be the clear leader; nobody had a lock on this segment.

CHAPTER 11

Products and the 'Flying Wedge'

One of the early strategic concepts we developed at Applied was the "flying wedge." What that meant was that we were going to use our existing successful products (at the time those in epi and CVD), to drive our relationships. We were going to make ourselves a top provider of service for those products as a competitive advantage, and then we were going to use our increasingly close relationship to our customers to give us insights to what other products they needed and wanted. Using the restaurant analogy, we were going to use high quality industrial ovens as our entry point with customers, then make sure we provided the best service of any oven company, and then use the good relationship we developed by providing that service to talk with our customers, understand their plans for new food ideas, and then figure out how to expand our product offerings and develop our relationship based on what we learned.

We were addressing only the deposition steps involved in making a chip. Another important element of creating a chip is to create patterns by selectively taking material OFF the surface. There were several ways to do this, and they fell into the category called "etching," or using a process that could selectively remove parts of a chemical layer to create channels and circuits.

It was no secret that etching looked to be the next important semiconductor equipment category, and by 1979, it was clear that our customers wanted this capability. It also was clear that we would have many competitors in trying to provide this tool. This was a different technology challenge from CVD and epitaxy. Getting into etch would require a total focus by an outstanding team. There were more than 25 companies with some type of etch effort. We decided to set up a development group in an independent building.

To be successful, we would need an effective implementation strategy. We would need a few game-breakers and we specifically would need key people with experience with etch processing and equipment. We needed to physically set a development team apart, creating what is often referred to as a "skunkworks." The term originated during World War II when Lockheed Advanced Development Group wanted to speed up work on a project to design and build a new jet fighter. Lockheed isolated a group of researchers in a circus tent that was set up near a Southern California plastics factory that periodically released foul-smelling odors. It reminded the workers of a bad-smelling "Skonk Works" factory in the Li'l Abner comic strip, so they started calling it the Skunk Works. Over time, the term came to refer to any secret or semi-secret project where employees are hand-picked and isolated, and usually they are relieved of other general or administrative duties and told to only focus on that project. It's a balancing act; if you have too many secret projects you can create paranoia and resentment, but when you have to get something technical done quickly, it is a very useful tool.

We knew what we wanted, but the team was having trouble delivering it. After more than a year of work, we were progressing but we did not have what we called a leapfrog solution; in other words, a technology that would jump ahead of the competition. Then, I got a cold call from someone at Bell Labs. I have a rule that I return calls the same day unless they are an obvious personal sales call. The person I called back said that a friend of mine from the venture business named Frank Bonsel had told a Bell Labs scientist he worked with named Dr. Dan Maydan that if he wanted to go into the semiconductor equipment business he should call me. Dan was educated at the Technion in Israel and then the University of Edinburgh. He had begun his career at the Israel Atomic Energy Commission, but for about a dozen years he had managed several new technology developments at Bell Labs. He had made significant contributions to developing the laser recording of data on thin-metal films, as well as doing research in photolithography and plasma etch — exactly what we were trying to develop into useful equipment.

As a result of that call I arranged for Bob Graham, our vice president of marketing who was on the East Coast visiting IBM, to meet Dan Maydan on a Saturday and talk to him. That went well, and I invited Dan out to California. We hit if off very well. He seemed to know how to take our technology to the next level and I immediately had a lot of confidence in him. It was an opportunity to change the dynamics and provide some better process capability to the industry. Dan is a brilliant scientist and good at product development. Over time he became a good executive, and eventually he was President of Applied Materials. Fortunately, Dan and I always agreed on the fundamental values of how our business should be run.

Dan decided that if he joined us, we could build a major company. He brought another key member of his Bell team, David Wang, and we added Sass Somekh from Intel (Sass had previously been at Bell Labs). It turned into a great multi-decade partnership. Strangely enough, the person who had originally called me on Dan's behalf decided that coming to Applied at the time would be too risky. It was very satisfying to me years later when Dan was interviewed for a video the company made to celebrate my 60th birthday. He recounted how in our very first meeting I had talked about the importance of partnerships and that to make them successful, you need to value your partner's success as equal or even more important than your own.

Game-breakers and milestones

Etch became a model for developing products at Applied. If we thought we had a winning concept, we would search inside and outside the company for "game breakers" to lead the efforts. Once satisfied with the process and product concept, we would provide resources to the effort as long as it was meeting its milestones. I had learned from watching many venture-backed companies that too often they would give a development team a budget, and as long as the team wasn't asking for more money, they would leave them alone. It's not helpful to be under budget if you are failing to meet technical or sales targets. I was fortunate that Dan completely bought into the idea that our products had to be commercial successes with an acceptable level of quality, not just technical advances.

We often tore up the original business plans for a product and managed by milestones. This was frustrating for the technical people in the early days, but it soon became a way of life. The team had to keep in mind a timetable for hitting certain technical, cost, and reliability milestones as well as product introduction schedules in order to keep its funding. We made sure to have a strong balance sheet with cash to fund product development even in the depths of a downturn. Dan and his teams developed product after product as we filled out our flying wedge.

A "flying wedge" approach is a useful tool in many business settings. When you provide good service, you become close to customers who will be willing to share their plans and desires, helping you anticipate their future needs. This is vital in high technology, but it works in many industries.

Leading Semiconductor Equipment and Services Company Worldwide

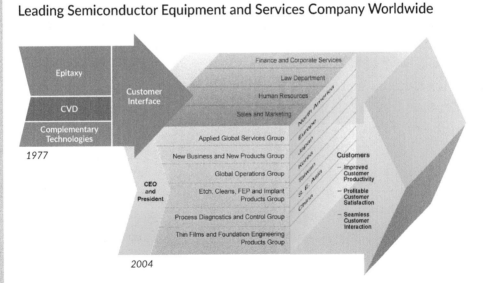

This diagram explains the "flying wedge" strategy we described in 1977 to become the world's leader (even though when we set the goal we had only one viable product and were emerging from near bankruptcy). By 2004, we used the same basic strategy to keep our leadership position despite a dramatic expansion of product lines, organizations, and global markets.

It took us less than two years before we introduced our first etch product, the 8100. Unlike the products most of the competition had developed, ours was a batch system instead of a single wafer system. We felt it gave the best process performance, and that proved to be true for a number of years.

When I first arrived at Applied Materials I had to get the company stable financially, get our basic business functioning, and take care of customers. The point of the wedge had to be excellent service on our existing products, but once the basic business was stable again, I felt it was critical to get new products as fast as I could. The field was wide open: I could see that whoever got new products out the fastest would be the leader in the industry. The second phase was whoever got the strongest global position the fastest would have long-term success. As you'll read in the next chapter, we succeeded in that goal as well.

In the early '80s there were some major companies like Perkin-Elmer, Varian, and Eaton who thought they were going to take over the equipment business as they undertook a series of acquisitions. We worked at it from the inside, building our products so that we had a powerful capability in terms of technology, but then we also succeeded in building global capacity. A particularly powerful aspect to how we used the flying wedge was that we made sure we understood what a variety of customers needed. Our competitor Perkin-Elmer, for example, aligned with IBM early; while P-E had a deep understanding of what IBM wanted, they did not understand other customers. They were in denial about some of the quality issues that we realized customers were concerned about. We also could see that top engineering talent was worth the Valley's pay scales that even in those days outpaced much of the country's. Companies like Eaton were trying to overlay Midwestern human resource policies and pay scales on Silicon Valley companies, and Applied was steadily winning the battle for talent. Together these factors eventually led us to become the leading company.

We built Applied Materials mostly through internal product development, not with mergers and acquisitions. At times we realized we had some gaps in our technology offerings and we did make a few strategic technology acquisitions. As you'll read in the next chapter, we also stumbled on some, such as a British company called Lintott, and a U.S. company in Silicon Valley in the photolithography market called Cobilt. Neither hurt us significantly and the Cobilt deal brought us some unexpected benefits and became a good example of what I call "protecting your downside." Prior to purchase much of the inventory was written down; it had extremely good lease terms on Silicon Valley real estate that we enjoyed for years; it provided space and operational talent quickly for the new etch product production ramp; and it had older equipment installed in China that later helped us develop a service business there that we leveraged. There was a lot of potential strategic upside that inspired us to do the deal; that didn't work out, but the lesson here is how important it is to protect the downside.

I also was very careful in deal negotiations to not get carried away with getting bigger at the expense of maintaining an intense focus on our strategy. This is what had pushed Applied Materials off course to begin with. For example, in the early 1980s I met with Milt Greenberg the CEO of GCA Corp., a company that had a product called a "stepper" that was becoming the preferred technology for printing circuits on wafers. We did not have a play in that area. He and I discussed merging our two companies to be able to offer customers a more comprehensive set of equipment products. Unfortunately Milt liked the idea of hedging risk by staying diversified. He wanted the merger to produce a large company with three unrelated business legs. I felt the rapidly growing semiconductor front-end equipment market was the driving force we needed to focus on and that he should get out of his other businesses. So we agreed to disagree and did not do the deal. Because he had not shored up his balance sheets when the financial markets were supportive of technology companies, Milt got caught later in a squeeze when he needed cash after the markets turned down. Not too much later, GCA went bankrupt and eventually disappeared. In a business that requires large capital investments to remain competitive, cash is king and you must raise it when you can, not wait until you need it.

CHAPTER 12

Going global

When I joined Applied, the company marketed its products through a direct sales force throughout the United States and Europe. Applied had been distributing our products in Europe through a Dutch company called ASM in the early '70s, but Bob Graham, who was head of marketing, set up a direct sales activity base in Munich, Germany to service Siemens, Phillips, IBM and others. Munich came to be one of my favorite cities and two of our most important senior executives, Franz Zanker from IBM, who eventually headed up global sales and marketing for us, and Manfred Kerschbaum from Siemens who subsequently led global service, were from there. Their global leadership and cultural discipline developed a powerful force for us. I remember an analyst telling me one day that he had congratulated a competitor on getting an order. The competitor said to the analyst in a serious voice, "Thanks, but you have never seen Applied fight," adding that his company may have won the first round but he was sure Applied would battle back furiously to regain a long-term position with the customer. Franz and Manfred were serious and competitive, but they had a great sense of humor. One of their favorite events for our customers was the annual Oktoberfest in Munich and sometimes I would join them.

Europe was especially important strategically because it enabled us to have a scale to do battle in Asia, and both U.S. and Japanese companies were expanding in Europe. As part of our commitment strategy to a region we looked for local capability beyond just sales and service. We thought we had found that in a new technology called high-current ion implant, via the purchase of Lintott. Lintott was located in Horsham,

England near Gatwick Airport, and we bought it at a very favorable price for the technology. In retrospect, though, I should have listened to the advice of Ralph Lee, a senior Hewlett-Packard Executive I had recruited to the Applied board. Ralph had had unfortunate experiences with companies in England, where he found it was difficult to get marketable products in a timely manner — essential in technology — and he was against the acquisition. It resulted in Ralph resigning from our board, which was unfortunate. Ralph was right; while buying Lintott expanded our base in Europe and brought us significant new sales, we could not get beyond a poor second in the industry. Years later, we eventually closed the company.

A funny aside to the Lintott deal was that the company had some interesting past experience with large wafer shapes. One day, walking out to the car on a visit to an ITT semiconductor plant in Foots Crey, England, I saw a large round object in the street that also had the name Lintott on it. It turned out Lintott was a foundry in the 1800s making large circular street sewer covers with raised squares like semiconductor chips on the surface. Eventually, the company evolved into government contracting, and the government had funded the advanced high current implant technology. We joked they were the first to see the semiconductor industry was headed toward large wafer sizes in the 1800s.

In Japan, Applied had had a distributor relationship since 1970 with what was called a trading company, Kanematsu Electric, a subsidiary of Kanematsu Gosho. I found out that the company had chosen this route to Japan because the Japanese historically had been reluctant to purchase equipment from non-Japanese companies and suppliers. By contracting with a Japanese trading partner, Applied Materials as a very small company was afforded access to what might have otherwise been a closed market. The trading partner provided the Japanese chip makers with an acceptable interface, while at the same time assisting Applied in navigating the unfamiliar nuances peculiar to the Japanese way of doing business. In six years of distributing through Kanematsu, Applied Materials enjoyed healthy, yet unspectacular growth in Japan. The company's most successful year there brought sales to a modest $3.8 million.

Kanematsu was a general trading company that sold a large catalogue of foreign products in Japan ranging from simpler testers to the most advanced equipment. Because of the complex technologies involved with Applied Materials' systems, I assumed that Kanematsu must have a very technical team of sales people who were specialists in the semiconductor processing field. The technology seemed to me to be too complex to sell without some degree of expertise. However, as I came to learn, this is not necessarily the case with a Japanese trading company. A salesman in the electrical group might represent anything from soldering guns to sophisticated processing systems like Applied's epitaxial reactors. At that point, I judged my best move would be to meet personally with Kanematsu officials to see how we should proceed. This required a trip abroad.

For all the travel and adventures I had enjoyed with the military and with Textron, in 1977 I was 38 years old and I had never traveled outside of North America. In comparison, my youngest grandkids, Lucie and Sophie, have been in over a dozen countries and speak multiple languages. I never had a reason to go for business, and Becky and I never had the time or extra money to travel abroad for pleasure. For some reason, in my mind's eye I thought foreign cities would just be like expanded versions of ethnic neighborhoods in American cities. I had visited San Francisco's Japantown and seen its pagoda-style roofs and sushi restaurants, and that was the extent of my imagination about what I would find in Tokyo.

Taking on the 'two Japans'

By now I had become involved with an organization called SEMI, which at the time stood for the Semiconductor Equipment and Materials Institute. Joe Ross, one of the SEMI board members, contacted me and said as the head of Applied Materials I should join the SEMI board. I had plenty to keep me busy at Applied, but I could see that with so many smaller organizations scrambling to invent new technologies and latch on to standards, I needed to be up to speed with what was going on. What's more, SEMI, which was just six years old, had decided to hold its first-ever trade show in Japan. We equipment makers were in an interesting position. While our U.S. semiconductor company customers would fight intensely with Japanese semiconductor companies, and both countries waged various trade wars, both sides actually were potential customers of equipment makers like us.

This trip was intensely meaningful to me both professionally and personally, and eventually Japan became very important to my family as well. My eyes were opened from the minute I stepped onto Japan Airlines in San Francisco. I flew coach in those days, and yet the service on JAL was exceptional, far exceeding any experience I had had on a U.S. airline. The flight attendants were completely focused on the customer and the customer's comfort; the plane was impeccably clean and every detail of the meal and amenities seemed carefully designed and presented. Later, I found the same focus in restaurants, in hotels, in taxi cabs, train stations, literally everywhere in Japan where there was a service to be delivered.

On the other hand, there was an immediate paradox because from the minute I arrived in Tokyo Haneda International Airport, I also felt like an outsider, even shunted to a passport control area marked "aliens." Passport Control and Customs agents were polite, but not welcoming or friendly. This seemed incongruous, and yet I came to understand and learn to deal with the notion of "two Japans," one that lets you in and can be very accommodating and attentive; but another that is suspicious of foreigners and even resentful. Over and over, the two Japans would collide; I would attempt to walk around and get my bearings, yet there would be no effort at all to make signs or navigation accessible in any way to international visitors; on the other hand, looking confused or frustrated, individual Japanese people would go out of their way to come over and politely ask if they might be of service, and even take quite a bit of time to walk with me to my destination.

The trade show that December was mostly a bust. There were a few undistinguished booths in a very large, cold domed exhibition hall at the Harumi Center on Tokyo Bay. We learned a lot over the years and the shows became increasingly popular and well-attended, but year one was not of much value.

The visit to Kanematsu was even more discouraging. I had gone in with a set of expectations; in retrospect they were typically American in thinking that being straightforward and direct in a short meeting would achieve my goals, which was to improve our sales in Japan. I felt we should be able to get better market share and profits, to the benefit of us both.

On arriving at the trading company's offices, I was taken through the usual ritual of being introduced to each of the key people on our account and being briefed on the status of their activities. I spent most of my time with the head of the equipment sales department Ikuro Yusui, and an aggressive young salesman named Tetsuo Iwasaki. They were polite and cordial, and they outlined some of the problems and opportunities we faced selling products in Japan. At first, it was fine. But once the initial pleasantries were done, they began speaking in Japanese, which of course I could not understand. I tried to bring up some substantive concerns about operations and customers. With some condescension they stiffly explained to me that I was going to have to understand that the Japanese way of doing business was different than the American way, and any progress I was seeking was only going to come slowly. The meeting took five hours and as far as I was concerned, did not advance the ball. There was another Applied Materials executive with me who said as we finally were ushered to the elevator, "We're going to have to get everything in writing." At the time I was so discouraged by the hours of time wasted with no progress I was not sure that it mattered to get *anything* in writing.

The paradoxes of my very first trip ate at me. On the one hand I had seen the meticulous attention to detail and the high standards for service the Japanese valued; on the other, I experienced what seemed like a deliberate fog blown my way that kept me from getting a clear picture of the market, the customers, and the distribution system that was handling our products. I came away with little or no confidence that Kanematsu was the right partner to develop a broad-scale technical systems business like ours. Yet, what choice did we have?

I started talking to as many American business people as I could about doing business in Japan. We also sat down with some of our Japanese customers who visited us in Santa Clara to try to better understand the market and other factors. Basically, all that process did was confirm how ignorant we were and how nobody thought we had a chance to crack the market. The most difficult element of what we faced was that we had no model. There were some companies who had set up operations in Japan such as Texas Instruments, IBM, and General Electric. Virtually all had many billions in worldwide revenues. We were small. We had some cutting-edge technology, but we had little leverage.

Eventually, we would establish our own presence in Japan and we created a new model and inspiration for other high-tech businesses that wanted to enter that market. Becky visited Japan with me a couple of years later and she was as impressed as I was with the country's design sensibility, the subtleties and the beauty of the gardens and the country. My son, Jeff, also found Japan to be an interesting and challenging culture (he has an impressive aptitude for language and learned to speak Japanese; eventually he worked for one of the large trading companies, Mitsu Busaan) and we co-authored a book in 1991 with help from Tom Hayes, an executive at Applied Materials, called *Cracking the Japanese Market: Strategies for Success in the New Global Market.*

There were two driving forces that inspired me to keep pressing on and trying to figure out how to do business in Japan during the late 1970s. The first was simple: we wanted to be a global leader and I could see Japan was going to be an aggressive maker and user of semiconductor chips. Our industry was growing, but there still were a lot of companies competing to become the standard of various processes. With leading market share in Europe and the United States, we could not afford to pass up potential customers with the money and interest in cutting-edge technology.

The second driving force was that I had a sense that the Japanese interest in quality could work to our advantage in becoming their partners. By this period, U.S. manufacturing was widely seen as being pretty mediocre in a lot of industries, such as the automobile industry. Japanese cars were so much better engineered and reliable that they had gained huge market share. Japanese companies would buy non-Japanese equipment only as a last resort, but if we could maintain technological superiority, they would have no choice. The partnerships and more direct involvement we would have would extend the flying wedge — we'd understand their needs better and that would drive future successes in new products as well.

As our cash position improved, I knew we would be investing in top quality products that the Japanese would have to buy. The technology advantage was crucial, and the field was moving so quickly, we stood a good chance of getting out front and staying there if we developed good relationships with our partners. The trading company relationship was never going to deliver any of these benefits; it was too far removed from the actual customer. So we needed a direct operation that was designed in a style the Japanese customers could accept; it needed to be run by Japanese management and convey that it was a long-term commitment.

Striking out on our own

On the other hand, we were back in the black but still small — just $28 million in revenues in 1978. Then, we got a fortuitous break: Applied's Bob Graham and I had developed a good rapport with Tetsuo Iwasaki, whom I had met on my very first visit. He was young and aggressive, and about two years after our first meeting, he informed us that he and half dozen other Kanematsu executives wanted to leave and form their own company, Nippon IC. We decided to form a partnership with that company, and we launched Applied Materials Japan (AMJ) in 1979 with one of Iwasaki's partners as our president, and Iwasaki in charge of sales and service. For the first year, things went great, but then the Nippon partners came into conflict. We ended up backing Iwasaki, and the relationship changed again: In 1981, we decided to make AMJ a wholly owned subsidiary instead of a partnership. It was Japan's first wholly foreign-owned semiconductor equipment company, with Iwasaki as its leader.

He delivered immediately. After the first year, AMJ's revenues rose 100 percent over the previous year. Best of all, AMJ was building direct relationships with customers in Japan; our technology opened the door, but Iwasaki's leadership and understanding of the elements of trust and respect needed in Japan solidified the partnerships.

The most valuable insights we gained from this structure were often the most difficult to address. The Japanese IC industry was far more demanding than our U.S. customers. We had committed to offering excellent service and working with partners, and the Japanese demanded that we make constant improvements in process technology, process repeatability, and equipment reliability in high-volume production. The Japanese called this continuous improvement process *kaizen*. I mentioned above that we also used the term "leapfrog" to emphasize the importance of introducing products that were ahead of our competitors. Over time, we often talked about these ideas in tandem. You need to target your next product as a leapfrog, but you need to continually improve the existing product. If you don't get the timing right, you may invest development time and resources in a product that is not advanced enough beyond your competitors to win market share.

This is the essential tension of competitive technology industries. Some of our people were defensive and resistant to some of these changes at first, but over time we began to appreciate the lengths to which our Japanese partners were willing to go to help us improve these systems. Our U.S. customers were just as demanding, but they were not as helpful or willing to devote resources to working with us. In Japan, we had to prove that we were going to hang in there no matter what, and we did. The benefit turned out to be that what we learned in Japan would help us worldwide.

All in for the long haul

It's worth a quick flashback to the semiconductor industry in the early 1980s. At the time, leading semiconductor makers were U.S. companies including Texas Instruments, Motorola, Intel, and IBM. We were among perhaps 50+ companies working on semiconductor equipment. Both Europe and Japan had their own industries, but the U.S. was feeling pretty confident in its semiconductor leadership. What many didn't appreciate was that Japan was quietly implementing a long-term strategic plan with strong government support to ramp up production of not just semiconductors and semiconductor equipment, but of electronic devices as well.

Even we didn't realize how valuable the flying wedge approach was in dealing with what was happening in Japan. Our equipment was being used to re-engineer and build Japanese semiconductor plants; our epitaxial reactors, CVD, and eventually our etchers were going into the major production lines sprouting up all over Japan. Most of our competitors were still working through trading companies, and that was actually insulating them from appreciating what Japanese companies wanted from the next generation products, while we were working with them and hearing it directly.

A moment of truth came in 1982, when a recession hit the semiconductor industry. American chipmakers stopped buying, which hurt equipment companies who, in turn, bailed out of Japan because they felt they could not afford to keep investing when their domestic market was so battered. However, the Japanese government kept investing and guaranteeing demand, so the Japanese chip market grew 66 percent. We hung in there and our Japanese partners appreciated our loyalty and commitment. As they grew, they continued to buy our equipment and work with us in developing new generations.

These were complex relationships, to be sure. For example, some of our biggest emerging competitors in equipment were financed and spun off from our customer companies, such as Anelva, an etch company that came from NEC. It might seem like a recipe for disaster, but that is not what happened. Ironically, Japan's homegrown industry was limited precisely because it was so insulated from the global market. The Japanese chipmakers wanted and could afford to buy only world-class equipment; we were a company able to provide it because we had strong relationships with the entire global customer community, with all those resources and relationships helping us jump on the very best technology early. What's more, because we were independent, we were not limited to selling into one *keiretsu* or industrial group in Japan. So the flying wedge helped us stay current and connected to all of our customers.

AMJ amounted to 33 percent of Applied Materials' total sales by 1983, and we had begun to receive multiple orders from our Japanese customers as our systems were qualified and welcomed into full production facilities. With this head of steam and with other equipment companies struggling from the lingering effects of the recession, I could see that we had an opportunity to cement our leadership position in Japan. We needed to expand our commitment to doing research and development in Japan and manufacturing equipment there as well. To this point, AMJ was selling and servicing equipment made back in California. To make it easier to build to our customers' requirements, we needed to actually modify systems locally. We needed a significant technology center in Japan itself.

Again, our willingness to adapt to Japanese customs and invest in relationships would pay off. Our local Japanese bank, The Bank of Tokyo, encouraged us to apply for a loan from the quasi-governmental finance organization the Japan Development Bank (JDB), which to that point had never given any money to a wholly non-Japanese firm. The process took months and we were careful to place Japanese nationals in key positions on the new project, and even our global treasurer was fluent in Japanese. We also enlisted the help of the governor of the Narita prefecture, where we hoped to build the plant near Tokyo's Narita airport, to support and recommend us. Our project would bring valuable jobs and revenues to the region.

When months later we got word that we had been selected, it made worldwide headlines. We launched construction of a 65,000 square foot facility with a $3.2 million loan from the JDB. It was completed in 1984, the year AMJ's revenues surged from $34 million to $52 million, and it represented about one-third of total sales. The JDB loan was extremely important to us, as it meant we were accepted as a player. We had, to paraphrase the book Jeff and I later wrote, cracked the Japanese market.

> **To be successful globally, you must work to understand global driving forces and align with micro driving forces. Applied Materials succeeded where others failed by showing respect for local culture, investing in our partners' success, and doing business with an open mind and honest communication.**

MORGANISM

Beyond Japan

The early progress in Japan gave us a model for our expansion into other Asian countries. I visited Korea in the early '80s. My visit took me to Samsung's Research Center and a nearby factory. They had a few epi reactors and were having some problems. We finished our discussions and finalized a plan to fix the issues about 8 p.m. Saturday night. Walking outside the building, I could see extensive construction activity on new manufacturing buildings. Bathed by spotlights, the cranes and bustling workers were a clear sign that not only the "Japanese Are Coming" (which you frequently heard in the U.S.), but the "Koreans Are Coming" as well. The Asian tigers were waking up, and business was not going to get any easier going forward.

That was sobering but also exciting. I enjoyed Asia and I made good friends there. For example, a Korean named Y.W. Lee was head of research and H.K. Kim was head of business at Samsung, and, like most of the executives I met in Asia, they were tough, competent, dedicated, and collaborative customers. We eventually hired a North Korean who had escaped that country as a child and had spent some time in Japan being educated. He had worked for Fairchild Semiconductor and was an excellent leader. His name was Y.I. Lee and he helped us grow our business in South Korea to number one in that market.

Many connections developed that we hadn't anticipated. Applied Materials had a manufacturing site in Austin, Texas, for example, and in the late 1980s, Samsung would build its own site there as well. Samsung had a groundbreaking event including a mini rodeo. The night before, there was a big dinner at the Four Seasons Hotel and I was asked to speak on behalf of the U.S. equipment makers. My turn came after many local officials who were thrilled to have a major employer move into the area, and they heaped praises on H.K. Kim and Y.W. Lee. I looked at my old friends on the dais and said, "Well, I knew them before they were famous." That brought many laughs including from them. So much for the stereotypes that sense of humor doesn't cross borders easily or that Asian partners are difficult to read and hard to work with. If you respect and like people, you generally get that back, no matter where they're from.

During the 1980s, countries and companies in Europe and Asia felt it was important to invest in semiconductor technology. Sarawak, Malaysia, was even building a semiconductor facility. Naturally, Taiwan wanted to develop their technology and manufacturing base. Taiwan was fortunate to have Morris Chang who established a vision for semiconductors there. Morris had been at Texas Instruments for many years but went back to his homeland and eventually started Taiwan Semiconductor Manufacturing Company (TSMC). He was a great visionary and friend. As Dan Hutcheson pointed out, TSMC initially dealt with Japanese trading companies that were heavily marking up equipment; Applied established a global pricing program which forced the trading companies' prices to fall in line. Also, initially TSMC couldn't keep its tools running because it couldn't get parts rapidly due to U.S. export regulations. We set up a parts depot in Taiwan to help solve that problem, and we hired a highly competent Taiwanese woman named Cham Wu to lead the growth of our business in Taiwan. To this day, TSMC is one of Applied's top three customers, and it was another case where Applied set a standard for treating the customer's issues as top priority.

In Singapore, Khim Han Ng built our business on the same model we used in every Asian country, which was to set up a subsidiary and work directly with customers and invest in facilities and projects that demonstrated we were there for the long haul. Singapore later became Applied's operational base due to its competent government, investment in infrastructure, education level, and geographic location.

China was our toughest challenge. The Chinese semiconductor industry was at a much different stage than in the rest of Asia. U.S./ European export rules prevented the sale of advanced equipment. The Cultural Revolution eliminated a decade of engineers that could be trained in the newly emerging electronic world. There were older engineers who'd been trained before semiconductors, or young, inexperienced engineers emerging from school. There was little money to purchase anything. Restrictions on the kind of technology that could be exported meant that we could not even sell most of our products to China; however, they did have some older equipment that created an opening for us to go in with a service organization.

It might seem from all these factors that there was not much opportunity. But once again, alert preparation, contacts, and luck visited Applied, as I will tell you about in more detail in Chapter 14.

We hired R. L. Chen in 1984 who was from Tianjin, China and whose advanced education was from the University of Maryland. He was instrumental in our China success. Through a twist of fate, we also made good friends with the Chinese Vice Minister of Electronics who went on to be Mayor of Shanghai — and then President of China.

Later, Ashok Sinha, then Senior Vice President of Silicon Systems, and I made a trip to Delhi, Hyderabad, and Bangalore, India. We visited the President in Delhi to understand the government policies and two of the high-tech cities. In Bangalore, we dedicated the expansion of Applied's office there. India operations have expanded over time.

By necessity, our board traveled overseas every few years to be sure we understood both the opportunities and risks we were undertaking. The experience turned out to be more valuable than we would have imagined. We of course enjoyed the new learning experiences together, but also, the board was able to support us in taking the risks involved as we pioneered new technology and new markets in the midst of the challenging business cycles.

One Applied board trip was to Israel when we were expanding our Process Diagnostics Division, which was headquartered there. We toured and learned about the history, culture, and business in the region. Also, we celebrated something very unique. The Applied board and team, my family, the Maydan family, and a few other individuals and companies sponsored a statue of Einstein that was a smaller version of the Einstein Centennial Monument by Robert Berks, a renowned sculpture on Constitution Avenue in Washington DC near the Academy of Science. You can see the one we dedicated on our trip today in the Academy of Science and Humanities Garden in Jerusalem just off Einstein Square. As luck would have it, two weeks later Albert Einstein was designated Man of the Century on the cover of *Time* magazine.

CHAPTER 13

Culture, showerheads and the P5000

One late November day in the mid-1980s, I felt like I was watching a perfect display of the culture we had built at Applied Materials in a very unusual spot: a Hawaiian beach. The company was holding a sales and service conference at the Ritz Carlton Hotel on the Big Island of Hawaii. In addition to sales and product teams, we had worldwide business operations and product operation managers. These meetings were a good chance to bring together people who mostly communicated on the phone and (increasingly) by email. It was both a reward for good work and a motivating experience for successful colleagues to come together and get to know each other.

It's common at events like these to have team-building exercises. We hired a local company to manage and run the team-building, and this time, the event was a cardboard boat-building and race. The essence of the exercise was to get teams to take on different elements of a multi-stage project — to build a seaworthy (well for at least a few minutes anyway) boat, walk with it in a viewing parade, and then race it in a short course in the lagoon.

We had over 100 people there, and a local organizer gave each team cardboard, duct tape, plastic sheeting, and other supplies, in addition to a few tips on how to build the boat. It was a mix of engineers, sales, service, and marketing people. There were several different jobs involved for each team. You got points for the build, but also for showing the best in the parade, and then for the athletic feat of paddling the canoe in the race.

Since this was a worldwide meeting, there were men and women employees from all around the world who spoke many languages. But the common languages they spoke were determination and competitiveness. I remember watching the teams work together. We deliberately mixed up people from different countries and with different roles. What struck me was that nobody hung back; nobody was left out. It would have been easy for the engineers to take over, but they all realized other talents were required to chalk up maximum points. They appeared to go at this competition with the same intensity they brought to work.

It was fun, but it also was deeply satisfying to see the Applied Materials culture at work among people in Hawaiian shirts and flip-flops. It was a testament to our character and our culture. The best-looking boat might sink, the best-engineered boat might not have picked the most coordinated paddlers; all kinds of things went right and wrong. I can't remember who won. Years later, mention this race to people involved in it, and you'd get instant recall of either their elation at winning some element of it or frustration that their boat sank or they didn't have a clever enough display for the parade.

One of the organizers said it was one of the most intense competitions he'd ever seen.

The P5000 — 'I think I've got it!'

There were dozens of Applied Materials teams who went above and beyond what seemed possible in pushing to make deadlines and keep us ahead of the competition. We were known throughout the industry for investing in R&D in good times and in bad, for taking advantage of larger pull-backs to come on strong with new products when customers were ready to buy again. This was because of excellent execution across the board. The reason we could invest in R&D when others were cutting back was that we managed our cash so carefully when business was good. It was as much a function of the controller and finance department as the sales and service reps bringing in the revenues.

But there is no question that our technology developers were best of breed. One illustrative story involved a linchpin process at the heart of one of the most important pieces of equipment we ever made: the P5000 single wafer CVD System. This kind of achievement is the antithesis of the "diving catch." It is the result of determined, smart people motivated to work together on a worthwhile goal.

In the early 1980s, semiconductor companies were using what were called "batch" or "batch hot wall" processing systems to deposit semiconductor materials on the surface of wafers. But as chip designers packed more and more transistors on the wafers, and created more complex designs, it demanded new CVD processes to make sure the deposition was absolutely uniform or the chips wouldn't work. To draw a crude analogy, if you're just writing "Happy Birthday" in icing on a cake, you don't need the frosting of the cake to be smooth and uniform to read it. But if you're going to reprint a page of text in icing on the same-sized cake, the surface needs to be absolutely flat, or else even small variations or gaps will make some words unreadable.

We believed that the way to get even deposition on each wafer without ruining an entire batch would be to use a single wafer processing system. Dr. Dan Maydan and his team had confidence we could make this work as a brand new instrument. However, for that to represent a breakthrough, we were going to have to not only attain very even deposition, but also make it happen at a rate ten times faster than the batch systems. Since we were dropping from processing many wafers at a time to one per processing chamber, we knew our customers would not accept a drop in productivity.

In 1985, we set up another skunkworks-style team. There were 26 people on the project including chemical engineers, mechanical engineers, and other specialists in the technology this complicated machine would require. Cissy Leung was a young chemical engineer who had been born and raised in Hong Kong, but then studied engineering at UC-Berkeley. She was responsible for the critical process step: figuring out how to achieve the uniform deposition. The eventual tool would require a number of other innovations, such as the software and mechanics necessary to physically move the wafer around in the chambers for other steps. But if we couldn't get the deposition even, we couldn't move forward.

The teams went to work. The variables Cissy had to figure out included the gas flows and the pressures inside the system to create a plasma deposition of the silicon oxide film. "When we started, the uniformity was all over the place. It was coming out in concentric patterns, all kinds of issues," she remembers.

The critical invention Cissy focused on was what was called a "showerhead," and the name is helpful in explaining the function. It was the showerhead that dispersed the gas, so she started experimenting with the size of the holes, the pattern coverage of the holes, the depth of the plate. One issue was that this equipment had to be so precise — even for testing — that the showerheads had to be machined. Once Cissy's team determined the specs of a new head, machining it could take a week. Cissy got frustrated with those time delays, so she came up with a clever workaround: She ordered a very large plate with different-sized holes, and then she used tape to experiment with patterns on its surface. Instead of having to wait to get a new plate machined, she used the same one but tried a different arrangement of holes by using tape to create a new pattern.

This went on for a couple of months, and that involved nights, weekends, holidays, no vacations for anyone. Cissy remembers living on pizza dinners for weeks.

One day I made my periodic porpoising visit to the lab. Cissy matter-of-factly said, "I think I've got it, Jim." Through smarts, brute force trial and error, and lots of long nights, she had come up with the right combination of size of showerhead, size of holes, and pattern design. There were test showerheads all over the place; they had tried dozens of different patterns and hole sizes. But this was a key technical challenge we had to solve to move forward and she had, in fact, figured it out.

It took several months to optimize the design in the eventual piece of equipment, but we were so proud of that team. The tool went from concept to shipping in 18 months. In addition to the uniform, high rate of deposition, the mechanical engineers created powerful robotic innovations that became part of many future Applied systems. The day I walked past the folding scissor robot in the room next door to Cissy's lab, I knew we were ready to go forward. I authorized a spending level we needed for the final push, even through it would cause us to lose money for the next two quarters. I advised the board and Wall Street and the rest is history.

We introduced the P5000 in 1987. In the space of a year, it became the industry leader, and within five years the tool could handle 50 unique processes in its chamber. It was at this introduction that we began talking publicly about our leapfrog and *kaizen* approaches. I still have a wonderful sculpture of a frog on my desk that Applied executive David Wang, who managed the global introduction of the P5000, gave me to celebrate the power of leapfrogging. We even held a party at SEMICON in San Francisco and deliberately served Frog's Leap wine.

Today, one of the first P5000 systems is at the Smithsonian Museum of American History. Having a product included in the Smithsonian meant you could have an event there. In 1993, we scheduled several days in Washington DC of management meetings, a board meeting, and a celebration of the P5000 leaders, Drs. Maydan, Somekh, and Wang's leadership at the Smithsonian. We timed it for the Semiconductor Industry Association's board meeting and invited the people from SIA and legislators, staff, and agency personnel in Washington interested in high technology. It was a successful and wonderful experience. Everyone was able to tour the museum. We saw a model of the ENIAC, the code-breaking Enigma machine, the signal room of the Titanic, the first chips, the first PCs, and of course, the P5000. We held a reception and formally honored Dan, David and Sass.

In 2012, Applied calculated that 3500 of the P5000s sold had helped create one trillion semiconductor chips. Rapid single-wafer processing and the robot configuration led to the dual robot Endura product business driven by Sass Somekh and Howard Neff that also became the workhorse of the industry.

As of this writing, Cissy Leung still works for Applied Materials, now as a service business unit head.

Nothing is more powerful than perseverance.

MORGANISM

Talented, motivated people will always overcome technical challenges, language differences, distance, or time pressure. And nothing attracts more talented, motivated people like a critical mass of talented, motivated people. This is the foundation of an excellent organization.

Structure, process, people ... culture

When things are going well, as they were on that beach in Hawaii or in Cissy's development lab, it's easy to feel proud of the culture that surrounds and supports employee success. When things are not going well, many managers will suddenly decide, "We need to change the culture. We need to be more innovative, not so bureaucratic, closer to the customer, predictable, or show more trust and respect for each other." Or they focus on some other quality they believe is deficient. Slogans are developed and printed on mugs and banners, perhaps an off-site is scheduled, and the idea is suddenly worked into every memo.

Unfortunately, you will never change any organization's culture by just telling employees the culture needs to change. An offsite discussion might help get agreement from executives about what is desirable, but it won't create that permanent change. You must "do something," and not just once, but consistently and systematically. You must make real changes and communicate them. Those teams building cardboard canoes didn't exhibit teamwork because we announced that they would have to do that to win. Nobody had to tell Cissy Leung that she was going to need to be determined and creative to solve that problem. I like to think Applied Materials hired the right people, listened to them, and supported their efforts with resources and encouragement even when the going was tough. In return, all those elements produced a culture that valued and worked hard for success.

A strong and productive culture is the result of three elements that must be handled properly — and in order: structure, process, and people. If management and reporting lines do not support the presumed values of the company, and if your managers are not communicating and aligning with the same message at every level, you will have confusion. If you don't develop processes collaboratively, ideally requesting but also accepting input by all stakeholders, your culture will be plagued by simmering resentments and sometimes even sabotage; and if you put inferior people in key positions, no amount of management will spin gold out of straw.

If you want to build a certain kind of culture, or you want to rebuild a failing culture, begin by looking at the structure under which people are working and make sure specific managers are accountable for the changes you want to see happen; scrutinize the process for inconsistencies or unintended gaps; make sure your team is as skilled and focused as possible. If you do these things properly, the culture will change.

CHAPTER 14

Work hard, stay alert to new ideas, achieve goals, repeat.

Although I've traced a mostly chronological path through the phases of my life and career, I imagine it's obvious that I never intended this book to be a definitive history of Applied Materials. It would be tedious for anyone who was not intimately familiar with the company for me to go year by year and list everything that happened. But I hope stories about events like the cardboard canoe race and Cissy Leung's major innovation that made the P5000 possible, convey some of the excitement and dedication I experienced and witnessed almost daily.

In some ways this book's central mission for me is to answer the question: What drove Applied's consistently excellent execution and success? What made possible the "Wall of Firsts" celebrated at the company's history display area in Building 1?

When I look back at the team I worked alongside for three decades, I'm always struck by what I would call a zero-defect mindset. Our teams were empowered to make decisions, and they did. When they made a mistake or miscalculation, the "owner" of the problem was usually the first person to report it. "Sound the alarm and point with pride," i.e. identify problems and celebrate solutions, was what our outside Counsel and Corporate Secretary Duke Slichter used to say. All around us, we watched company after company get hammered by Wall Street or the hit teams of the legal profession when they were discovered doing something wrong by an outside party. Over one of our regular lunches, Dan Maydan and I recently reflected on the fact that we could not remember one time in the decades we worked together that a serious problem developed that we did not know about before the board, Wall Street, or the press. Good news is no news, no news is bad news, bad news is good news if you do something about it.

There is always luck involved in success, but one of the keys is to be attuned to the best psychological time to move forward and how you communicate the plan. There are always unexpected twists that can sabotage the best-laid plans. But you can't execute consistently by just being lucky, so I want to return to a few notions we've already talked about and also to the techniques we used to communicate the importance of good management to our people.

Let's start with building a culture that accepts values such as "bad news is good news." It does not occur overnight. For managers, it means trying never to shoot the messenger, even when human nature makes you want to do that. My overriding Morganism is: build and model a culture of trust and respect. That sounds pretty simple. It was pretty simple at the cannery. At a larger company, certain techniques like porpoising deep into an organization and asking straightforward questions build trust. It takes time, but any manager can and should do this.

But at some point, you get too big for a core group of executives to be able to effectively model and push all the desirable values and systems throughout the entire organization; you need to create processes to teach the values and you need to stay current with new thinking so you can adapt as times and situations change. Also, you will hit paradoxes within your own values. For example, treating people fairly and not punishing employees when a decision doesn't turn out perfectly, does not mean giving poor performers leeway to make mistakes over and over. Doing that, in fact, is disrespectful to your good performers who deserve to be surrounded and supported by competence and, ideally, excellence.

A culture of respect and trust begins with a commitment to hiring excellent people. Most things my team did, they did better than I could have. I spent very little time ever cleaning up after anybody or reversing dumb decisions. People who owned their work, both its successes and failures, knew that we had plenty of capacity to adjust to an honest mistake. Employees who needed babysitters or a clean-up crew, on the other hand, didn't last at Applied. Getting a critical mass of good people was not just luck; over time our hiring process and our human resource management came up with ways to assess candidates that meant we didn't hire weak actors to begin with, and we also created tools to assemble complementary teams. We then invested in figuring out the most efficient way to get large numbers of employees aligned in systems that helped us move forward efficiently.

When I was getting my MBA at Cornell, business schools were not paying that much attention to the science of good management and the techniques of effective hiring. We learned a lot of nitty gritty business skills like accounting, marketing, and finance, and I always appreciated the education I received in analyzing industries and the driving economic forces that would sweep through them. But for fundamental management leadership experience, the only place I could get any at Cornell was ROTC. At ROTC summer camp at Fort Bragg, North Carolina, we had a course on basic leadership. It was there I received a wallet-sized folding card that was the foundation of the Infantry/Airborne leadership training that included Leadership Traits and Principles. That was probably the beginning of my collecting management tips. Everything else I learned I mostly picked up on the job, whether in the cannery, in the military, in business, or in venture capital.

People often ask me about mentors. I didn't have one mentor and I believe it's not practical to attach yourself to one role model or manager. I tried to learn from everybody I worked for. When you sincerely want to learn, not just get ahead, successful people are happy to help you. I don't view the notion of a mentor as being someone who advances your career. That may happen, but I think it's more important to realize that the most valuable thing successful people have is their time and they will only invest it in someone who really wants to learn and grow. Nobody is sitting around waiting for someone who needs help to appear.

I was never shy about talking to anyone regardless of their status, but I didn't waste their time making small talk or just "hanging out," as my grandkids like to say. I would ask questions about the work and how and why certain elements were the way they were so that I could

Leadership Traits and Principles

LEADERSHIP TRAITS

- *Flexibility*
- *Knowledge*
- *Initiative*
- *Decisiveness*
- *Tact*
- *Dependability*
- *Enthusiasm*

- *A Lot of Perseverance*
- *Integrity*
- *Judgment*
- *Courage*
- *Bearing*
- *Unselfishness*
- *Loyalty*

LEADERSHIP PRINCIPLES

- Be technically proficient
- Know yourself and seek self-improvement
- Know your subordinates and look out for their welfare
- Keep your people informed
- Set the example. Behave as you espouse. Follow ethical business practices and set high standards.
- Develop your people (coaching, training, delegating)

LEADERSHIP PRINCIPLES

- *Make sound and timely decisions. Delegate — you can't do it all.*
- *Seek responsibility and take responsibility*
- *Be sure that the jobs can be done by you and your group, and are understood, supervised, and accomplished*
- *Lead and train your employees as a team*
- *Develop a sense of responsibility among your subordinates*
- *Adhere to corporate standards for equitable treatment of all employee groups*

For years I carried a pocket reminder of "leadership traits and principles" modeled from my service in ROTC; its advice proved valuable throughout my career.

do my job better. In fact, I had not been at Applied for a very long time when I decided to do something unusual. Although we were a small company, we had some very significant global corporations as customers, including IBM, Texas Instruments, and Motorola. As a supplier of very expensive and precise equipment, I had an out-sized ability to get the attention of the leaders of these companies. I decided I was going to do the equivalent of a CEO walkabout; I was facing some important decisions about how to grow Applied Materials' global business and I wanted to know what executives who were running large global companies thought about where the world was going. How intensely should I focus on global markets and global partners? What were the trends they saw as shaping their companies?

I sent letters (there was no email yet in the early 1980s) to the CEOs of about a dozen major companies such as GE, HP, and Sony as well as some of our major customers like IBM, Texas Instruments, Intel, and Motorola, and I asked for an hour of their time. Almost all agreed, and in almost every case our meetings went much longer than our allotted hour once we started talking. In most cases, the CEO and usually one or two most senior executives and I would meet alone. I did little to almost no talking in these meetings, except to ask questions.

The upshot of those meetings was that I realized business had evolved to a point where every company large and small was grappling with a set of paradoxes that created tremendous tension, both inside the company and between companies and their customers. I asked these seasoned executives about the five or ten most significant issues and trends they were seeing. When I distilled all their answers, I realized that regardless of their primary business, every company was feeling the simultaneous pressure to speed up product cycles, but also improve the quality of their products. They needed to go global to find growth, but in every market where they sold they needed to create a "local" feel among their customer-facing employees in order to build trust. For that matter, our core belief that good news is no news is actually a paradox as well: Although we need to be optimistic and can-do people, we can't bury problems or refuse to deal with quality or other negative issues.

By being sincerely interested in their answers to some of my questions, I developed another set of friends and advisors that helped me and Applied going forward. I added their ideas to the collection of insights and sayings that rang true based on my experience. I found that in talking with some of the leading business people in the world, the fundamental tips that are the basis of the business thinking I'm sharing in this book held true for organizations of any size.

Regardless of the industry or sector, all modern organizations must learn to operate within and overcome paradoxes. Poor leaders tend to be dismissive of difficult and/or opposing forces. Good leaders convey to employees that they understand the paradoxes, but that by managing the consequences of decisions carefully and striking a wise balance, the organization can succeed.

Management science and systems thinking

Fortunately, early in my tenure at Applied, business schools and consultants did begin to think about various management challenges in a more systematic way. A lot of management styles previously were based on hierarchical military or Sloan General Motors structures; the problem was the world was becoming more interrelated and complex — and thus the paradoxes became more significant. Management had to inspire innovation and creativity in aspects of the company's business that a CEO might not even understand, or seek growth in foreign markets. Over time consultants like Phil Crosby, who created the "Zero Defects" quality approach, W. Edwards Deming (*Out of the Crisis* and *The Deming Management Method*), and later Tom Peters (*In Search of Excellence*),and people like Geoff Moore (*Crossing the Chasm*) created a new management science that was much more nuanced than basic command and control. They focused on repeatable systems to achieve objectives and motivating people, not just ordering them around. They looked at entire systems rather than treating each link in a value chain separately. They factored in creativity and the challenge of innovation. There was discussion of values and corporate culture and how that could be an asset. Before Peters became famous and routinely commanded five- and six-figure speaking and consulting fees, I remember that we once had him speak to some managers at Applied for, as I recall, $1000 and a pizza dinner.

I was attracted to systematic thinking for technology, sales, manufacturing, logistics and finance, as well as for factors that did not fit easily on a spreadsheet. I had a director of planning that helped me with strategy and acquisitions, Dennis Hunter. He was a very smart and creative Harvard MBA who excelled at finding leading edge ideas, and he organized our annual long range planning meetings.

I thought Dennis did a good job finding us new insights and strategic thinkers from this emerging curriculum of management ideas, people like William Davidow who wrote *Marketing High Technology*; Regis McKenna *(The Regis Touch)*; McKinsey's Kenichi Ohmae *(Triad Power)*; George Stalk of Boston Consulting Group *(Competing Against Time: How Time-Based Competition Is Reshaping Global Markets)*; Gary Hamel *(Competing for the Future)*; Harvard Professor Clayton Christensen *(The Innovator's Dilemma)*; and others.

It's essential to educate and support the development of your managers as an ongoing activity. As your organization grows, the demands of your industry and the dynamics of the larger world change and you have to stay on top of that. You're never "done" putting management systems in place because the challenges change, people come and go, new tools emerge. You have to constantly battle complacency and the idea that your success validates what you are doing today, creating a bit of a fog around your potential vulnerabilities. But I recognize that there is a paradox in providing training in these systems: employees must perceive the value of the training to compensate for the interruption of their work processes, or it is counterproductive. This is a tension that demands management. The heads of each organization and the units underneath must take responsibility for management development and not just delegate the job to human resources.

Dennis vetted the programs so we didn't just sign on to every "new idea of the week." But we also thought a lot about how to integrate new systems into what we already were doing. For example, in the 1980s, the head of our global leadership training team would sit down before a new training program was implemented and align the terminology with what we already were doing. A consultant or new human resources manager might be excited about bringing in this brand new idea or way of thinking, but we tried to make sure we weren't just renaming ideas we'd already invested in teaching our people. This was particularly important because of our multi-cultural workforce. Our employees were at the cutting edge of their engineering and scientific disciplines, but many had virtually no management experience or training at all, and in many cases, English was their second language. In teaching management concepts, we were asking them to cope with two new languages at once.

Leadership vs. Management

Effectively running an organization demands both leadership and management, which are closely related but not interchangeable.

As the chart that follows shows, the leadership function is about setting the vision, mission, and strategy. A leader establishes the opportunity for the organization by pointing it in the right direction and hiring the people it needs to make it a success. Successful start-ups tend to be led by charismatic leaders who are good at raising money and positioning the value of the company's product or service.

Leadership is essential but not sufficient for success, however. Every person running an organization, a division, or a team must accept responsibility for also managing less-glamorous duties, such as the implementation of strategy through planning, budgeting, organizing, staffing, problem-solving and follow-up. Both leaders and managers need to be effective communicators, decision-makers, and influencers — or at minimum they need to add those capabilities to their teams so that those functions are addressed and they accomplish the whole job.

Not every manager possesses all these skills equally, especially early in one's career; however, every manager needs to understand and accept the importance of each of these responsibilities and either work on developing them, or assemble team members to make up for their weaknesses.

Applied had two Japanese executives heading up our subsidiary in Japan, and they were a perfect example of doing the whole job of management in team fashion. Tetsuo Iwasaki was an outstanding leader and a compelling salesman. He had the initiative and courage to take on a new idea like our subsidiary and drive its success. But he also wisely brought on board a man named Seitaro Ishii. Ishii was the administrative and management complement to Iwasaki; as talented as Iwasaki was at the big picture and inspiring his people to deliver on the strategy, Ishii was right next to him every step making sure all the administrative, operational functions were on track. Eventually, Ishii became head of Global Human Resources for Applied when we were developing the Asian organizations. In that job he focused on building complementary teams as well as implementing processes and consistent quality in our operations.

It is sometimes human nature to emphasize what we do well and ignore or put off working on what does not come as naturally. A good manager must fight that instinct, understand what key leadership or management attributes he or she may lack, and either develop those skills or hire them onto the team.

Leadership/Management Model

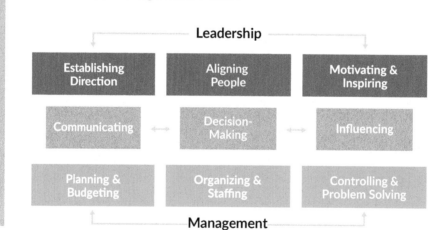

Situational leadership

When I was a student at Cornell I became friends with a student named Ken Blanchard, who later would become a very well-known management consultant and author. He wrote the book *The One Minute*

Manager, which was a business best-seller for many years. In 1981, our Chief Financial Officer Steve Pursell and I attended a seminar in San Francisco that Ken presented; he had developed a model of leadership he called Situational Leadership, and Steve and I found it very insightful and useful. In essence, the term referred to managing individuals using different styles based on each objective for that person, and the person's maturity relative to each objective.

Every job requires several different skills and levels of maturity. You may be a very fast and efficient canning line employee — maybe the best in the cannery. But are you a mature manager of canning line employees? That's not necessarily a yes or no answer; you may be good at anticipating schedules and talent needs, but not so good at motivating people with very different personalities. What often happens is that individuals develop a "management style" that they use in every situation, but it eventually fails them because of uneven experience or maturity levels in different objectives.

Situational Leadership

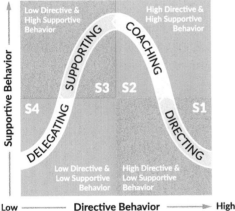

Ken Blanchard's Situational Leadership model is calibrated according to an employee's experience, maturity, and personality, and can vary by tasks. An S4 is a highly developed and mature employee who needs little overseeing; an S3 understands the challenge but will need some feedback and support from you as the task develops. An S2 requires considerable interaction to monitor the employee's priorities and work progress. An S1 is functionally capable and primarily needs guidance in setting priorities and performing to specific objectives.

In an exercise we did at the seminar, Steve and I had to list five objectives for the next six months and what management style we would expect to use with each. We were completely aligned with both our objectives and the management style that we thought we would use for each objective. A common complaint of employees is when a manager uses a "leave alone then zap" management style. That means the person gets little oversight until a mistake and then *zap*. The Blanchard Situational Model lets you use the full range of management styles depending on the experience relative to each objective. The employee knows the management style for each objective and can expect close or loose management based on his or her own strengths, so there can be trust and respect. I think it is a great way to conceptualize your management style.

New manufacturing systems incorporating quality

A critical management challenge for us at Applied was figuring out two changing elements of manufacturing: inventory management and quality. U.S. manufacturers had evolved to optimize their systems to obtain volume discounts on specific parts and to have sufficient parts inventories on hand to meet fluctuating demand, but they had not paid enough attention to the amount of capital tied up in inventories. The Japanese on the other hand, had embraced "Just in Time Scheduling" which was a different way to schedule material deliveries to arrive close to when they were needed that gave them more flexibility, better quality, and prevented them from getting stuck with extra inventory. I felt we had to understand this in terms of supplying our customers, but also in terms of our own productivity.

We saw "just in time " first hand in 1983 when 23 of Applied's global executives gathered for ten days in Japan with the five top executives there to better understand the Japan market, the Japanese culture, and their business practices. A visit to Honda City made very clear what "just in time" meant — no warehouse, no receiving center, no inspection for quality, and little office overhead. We immediately began overhauling engineering and manufacturing. Fortunately, Applied was helped by world class companies Komatsu and Toyota. We also went to the

SEMICON Trade Show, legal presentations, a tea ceremony, Tsukiji Fish Market, a Geisha party, a middle school at 8 a.m. Saturday morning studying English or math and other experiences. Near the end of our time there, we went to a hotel near Mount Fuji for a strategy session on competing against a Japanese company. It was clear to all of us "the Japanese were coming."

At the Geisha party, Howard Neff, an operations executive who, like me, had grown up on a farm in Indiana, was sitting near me at dinner. I asked Howard how he liked the food — raw fish, etc. He said, "I can almost watch Art Noeth across the table eat and not get sick." Yet Howard later moved to Japan for an extended period of time to build Applied's operations there (and came to like Japanese meals!).

I felt that a complex technology systems business like Applied must have a quality process in all departments, not just manufacturing. We had a global team of six people — two Americans, one European, one Chinese, and two Japanese — review all the quality programs worldwide. They selected a program developed by Phil Crosby *(Quality Without Tears)*. This was hard, sometimes even tedious work, but it paid off because it was a vehicle to drive a desirable foundation culture throughout the company. Many of us who were veterans of Applied have never found the responsiveness and probability of the right response in any other organization. We usually comment that we were all spoiled.

Hiring and team-assembly tools

Early in my tenure at Applied we began using a specific personality test called the Winslow Profile. It was based on a theory that beyond intelligence, education, and training, what makes a good employee in a setting that requires teamwork is how that person's personality tends to mesh with the personalities of others on the team. These are factors you appreciate from an organic or observational point of view as a manager, but we didn't have time to wait for that. We had a complex, diverse workforce and we were racing to develop new products before the competition. We needed to have teams hit the ground running.

I found the Winslow test enormously helpful and insightful. I felt its assessment of me and members of my team was both accurate and eye-opening. The tests weren't foolproof, but they raised important questions about how people were likely to work with others. I had several executives I inherited when I joined Applied that I misread; the Winslow Profile made me see that I needed to manage and deploy them according to their needs for attention and support, and they turned out to be very strong performers.

MORGANISM

You don't balance a team with "strong" and "weak" players; you insist on overall high competence, then look for complementary strengths of personality, strategic thinking, attention to detail, and other more subjective but important qualities.

I also used Winslow to help me choose an administrative assistant. Betty Moyles was outstanding in every way and ended up working with me for more than 25 years. Everyone at every level in the company trusted and respected Betty's can-do and pleasant attitude. She set the standard of zero defects for the administrative staff all over the world. I do not think I went into an office on my travels that someone did not mention her. When Betty was weighing whether or not she wanted to work for me (I had had a number of assistants prior to Betty who were not the right fit for my working style), we sat down and compared our Winslow Profiles at an interview we did at the San Francisco Airport before I boarded a plane to Japan in the early 1980s.

Betty still remembers me pointing out that her profile showed she liked to have a certain amount of encouragement and praise, while I did not value that kind of reinforcement as highly as she did. I mentioned that I was concerned that could be an issue for us. Betty appreciated knowing what she was getting into. She says today, "We identified that and that's who I became — a person who did not need a lot of compliments and praise. We were just all business every day, getting one thing done and then on to the next thing."

Winslow is not about "good" and "bad;" it's about understanding differences and complementary traits. Some people value success, but don't care much about credit. They work fine on a team led by a very ambitious extrovert, while a team with too many ambitious extroverts will clash and compete with one another. Others are introverts who are not likely to raise an alarm or draw attention to their concerns easily. That is not a fatal flaw, but you have to be careful not to have too many people like that on a team that has to move quickly. That reticence can mean problems get kicked down the road instead of fixed.

The only trouble with the Winslow tests was that eventually, after Applied went through a series of boom and bust times for our industry where we had to lay people off, some employees mistakenly thought we were using these tests to cull the ranks, dividing people into lists of desirable and undesirable traits. In fact, that was not how we used it. We did trim off the lowest-performing employees when we faced a downturn and had to cut costs, but it had nothing to do with Winslow Profiles. Winslow didn't tell you whether someone was competent; it told you how the person was likely to perform and get along in a particular constellation of other personalities. We laid off people who had shown by their performance that they were not succeeding, despite our efforts to coach them to success.

Life cycle management

Keeping everyone on the same page was one of the most difficult challenges we faced in a cyclical global industry. One of my sayings used to be that I wanted Applied to always be "facing the elevator door." In other words attuned, to the economic momentum that either propels or slows your revenues. You must anticipate how you are going to move when the momentum in either direction reverses. When revenues are strong, for example, watch your spending. Set aside resources for R&D. When the cycle tops out and competitors are forced to pull back, you will be able to afford to double down on product development and be ready with new products, leapfrogging the competition when the sales climate recovers.

That's how you capture market share when others are recovering from a downturn. When you are managing a cyclical long-term technical growth company, you need to develop a culture that realizes change is the medium of opportunity. You need to be able to quickly organize a new initiative when an opportunity arises and then move fast to capitalize. Getting an entire company in sync to do this is not easy, however.

A UCLA professor and consultant named Ichak Adizes, came up with an analysis and a system for managing through what he called "Corporate Lifecycles." I first met Adizes (which is what we all called him) when he spoke at Japan Young Presidents' Organization (YPO) University that Becky and I attended in 1984. An additional capability he brought was he had spent time in Israel and had consulted and taught in many cultures all over the world. Since several on our team needed very basic management training and two of the key members were Israeli, he brought a valuable familiarity with their cultural background that won their trust and gave me insights.

Adizes helped us in several ways. Recently, I was discussing some of the management programs we used with a long-time Applied executive named Manfred Kerschbaum, and he said he particularly valued the tools Adizes came up with in terms of organizing and deploying teams that are matched to the challenges at hand. "What people tend to do when they have to create a team is look around and hire their friends," Manfred observes, adding that the problem is your friends may all be very similar. "No one kind of person can handle all the elements of the whole job. You need an administrative component, an entrepreneurial contribution, an integrator to make things work together, and you need producers – people who are determined and focused on getting the job done."

Manfred is trained as an engineer in "technical physics" and he started at Applied as a process engineer. He eventually rose in the organization, taking on many different responsibilities for which he was not specifically trained, including account and regional management in the U.S., Manufacturing and Operations, and the Global Services Business. When he retired in 2013, he was Senior Vice President and Chief of Staff for Applied Materials.

In the 1980s, we decided we had to deliberately and formally push decision-making power into our global divisions. As we grew, it was taking too long to have divisions waiting for approval from headquarters on business decisions like process specifications, pricing, and support.

Manfred was in Germany and had to put together what we called a Business Center Team responsible for all aspects of our CVD and etch business in Europe. "If I hadn't had this training, I would have done the thing you shouldn't do — recruited just my loyal friends to the new team. This training motivated me to systemically scope out the skills needed to successfully execute the whole job and then build out the team based on complementing each other's skills. I had to look both outside the company and to a wider circle inside the company to get this done. That takes more time and patience than just recruiting from the inner circle."

According to the Adizes model, Manfred says he is a high "Integrator" and "Producer," medium high as an "Entrepreneur," but low as an "Administrator." Therefore, he brought in individuals stronger in administration skills to complement the team. "Once you do it right and it works, you get hungry to take on more and bigger challenges that you otherwise might have shrunk away from in the past."

To teach this, we had to spell out exactly what the responsibilities were, and what should happen if an employee hit a roadblock that was holding up a decision. But it's a misconception that this exercise creates bureaucracy; in fact, we found that by investing up front in a structure, then a connect-the-dots process attached to that structure, we could decentralize decision-making and thus give our people confidence to make decisions at the lowest possible level. Success bred more confidence. Correct, rapid decisions throughout the company most of the time enabled us to grow to become number one in our industry.

MORGANISM

Once an organization grows beyond your executive team's ability to touch every employee, you must systematically teach and reinforce good management practices. When you find programs you believe in, you must personally invest the time to reinforce their importance so that employees take them seriously.

Paradox management

Rapid ups and downs are rough on people. Employees can fall into predictable patterns where they deny what's going on, become depressed and discouraged, and resist change (these are elements of the Bridges model I discussed in Chapter 10). I found that it was important to validate employee concerns by talking about the paradoxes of business in our sector so they realized that I did understand that certain directives created tension and demanded situational judgment. I have also seen this theme reflected in the writing of generals and military leaders. If you issue orders and gloss over that you're asking for something difficult, employees get insecure and resentful. You may end up with 80 percent of your people privately asking themselves, "Am I the only person who is confused here?" If you do it right, if you convey that it's tough but it's up to every one of us to do his or her part to work together, you can build on positive momentum and blast out of the elevator, regardless of whether it is going up or down.

Cultural Conscience

Before I end this chapter on elements of the special management culture we developed at Applied, I want to say a few words about a man I have said many times became the "cultural conscience" at Applied, because of his unique talents and his unfailing integrity.

Dr. Glen Toney was our group vice president of human resources and corporate affairs. Glen's prior position was assistant superintendent of schools for the Palo Alto Unified School District, but he became interested in switching to industry. I met him at a dinner when Becky served on the Palo Alto School Board. She shared how impressed she was with him, and even though jumping from educational administration to business is not all that common, I quickly saw that Glen was a natural executive with a solid management education and prior experience at Lockheed.

Glen and I were completely in sync about the importance of all the key elements I've discussed so far, and we adopted a metaphor for working at Applied as a manager: "plate-spinner." A plate-spinner is an old county fair act where the entertainer would start plates spinning on thin poles and keep running up and down the line giving ones starting to wobble a quick boosting spin with his hand. Every manager has many plates or projects "spinning" and managing them means constantly watching them all while running to the individual plates that need attention and energy to keep them from falling off their sticks.

In a way Glen had thousands of plates, but he built a team of problem-solvers who had tremendous credibility and respect within the company. Glen was an excellent confidante for executives who were having difficulties with colleagues or experiencing personal issues, and he taught his team to be a positive influence at every level of our workforce and in the community. The result was that we were able to keep great people to continue leading the company forward. Applied Materials often appeared on lists of the most admired companies, the best places to work, the most diverse companies, and one of my favorite recognitions, *Business Ethics* naming us to its list of the "100 Best Corporate Citizens." The management team and Glen reinforced through our leadership development Applied's three most basic values: 1) Close to the customer; 2) Mutual trust and respect; 3) World-class performance.

I will always be grateful that I didn't find an excuse to duck out of that Palo Alto School Board dinner where I met Glen and found the perfect human resource and community executive to become the conscience of Applied Materials.

CHAPTER 15

The larger context

When I was about 16, my dad took me to Chicago with him for a meeting of an organization of independent canneries. He explained to me that we had common concerns and all of us would benefit if we worked together. An important element of any food producer's business, for example, involves complying with government standards regarding safety and quality of products. Canners had preferences and concerns about being certified and inspected, and the canneries worked together to make recommendations and lobby as one voice with government regulators for grading standards, safety rules, and facility requirements. My dad made a point of telling me that he was impressed by how seriously the canners took their role in representing the entire group and would vote for certain actions even when those actions did not benefit their own companies.

I thought about this when I first joined WestVen and I was attending meetings of the Western Venture Capital Association. We had some issues we organized ourselves to advocate for in a united way, such as tax treatments for venture investments. But I also appreciated the opportunity to network with other people trying to do what I was trying to do. One month, I might sit next to somebody at lunch with whom my firm was actively competing to get in on a deal; the next month we might be co-financing a start-up together. Or, we might both have decided to pass on a deal and when we talked about that, my instincts were reinforced in a useful way. Or, we'd talk about some new innovation or advance announced by a university. In any event, these forums were a plus for all of us. This was long before social media, and this form of shoe-leather based networking built relationships of trust among people who were part of an economic ecosystem. I've enjoyed the benefits of those friendships and relationships for decades.

When I tell people I have never had much interest in doing a start-up, it surprises those who think all of us in Silicon Valley are cut from that pattern. But one reason I feel that way is that in the early days of a start-up you need almost manic fixation on gaining traction. You need to raise money and manage product development; your team's strength is developing but uncertain. In the early days there are so many small, unpredictable curveballs that can throw your team off track or create delays. Fires break out constantly. You can't think too much about long-term strategy because there aren't enough hours in the day.

Past a certain point, however, even companies with great teams and good products can fall apart if you don't have a leader who is not only keeping a close eye on technology, sales, and operations, but also on the larger context. By that I mean global trends, competitive threats, and strategic opportunities. Almost overnight, producing the best buggy whip in America just didn't matter much anymore for reasons that had little to do with buggy whip design or manufacturing. One reason Apple fell into a long slump in the early 1990s was that the company was so inwardly focused; it was difficult for outside developers to work with Apple at a time when the PC world was moving toward openness. Apple had a small loyal customer base but could not break out. Apple reversed that posture over time, and the "Apps" written by thousands of third-party developers have become one of the iPhone's most powerful competitive weapons.

Again, it's about court sense. Your basketball team may have strong ball-handlers who love to drive to the hoop, but if you are playing a much taller team you may need to emphasize outside shooting and getting the other team in foul trouble early in the game. Earlier, I mentioned the film *Hoosiers*. Not only does it offer a look at what my town was like in the 1950s, it is a story of how flexibility can help you be successful. It was based on a true story of how a small town basketball team from Milan, Indiana won their sectional, regional, semifinal, and eventually the Indiana State Championship. They had a small number of players and were shorter than many of the big city teams. They won by intense teamwork, ball control, patience, perseverance, and only shooting when they could score. For almost eight or nine games, Milan (as I remember), shot 75 percent from the field and 85 percent from the foul line and won the final against Muncie Central at Butler Field House in Indianapolis 32 to 30. They did not have a shot clock in those days, and Milan controlled the ball for over four minutes before taking the final shot to win the Indiana State Championship.

Success often is not just about your strengths, as Apple learned, but also about the adjustments you make to the competition's strengths and to exploiting other dynamics and trends. To appreciate these dynamics, you have to get out of your comfort zone and the weeds of daily details and immediate issues.

MORGANISM

Understanding the larger environment around your organization will give you early clues to changes in momentum and new driving forces. You can't hone your court sense in a vacuum — or an echo chamber.

When I joined Applied, there were barely enough hours in the day to focus on the details of the turnaround. But I could see that aligning our future with the larger driving forces affecting our industry was going to determine our fate. Part of the reason I went to Japan in 1977 was that I was asked to join the board of directors of an organization a few years old called the Semiconductor Equipment and Materials Institute (nicked SEMI, although we later swapped "international" for institute). One of the advantages of SEMI was that it had held a trade show close by in the all-purpose county fairgrounds in San Mateo, California. We literally set up very sophisticated reactors and other equipment in the cow barns and paddocks. For a young industry working in such a complicated technology, this was an important resource. SEMI charged money to attend, which gave us some operating funds, and it brought customers together from all over the world. Like at the cannery industry annual meetings, the members were focused on making the industry a success, and I had conversations that gave me important insights about global trends and customer desires.

SEMI was small; there was an executive secretary, two clerks, and eight board members. I learned so much from the other board members that I made time for the meetings even when I was very busy. One of the most important things we did was discuss and try to settle on standards. This is always a very intense and important period in a capital-intensive technology's development. Companies understandably believe their own designs have advantages over competitors', but at some point competitors need to coalesce around a standard or they lose the opportunity to innovate the next leap forward.

What has become a classic example of a standards battle was occurring right around this same time: The mid-1970s were the early days of the home "video cassette recorder" or VCR industry. Sony invested in the so-called "Betamax" format, while JVC developed the "VHS" format that was slightly lower quality but also cheaper and could record for two hours instead of one. Customers preferred the second. Sony battled for years to try to make Betamax the standard, but the market spoke and gradually Betamax just disappeared. Sony should have conceded the standard and spent the energy and resources it spent on Betamax on a next generation VHS system, instead.

The neutral advantage

SEMI, on the other hand, reminded me of the cannery association in a good way. I don't recall any member ever voting for a purely self-interested initiative. We took our obligation to develop the industry seriously. In part because of the maturity and long view of its members, SEMI took on a very special role in the larger semiconductor industry that we had not anticipated: U.S. and Japanese semiconductor companies in the 1980s fought an all-out trade war that both governments got involved with. However, as suppliers of semiconductor equipment, we counted both of those combatants (in addition to European semiconductor companies) as important customers. We voted to remain as neutral as possible, and that would prove valuable.

By 1981, a couple other board members and I pushed the idea that SEMI should take its neutral posture to a new level and actually invite Japanese semiconductor equipment companies to join us — that's when we switched the "I" in our name from Institute to International. The conventional wisdom at the time was that this was a dangerous move, that the Japanese would use us and contribute nothing in return. But I had been operating for a couple of years in Japan at that point and I disagreed. I had seen what good partners the Japanese could be if you made certain concessions to their culture and style of operating, concessions that were dwarfed by the overall value of the relationship. I also was involved with Japan Western Association (JWA), for which Stanford Research Institute (SRI) located in Menlo Park, California, was the secretariat. Bill Miller, head of SRI, was a friend and he asked me if I'd co-chair JWA and I did that for several years with Akio Morita of Sony. He was one of the few real global Japanese executives at that time. As a result I learned a lot and we worked really well together.

So, the board made SEMI the first international trade organization. That put us in a neutral position with customers all over the world, and with governments all over the world. Not many years later my friend Shoichiro Yoshida, the head of Nikon Semiconductor, became the Chairman of the SEMI board. For a small industry that wasn't too visible in those days, we ended up having a disproportionate amount of influence. Customers and government organizations would look to us for advice and work with us to help resolve some of the issues, such as standards, trade shows, and government rules.

U.S. companies as a group were obsessed with the fear that Japan would steal our intellectual property (IP). The irony is that it's been my experience that the bigger threat to U.S. companies' IP tends to come from within a company's own ranks. Especially as start-up fever escalated over the years, what your own people had learned in the R&D labs would sometimes appear in a competitive product down the road.

The Japanese are intense competitors, and sometimes they will cross a line. But integrity and loyalty in partnerships are incredibly important values to them. There were a few times when the degree to which we had worked with our customers to resolve problems raised issues, particularly in companies where our customer might actually be a sister division of a semiconductor equipment division. We always found a way to resolve these difficulties without lawsuits.

For example, once I was co-chairing a JWA conference in Japan with Morita and we were on a bus moving from one venue to another. I told him about a problem I was having with one of my Japanese customers: One of its subsidiaries was making an exact copy of one of our products. I was upset about this, and I asked Morita if he had some advice.

I could see Morita was troubled by what I told him, even though it was not a Sony company. This was before cell phones. What he did was to get off the bus at the next stop and use a pay phone to call the chairman of the company whose division was copying our product. The next day when I got back to Tokyo, three of that company's top executives appeared in our office. The next day after that, two top executives from the parent company and the head of their semiconductor division met with our executive Iwasaki and myself in a Tokyo hotel room and resolved the dispute in about two-and-a-half days. We asked for compensation for lost profit, agreement not to copy our technology again, and would they work to help us be a preferred supplier. Going forward, we never had another problem with them. They carried their side of the bargain and we carried ours. We eventually became one of their leading suppliers.

Also, it's worth pointing out the way we learned about this copycat situation. Japanese engineers who worked for the sister semiconductor company that bought the reactors from the group copying our designs brought us the drawings of the copycat product (it was likely the semiconductor equipment maker had just reverse engineered one of our machines). They were offended that their sister company was treating us unfairly. This is the value of building relationships of trust and respect.

To be a truly global company I felt we had to continue to forge the best possible ties with our partners. In another unusual move, we set out to get a Japanese board member in the early '80s, and we invited Dr. Hiroo Toyoda, who was head of NTT Research and a customer — but a neutral party to our customers — to join Applied Materials. He became an important contributor to our success. I think we literally were one of the first public companies outside of Japan to have a Japanese board member in any field. Later he encouraged us to get into the flat panel display business. The display business later turned out to be a very important, roughly $ 1 billion business for Applied.

Today's flat panel screens are quite large, but at the time they were relatively small and the technology was the same as the CVD deposition process we had developed. It used the same robotic concepts, and it looked like a good extension product for us. With Dr. Toyoda helping us, we were able to get the head of Sharp and Toshiba Semiconductor to agree to partner with us; we developed the product and they helped us get it into production. Similar to how we worked with our semiconductor partners, the development phase involved a lot of feedback and discussion about optimizing the product. Komatsu, an outstanding Japanese company, became our partner and helped develop the business. We were the only American company that ever made flat panel CVD equipment; eventually Taiwan and Korea moved into the industry.

In this deal, as in any partnership we undertook, we operated under some basic guidelines, both in setting up the partnership and in managing it. First, it's important to bring a certain mindset to the collaboration — the same one I used in my discussions with Dan Maydan when he was considering joining Applied. I also circulated the list among my executive team members.

- Agreements must be perceived as fair by both parties. Goals should be attainable and payoffs realized.
- Long-term relationships have greater payoffs financially and in personal satisfaction than quick reward of advantage.
- I don't expect to make money before my partner makes money.
- I keep my partners apprised of both the success and failures of my efforts.
- I believe my contribution is critical, but that my partners can be successful without me.
- All business relationships require open and honest communication, teamwork, and patience.

The second aspect of collaboration is one that is increasingly important in a world of technology that allows constant communication, text-message interruptions, remote video-enhanced meetings, and other interactions that may or may not be productive. I developed a presentation I used to give inside Applied that I called "C to the 6th." It focused on six tactical elements of collaboration that I felt were important to actually make collaborations work:

CONTACT — Network for points of contact
COMPROMISE — Intelligent compromise
CONTRACT — Agree to work together
CONCRETE — Clear objectives and measurements
CHECK — Streamlined collaborative processes
CLOSE — Meet your commitments

The list is self-explanatory, but I'd draw your attention to the last three — Concrete, Check, and Close. I'll revisit this idea again in Section III, but for now I would just point out that when I advocate collaboration, I do not mean schedule a lot of meetings. Collaborating often means aligning and combining the efforts of teams that do much of their work separately and that, to be productive, must be allowed to focus on the clear, high-value deliverables needed to make a project succeed.

These were the values Applied brought to all its interactions with partners. They may sound fairly simple, but they require serious commitment. It's easy to rationalize small actions, small variations in those values that can undermine a partnership. If you are having technical problems and may be late on your deliverables, you may want to hold on to that information until the eleventh hour to avoid upsetting your partner. Unfortunately, your partner can't develop a good Plan B if he or she doesn't realize Plan A is in jeopardy.

Going back to the value of industry groups and associations, there are times when your competitive issues poison the atmosphere of an industry group. As good as SEMI was at being neutral and international in attitude, that was not the prevailing spirit of Sematech, an industry group launched in the late 1980s. Sematech was started in response to the trade war with Japan, and the U.S. semiconductor industry set up a consortium to encourage collaboration between U.S. chip companies and equipment companies. In theory, it was a good idea to improve communication and streamline certain kinds of development.

Right around this time, Applied had introduced the P5000 system and our customers were very pleased with it. However, some of our competitors tried to work through Sematech to develop a robotic wafer-handling standard that would exclude our approach. I offered to allow our wafer-handling design to become the standard, which meant giving up some potentially valuable intellectual property rights. Per my list of collaboration basics, that offer was about taking a long-term approach that was good for us and good for the industry.

As we saw it, Applied had the VHS; our competitors were working on Betamaxes. The problem was that fighting over standards once customers have voted with their orders wastes energy and resources. Our product's approach was gaining a lot of traction, and I figured we would benefit from it becoming the standard. But it also stood to help the industry hit new performance and feature advances if everyone focused on the next generation instead of fighting over the basic plat-form. Our P5000 used the platform but was an integrated system with processing chambers and processes.

Instead, other Sematech members voted to build a different main-frame to become the standard. That development took time and it turned out that it was never optimized. Once they turned down my offer to let them use our standard, we chose to prove our point in the market. We raced to place as many mainframes with different processing chambers as possible. Ours became the de facto standard and supported the most successful series of products in the history of the industry.

Board seats

A second outside activity that I felt brought value to Applied was serving as a director of an outside board. When I was a venture capitalist I had held several board seats, and in other situations I served as an observer on boards. At Applied I spent a number of years on a very limited number of boards of major companies (always only one at a time) including the networking giant Cisco, the biotechnology industry pioneer Genentech, and Komatsu, the large Japanese competitor to Caterpillar. These were interesting experiences in several dimensions.

Cisco is a leading company in the overall value chain that Applied was involved in. The ability to connect computers over networks was one of the most important advances of the 20th century and it drove the use of semiconductor chips in many ways. Networking drove the adoption of smartphones, for example, and also the hundreds of millions of sensors and instruments used around the world for everything from military defense to weather forecasting. All those pieces of equipment use chips, and all those chips have touched a piece of Applied Materials equipment at some point in their lives. Genentech is also a hard-driving technology company, although it is outside of Applied's industry in the pharmaceutical and healthcare space. I joined at the request of my friend, the late Bob Swanson, the chairman of Genentech. Komatsu was a very good partner in our joint venture to build equipment for the flat panel display market.

I don't want to say anything too specific about situations on those boards, as it is an important responsibility of a director to maintain confidentiality about the dilemmas a board weighs and the choices it helps chief executives make. Over the years, the responsibilities and liabilities of board members have changed and in some ways became more onerous. In my early years, the meetings were focused on markets, products, and people. Meetings today use a lot of time on legal, finance, government, and administration.

But there are a couple of general observations and lessons I came away with. The first reinforced our saying at Applied that "good news is no news and bad news is good news if you do something about it." Some chief executives use board sessions to do a lot of cheerleading and pointing to all the accomplishments they've presided over. Since the CEO serves at the pleasure of the board and by extension the company's shareholders, it's understandable that they want to remind the board of their successes. But when you have a board meeting agenda that is 75 percent or more about the discussion of good news, and then a quick run-through of issues in play or challenges that they're working on that does not even invite much discussion, "Houston: we have a problem."

In my opinion, board meetings should be focused on bad news. You need to hash over what isn't working and dilemmas you hope the combined wisdom of your board and its experiences in difficult situations can contribute to helping you solve problems. At Applied I would usually have my executive team present technology quandaries or market dynamics that concerned us, and I would encourage the board to ask questions directly of the people who were closest to the problem. On some boards, the CEOs carefully screen and control directors' access to operating executives. Particularly in start-ups, this can be the sign of an insecure or paranoid CEO who does not trust his or her team and is worried a frank conversation will raise issues about the company's leadership.

The second observation I would make is that most CEOs of start-ups tend to be headstrong people who listen only to the people they need to help them raise capital. When they have a lot of money in the war chest, they don't listen to anyone. When a major investor has one or more seats on the board, the CEO will tend to direct all his or her attention to the investor. This is another waste of an outside board member's time. The whole idea of having a diverse set of people with experiences in different industries or stakeholder segments capable of independent thinking is a good one. It's a cliché that when you're only talking with people who know exactly what you know, and whom you value because they agree with you, that you can be oblivious to major problems or opportunities that are staring you right in the face. The slang for this kind of situation is "the echo chamber."

Fortunately the Applied board always had highly intelligent, functionally competent, independent, and experienced executives. They came from different-sized organizations in different markets. Their expertise can be illustrated by some of the early members like Herb Dwight of Spectra Physics, a growing technology company; Paul Low from IBM; Dr. Hiroo Toyoda of NTT; Gerry Parker, technology and manufacturing at Intel; Debi Coleman, an Apple executive who went into venture capital; Phil Gerdine of Price Waterhouse, GE Ventures and our excellent long serving Audit Committee Chair (Our CFO reported to Phil and the CEO); Cees Krijgsman who came from international and government from Phillips Europe; Tsuyoshi Kawanishi from semiconductors in Toshiba Japan; Charles Liu, experienced in investments in China; Mike Armacost, career U.S. government service and Ambassador to Japan. Several agreed to serve when they had retired from their positions. They identified with the Applied culture in a fashion I thought was important. For example, they always voted to cut their board compensation at least 10% when the management did not get a bonus and they reduced their salaries during our cyclical sales declines. They came to know and trust each other, were outspoken, and felt their job was to advise the management team and hire and fire the CEO. And I knew they were perfectly capable of doing that. My job was to be sure they trusted the management team and not to surprise them.

One of the early board contributors was a gentleman named George Farnsworth, a seasoned General Electric executive. He was there when I joined Applied as a result of GE's 20% ownership of the company by GE's Venture Capital Fund before the company went public in 1972. George ran various divisions of GE including the Semiconductor Division and before he retired, headed the Aerospace and Defense Group. I credit him with always reminding me and our executives that as difficult and preoccupying as any particular situation might be, we should never forget that we had to do what I have now referred to several times as "the whole job." In other words, we had to be superior in every dimension of the business — the R&D, the marketing, sales, operations, and also finance and legal departments. A weakness in any one of those key functions could obliterate successes in the others.

As an aside, one of our otherwise-outstanding executives sometimes would react defensively when George would begin to probe some issue. I realized board members would raise issues on their minds and it might not be an exact probe of what an individual specifically had said. I then coached him and other executives presenting to use the board member's question to understand the concerns rather than argue why it should not be a concern and take the opportunity to learn from that wise body.

George had been a carrier pilot in WWII and flew WWI biplanes as a hobby. As a retirement gift, we gave George a beautiful wooden replica of a WWI biplane and on its side we wrote in script "The Whole Job." He was still flying his WWI biplanes when he attended a reunion of our early management team and board at 92.

George and I belong to a school of doing business that puts its faith in honesty and integrity. There are many examples of high-flying companies who crash because their CEOs mistake the importance of fundamental optimism, which is important for a leader (otherwise, why are we bothering to go forward?), with refusing to listen for those odd sounds in the canning line or dealing with bad news promptly and seriously before problems escalate.

In the early years, Applied had a difficult relationship with Wall Street. Our technology was hard to understand and our strategic misfires led to a miserable stock performance that did not endear the company to investors. It went public at $18.75 per share in 1972 and in October, 1976 when I joined, the stock was about $3 per share. However, over time we built credibility by meeting with selective analysts and investors and telling them the straight story: we had a lot of work to do and challenges to overcome, but we had tremendous potential. We were aligned with larger forces promising to revolutionize the way the world worked and communicated.

As time went on, more and more shareholders became what I call "renters without owners' objectives," but we made it clear we wanted to be a company built to last, that all stakeholders were critical — customers, employees, shareholders, suppliers, and communities — not just shareholders. We conveyed to investors a focus on providing excellent products and operations, a respect for cash, and a consistent record of truthfulness. Mark Haines, the long time great morning TV anchor for CNBC wrote in a note to me on my 65th birthday, "Over the years I did my best to come up with a killer question that would catch you or make you stumble. But when times were bad you said so, and when times were good, there were no gotchas to find." We built credibility with investors and in 2001, we were asked to initiate the opening of trading on the NASDAQ at Times Square modeled after the New York Stock Exchange. It was a special week of board, management, and investor meetings, and it culminated with the morning opening of NASDAQ. As the management team put our hands on the ball starting NASDAQ trading, it was a testament to the hard-working employees of Applied and the reputation we all had built together. By paying attention to the trends and dynamics of an increasingly complex world we had put ourselves in a position to shape that world. We had come a long way from selling "anything we could get an offer for."

CHAPTER 16

Business and government

> **"I don't want to get involved with the government, I just want the government to leave us alone."**

The sentiment above is one you hear expressed around Silicon Valley and sometimes more broadly in the business community. I understand where it comes from. Like a lot of business leaders, I can get frustrated with government's tendency to look at business as a source of tax revenues, but not necessarily a resource that needs support as well.

However, I want to talk in some detail about my feelings about business and government, in part because I am disappointed at the atmosphere in Washington and in state houses today, and yet I also feel business leaders take a short-sighted approach to dealing with government. My involvement in government issues is in some way an extension of the outside activities I wrote about in the last chapter, but it also has unique aspects that I want to address in more detail.

I'll start by saying that I am a lifelong Republican. I am pro-business and I believe most good things in life begin with a good job. For reasons I'll explain, I dislike a governing style that emphasizes regulation at the expense of common sense and flexibility. But I also reject the idea that party loyalty is a value in and of itself. Once, after Jeff's and my book was published, I visited Austin, Texas on the book tour. We had a large facility there and were popular with the local Chamber of Commerce. They took a picture of me in a ten-gallon cowboy hat and later without our consent used it in a marketing campaign to promote Austin among California companies. Becky was a Republican State Senator at the time and I would not have willingly participated in that promotion, but the fact is that for years in public forums I had said, "Companies will go where they are wanted and stay where they are appreciated." Becky took a lot of ribbing in the State Senate because of the press over the picture, but I never apologized for speaking my mind on this point and Becky was re-elected!

I have plenty of frustrations with government, but I also don't agree with the sentiment "just leave us alone." I think it's worth thinking about from a couple of different angles. First, define "alone." Would there be a Silicon Valley without the U.S. Government? There would not. Spending from the Dept. of Defense, the Dept. of Energy, and other taxpayer-funded agencies laid the groundwork for every key element of what has created "Silicon Valley," from materials science to semiconductors to the Internet. The private sector could not have afforded to spend what it took to drive the research underpinning these advances. Business unquestionably improved upon that early research, and it accelerated what was possible. But basic, government-funded research is essential to not only a healthy technology sector but to a healthy economy.

Secondly, I appreciate that companies get fed up with regulations or taxes that they feel impede their progress. I have a vivid memory of a problem we had at the family cannery involving federal workplace regulations. We built brand new, modern restrooms in the cannery and were pleased to upgrade these facilities for our employees. Then, the Occupational Safety and Health Administration (OSHA) came in for an inspection. The inspector said we had violated the government standard in the remodel based on our company's headcount and we should have built several more restrooms.

What the calculation ignored was that about a third of our workforce did not work in the factory, they were out in the fields planting, harvesting, and doing farm work. They never used these restrooms. The second issue was that we did not have scheduled breaks at the cannery. We used a system where any employee could take a break whenever he or she needed to, as we had floating workers who could fill in on the lines. Therefore, there were plenty of restrooms to accommodate everyone because the workers never all went to the restroom at once. The OSHA inspector was not concerned with those details and filed a complaint against us. The complaint was no trivial thing — it prevented us from bidding on government contracts. My dad had to go to Chicago to speak to the OSHA region head in order for us to be certified to sell to the government.

This is a classic issue with regulations — they may be well intended, but the people who write the regulation often don't understand or consider actual field conditions and economic realities. Or, a regulation used in a straightforward manner by one administration can be co-opted for a different purpose in the next. You can have regulations that stifle innovation because the reporting requirements were designed for a major corporation, while a start-up just can't afford that. You can have bureaucrats with an agenda that stalls permit applications or otherwise uses legal means to stop a new facility from going up.

For all those reasons, an executive saying government should "just leave us alone" makes as much sense as a professional sports team owner saying, "We don't need referees. Just let us play the game." In business, you have to play by rules that affect other constituencies and they have the right to oppose or influence what you want for their own reasons. As a corporate leader, "Just leave us alone" is not rational or even intelligent thinking, and it's not going to happen. What is going to happen is that government is going to respond to the people and groups that engage with it.

Multiple communities

At Applied Materials we had an active government affairs group led by Joe Pon that was excellent in positioning and involving Applied in the U.S. and various countries in which we operated. They had my blessing to engage with the governments around the world and at the local and state level anywhere we had facilities. We seemed to resolve almost any issue. I observed their respect for and the respect they received from the staffs of officials all over the world and it was an important factor in their success. Maybe it was our cultural edge. Also, Applied paid attention to being good citizens of those communities in general.

We did not shirk on supporting education and local philanthropy. We got out in front of issues of pollution or toxic disposal and would react and fix them before being told to. This was just common sense, good neighbor behavior as far as I was concerned, and I felt overall it meant we were treated fairly in the communities where we operated.

As for me, along with industry associations and board seats, the third activity beyond my duties at Applied that I usually pursued at any given time was serving in some kind of capacity in government, usually on a committee or council. I felt it was the responsible thing to do and I also found it reaped a lot of benefits for us. Maybe I was willing to do it because I've had some unique exposures to government. Seeing General Besson overseeing the Army Materiel Command Board meetings was a good learning experience and I was impressed with what an efficient and effective leader he was. As my career progressed when I worked in Textron's Washington DC Office and then later managed projects at Dalmo Victor integrating new technology into defense work, government was part of the process. The government was our customer and we dealt with competent people by and large; it was important for government to set basic rules and that provided us guidance in how to operate.

Some of my colleagues in business complain that when you sit on a panel, nothing ever gets done. You do a report that gets put in a binder and nothing happens. Well, it's true that you're never going to see government implement a report with the speed a private corporation can muster when the CEO orders something to happen. But speed isn't everything.

One of the projects at the AMCB we did was a report on a strategy to strengthen U.S. arsenals and make them more effective. General Besson got buy-off from the Army; it was sent to the Department of Defense. John F. Kennedy was President at the time, and one recommendation was that the Watertown arsenal in Boston should be closed. Well, taking jobs from Massachusetts was not likely to happen during JFK's Administration. Defense put the report in the bottom of a drawer.

However, the politics of the White House shifted after JFK's assassination. Johnson became president and he was not interested in protecting jobs in Massachusetts. Ours was a well-researched, well thought-out plan and Johnson's administration implemented the plan to the letter.

If you take the long view, getting stakeholders and experts focused is an important exercise and, when the time is right, it is much better to start with a plan produced in a thoughtful way than to respond to whomever is shouting the loudest during a crisis.

In 1988, I joined the National Advisory Committee on Semiconductors (NACS). The NACS Committee was set up during the Reagan Administration but it was mostly active under George H.W. Bush. Vice President Bush had come to Applied in a campaign stop two weeks before he was elected President. Our team did an outstanding organizational job — circus tent for over 1000 people, at least 30 camera people plus reporters, and a large multijurisdictional security detail as we hosted the Vice President and Governor Deukmejian and my favorite Republican leader, Senator Becky Morgan. I remember the next day I ran into one of the Applied employees from the drafting department who appreciated getting to see and hear from these leaders during a workday. She said: "Jim, I am a Democrat but yesterday was one of the best days of my life."

George H.W. Bush was a seasoned executive before he served in the White House; he was a World War II veteran, businessman, congressman, representative to China, and director of the CIA. His White House was organized, competent, and easy to work with on trade and international issues. Applied and other high-tech companies benefited because his Administration listened.

NACS was set up for us to try to compete better with the Japanese. Companies started to work more closely with suppliers, and the result was Sematech. Those meetings allowed me to meet key people — Bob Galvin, head of Motorola, and others. I'd use my time in Washington to brief people who I wanted to understand our technology and our business. In the 80s, there weren't a lot of people in Washington who really understood technology and certainly not semiconductor manufacturing equipment. I was still active in SEMI as well, and I probably had the most financial experience and the most experience with Washington, thanks to the committee. The upshot of NACS for me was that at SEMI, although we had a small staff, we had good access everywhere in the world because people were trying to learn about technology. We had insight into Europe, Japan, Taiwan, Korea, even China, which most people didn't have. So, we had a global perspective and direct contacts and we collected feedback that allowed us to develop the right insights ourselves.

I left NACS in 1992, but then in 1996 I was asked to join the Commission on U.S. Pacific Trade and Investment Policy to advise President Clinton and Congress, and later the U.S.-Japan Private Sector Government Commission.

President Clinton and his Vice President Al Gore were engaged and were supportive of technology and Silicon Valley. In February, when Clinton took office, the two of them visited the Valley and I was fortunate to be invited to a small, four-table dinner and I sat with President Clinton. As we all learned over time he was smart, engaging, as well as surprisingly knowledgeable about technology and the issues we faced as an industry. He probably was one of the most amazing politicians I have met; everyone at the dinner was impressed at his ability to remember people, names, and details of issues.

One of the efforts by President Clinton to get the U.S. more engaged with Asia was to establish the Asia-Pacific Economic Cooperation (APEC) made up of 21 country members almost all touching on the Pacific Ocean. In parallel there was a business group that met in conjunction with the leaders meeting sponsored by the National Center for APEC where I was a board member. Each year the Secretary of State in preparing for APEC Leaders Fall Meeting would host a day-long meeting for the active APEC company executives. Key department heads, the President's Chief of Staff, and of course the Secretary of State would participate. This provided great perspective and contacts important for a growing global company like Applied.

The most significant personal experience I had with the government was being awarded the National Medal of Technology in 1996. It was a personal reward but it also was recognition of the outstanding Applied Materials Global Team. Becky, Jeff, Mary and her husband, and I went to the Award Ceremony in the White House. Our Godson Alex Martin later joined us for a Legal Seafood lobster dinner. At the ceremony Mary wanted to take a picture from the audience. I think I was the last one to go up to get the medal put around my neck by the President. I asked him if Mary could take a picture. He looked over at her and gave a thumbs-up and we have a great picture of the two of us and the medal. Walking out a couple of the Cabinet people I knew asked, "How did you get him to take the picture?"

In 2003, I took on my most significant government-related assignment when President George W. Bush appointed me as vice-chair of the President's Export Council. This marked me working with three different U.S. Presidents and the council run under the auspices of Don Evans of the Commerce Department. It was another good experience for me and for Applied.

Don Evans was a good friend and he also was Campaign Chair for George W. Bush. Our Export Council meetings were scheduled when the President was likely to be in town. Usually, later in the day the council met with the President. They were planned for an hour but I cannot remember a time it did not go much longer. He had a real interest and understanding of the issues

In 2004 the Export Council took a memorable trip to China. The main focus of the trip was to lead a trade mission. Executives on the trip included Bill Marriott, Chairman of Marriott Hotels and Chairman of the Export Council. In a funny aside, Marriott Hotels was expanding in China and when we went to Beijing and Shanghai, we stayed in J.W. Marriott Hotels. In Beijing and Shanghai about 24 people came out and met our bus and fussed over us, as we were with Marriott, himself. We each had a butler as I recall. Maybe a year or so later I went back to the same hotel. I wrote a note to Bill after I returned, "For some reason I didn't get all that great service in your hotel — I didn't even get a butler this time."

It felt that during those periods when I worked in Washington that people, regardless of their politics, seemed to be working to solve important issues for our country. It is a terrible disappointment that with the intellect, our amazing resources, and the good will of ordinary people throughout the land that our country's politics have become so dysfunctional.

Engage personally

At the time of the China trip, I was involved with The Nature Conservancy (TNC), which I'll talk more about in the final section of the book. The Nature Conservancy had prepared a memorandum of understanding that Rose Niu, head of TNC China and I signed with Jiang Zemin's sister, a Vice Minister of Forestry who was very committed to conservation. It called for a joint partnership with China's Ministry of Forestry to assist in reforestation strategies. Also, on that trip we discussed with the Ministry of Commerce a strategy to assist in preparation of a long-term environmental plan for land representing 1/5 of the land mass of China.

I promised to give more insights on how we came to operate so successfully in China. In 1983, China was still mostly a mystery, and a complicated place to do business, but members of our team had had some contacts with the Chinese Consulate in San Francisco. The Vice Minister of Electronics Jiang Zemin visited the United States, mainly to stop at a few companies on the East Coast and Texas. But when our team learned that he was stopping on his way back to China in San Francisco, they invited him to visit us. While he was on site taking a tour and meeting with me, we received word that he had been promoted to Minister of Electronics. On the spot we invited him to a celebration and we took the delegation of about 12 to Ming's Restaurant in Palo Alto for a Chinese Banquet.

It was a memorable dinner in many ways. He and I sat together and talked for about three hours. We discussed the outlook for Asia, the Semiconductor Industry, and the difficulties facing China. I was truly impressed with his experience; he had been educated in electrical engineering using English textbooks; he had gained experience in industry, and also worked for a time in the Russian auto industry. He spoke not only English, but Russian. In the three hours of discussion, I perceived that despite our very different political orientations, our views about the future of technology were about 95% aligned.

He invited me to China. The next year, I planned a trip there which he hosted. He was a few minutes late to the Banquet in Beijing. He said he had been visiting some farm towns outside of Beijing. The townspeople were giving him a hard time because they wanted colored TVs and his capacity was for black and white TVs. When Deng Xiaoping began to loosen government control he allowed the farmers to farm individual plots of land much like tenant farming in the U.S. The farmer had to give the government a share of the crop equal to half of the crop the year before. With more fertilizer and more attention to the plot the farmers doubled the output but only had to give 25 percent of the current crop. Therefore they could afford colored TVs and were angry they were not available.

We set up a joint venture to do service in China for older Applied Materials equipment; over time we built our own capability there. In 1986, Mary was selected by Dartmouth to extend her Chinese language skills through a program in Beijing. She was finishing the program about the time Applied Materials was dedicating a Service Center, so we had a memorable family visit together. The ceremonies were outside and as we dedicated this technically advanced building two donkey carts went by on the dirt road. To witness that incredible contrast and subsequently see the changes in China is a powerful indicator of the importance of aligning with driving forces. They move mountains.

Later, Mary took a picture of Becky and me seated at the edge of West Lake in Hangzhou of Alibaba fame. We sat against a beautiful sunset. About ten years later I learned one of our outstanding engineering executives grew up there. I showed him the picture and he showed me that his house was across the lake in the distance.

These personal connections and reminders of how small the world has become in my lifetime are powerful for me. Applied was such a special place for those open to the changes taking place globally, and those connections allowed us to participate in interesting ways. For example, many people we met in China in the 1980s moved into the hierarchy; Jiang Zemin became Mayor of Shanghai…and later, General Secretary of the Communist Party and President of The People's Republic of China.

Being married to a true public servant was another reason why I always considered it important for me to engage with government at different levels. Becky grew up in a small community in Vermont where her father, a dairy farmer, was deeply involved with the community and held local office. After we moved to Palo Alto, Becky began volunteering in schools, which eventually led to her being elected to the school board. She then was elected Santa Clara County Supervisor, and she was involved in critical issues for the region at a key time of growth for the local technology industry. Eventually, she was elected to three terms as a California State Senator, and was highly respected by both parties for her integrity and service.

MORGANISM

A company cannot thrive in a community that is not thriving. Engaging with local communities and government is not a distraction or luxury. It provides a leader with a better sense of the big picture, protects the interests and welfare of employees, and makes for more intelligent and practical advocacy.

My family was not active in local politics in Indiana. However, we often worked in partnership with government in a number of ways, not just through the cannery but as you do in small towns. Government played an important role in critical infrastructure support for roads or rural electricity, and when the Wabash would flood and we'd need emergency support to rescue friends and neighbors and restore the town to functioning. Government was not faceless, nameless bureaucrats, it was the postmaster, the emergency service personnel, the planning department — people you knew personally and saw every day.

Dangerous extremes

I never had any desire to run for office myself, but I respected the attitude that Becky took toward her public service; she didn't do it for the attention or admiration, she felt a sincere desire to serve and to fix problems and create opportunities. When Becky was a State Senator, it was during a time when you still had some moderates on both sides of the aisle. Even though Becky served as a Republican, she enjoyed the support of the Democratic leadership in obvious and not so obvious ways for important projects. If it weren't for Becky's legislation and hard work, for example, we would not have the Caltrain commuter system that is a linchpin for public transportation in a region that has grown phenomenally since the 1980s. She managed to get bipartisan support to save and expand Caltrain and now it seems absurd that we came so close to losing that valuable transit corridor in the mid-'80s.

The problem these days is that the extreme factions of the parties have driven so many moderates out of power. When I was in Washington, I was impressed with the politicians and the bureaucrats. As Majority Leader and later as President, Lyndon Johnson got a lot done. Presidents Reagan, Bush Senior, and Clinton were effective at accomplishing policy changes that made peoples' lives better and made government work better.

I also see a big shift at the Cabinet level. Cabinets used to have people with solid experience. You don't often see senior business people with global experience in Cabinet positions anymore. There's been rising influence among political consultants, pollsters, and young White House staffers. Somebody who's been a CEO of a global company has a problem not being heard by the President and dealing with snarky staff people. It's a weakness that's evolved at the White House. You think about Lincoln and his "team of rivals." He surrounded himself with people he knew disliked him and competed with him, but it worked because he actively sought the full spectrum of opinions, he managed the process, and he produced decisions that reflected all that input. We don't have that today.

Government is supposed to figure out solutions for people and must collaborate to do that. I again stress the importance of my rules of collaboration. You can't achieve the most basic element of those rules, mutual respect and trust, when you put extremists in key jobs. They don't want to compromise to get effective solutions for the majority. I like to see groups work collaboratively, whether at the small unit level, corporate level, industry level, government level, or global level. I don't care too much who gets credit, it's about moving forward, accomplishing goals. Unfortunately, the culture of a government bureaucracy tends to be such that rapid change puts people at risk. Unlike the culture we created at Applied, government staff often are scared of bad news. They don't want to go through the transformation exercises; change is not a medium of opportunity, it's a risk to your job and promotion.

I believe a strong and fiscally responsible economy is a paramount goal, without borrowing from our grandchildren. The extremists today make me concerned that both parties are leaving moderates like me out of the process. Parties can't just be against everything the opponents are for; parties have to be fiscally responsible and lead, govern, and solve problems for all Americans.

CHAPTER 17

The founders' legacy and The Tech Awards

At the height of the "dot-com" boom around 1999, a number of us in Silicon Valley were concerned about the way the culture of the Valley seemed to be changing. The pioneers of the Silicon Valley we'd grown up in were no less smart or driven than the new generation. But they were curious, creative engineers who were obsessed with solving real world problems. They wanted to create useful products, build companies, and break technical barriers. They weren't fixated on the daily stock price or competing to see who could get rock stars for their company Christmas party, as many dot-commers seemed to be. As time went on, many of the early pioneers made considerable fortunes, but they were still putting in 60+ hours every week because they saw so many opportunities to make the world run better, faster, and more efficiently.

I was well rewarded for my work at Applied Materials, but I was not motivated by trying to become wealthy for wealth's sake. The way I have always thought about my salary was that I wanted to make enough money so that I had the freedom and independence to make what I thought was the right decision for the company without it hurting my family. In other words, I did not want my fear of losing my job or not getting a bonus to give me a selfish, short-term mentality.

When your primary focus is solving a problem, it shapes your attitude to new ideas and how to put them to work. It's more than a can-do attitude, it's a let's do attitude. Let's put our heads together and make this work. It was common in Silicon Valley for companies that might battle tooth and nail against each other in one market to collaborate in another market segment and function very effectively as partners. I can tell you that these early entrepreneurs also would come together with that same creative, generous passion to work on community problems. Becky and I experienced that personally when she began her career as a public official dedicated to education, transportation, and other issues vital to the health of our region. She enjoyed the strong support and encouragement of people like Dave Packard and Bob Noyce.

This atmosphere was a vital part of what created the incredible foundation on which Silicon Valley was built. We celebrated invention and innovation, but mainly because it produced tangible, important results for people, for businesses, for communities. I eventually spent a lot of time in Japan, and while the Japanese had a lot to teach us about quality manufacturing and being good partners, I could see that the Japanese were frustrated that they could not figure out how to inspire creativity and innovation the way we did it. Their culture valued humility and teamwork. We celebrated the individual determination of innovators, inventors, and dreamers. We celebrated risk-taking.

By the end of the century, the Internet changed many dynamics for start-ups and that continued into the 2000s. You didn't even need a garage anymore, all you needed were clever programmers networked together. Dot-com fever and IPOs spread throughout the technology world and fueled an investing bubble on Wall Street.

What was getting lost in all the financial froth was the idea of human progress as a worthy application of technology. Not just the improved capability to order goods online and share photos in social media, but the potential of innovation to solve persistent problems that created suffering in the world, or that held large numbers of people back from achieving a decent, sustainable quality of life.

At the time I was involved with the Tech Museum of Innovation in San Jose. "The Tech" as it came to be known, had been modeled after the Museum of Science and Industry in Chicago but it was geared to products and technologies relevant in the 1980s. Over time, it has evolved to focus on more current technologies and on teaching and encouraging young people to engage in science. Applied was an early supporter and it was a very positive resource for our community. For a few years the San Jose Chamber of Commerce combined with The Tech for a fundraising speaker's dinner. But around 2000, the Chamber decided to do the speaker's dinner on its own and The Tech was looking for a new event to showcase and promote innovation.

About the same time Father Paul Locatelli, the president of Santa Clara University, had created three new centers at SCU, one for ethics, another for business, and a third for "Science, Technology, and Society." I sat on the advisory committee for that third group. Well-known inventor and technologist Doug Engelbart showed our committee a report that offered recommendations for achieving Millennium goals, and one of the factors was recognizing people who were using technology to benefit society. It seemed to me it could be a useful role for The Tech to begin sponsoring awards in that vein, and we could give them out at an annual dinner. Dick King, vice president of The Tech developed a plan and Peter Giles, then president of The Tech agreed. Santa Clara University would make the selections, and The Tech could host the event. Applied gave some seed money to pull this together. And our first dinner was scheduled for what would turn out to be an extremely challenging period of time: November, 2001.

We scheduled the dinner, but we got a late start organizing for an event of this complexity. In July, we signed former President Gerald Ford (who was 88 at the time), whom I had met and liked as the dinner speaker. But after the September 11, 2001 attacks on our country, a lot of folks just stopped traveling and the mood of the country was not celebratory to put it mildly. We were concerned President Ford might not be a strong enough draw to get people to travel to the event. We wondered if we should just postpone it, as many events had been postponed in the difficult weeks after 9/11, especially when the anthrax scares kept the public on edge.

Finally, we decided, let's just go ahead and do it.

The Tech Awards event was actually one of the first major public events in Silicon Valley after 9/11…and the evening could not have gone better. President Ford was a strong speaker and perfect for the times; he had stepped into the job of President of the United States after the Watergate crisis and so he had leadership experience and perspective that was inspiring and uplifting. He spoke of his military service during World War II, but far from seeming behind the times or beleaguered by recent events, President Ford's observations about how Americans rise to challenges and his comments about technology were inspiring and hopeful. This was exactly the spirit we wanted to ignite with these awards.

The variety of projects The Tech Awards recognized and supported amazed me that first year — and every year since. We interpreted technology broadly. We gave one award to a small company that had invented inexpensive prosthetic limbs that could be fitted without medical experts, a big advantage in developing countries where individuals recovering from landmine injuries and other mutilating experiences had few resources, including medical services. We gave another award to an academic studying the genetic structure of malaria.

Life-saving information networks

A moving moment in the first ceremony was when a woman named Kristine Pearson accepted an award for a project she was running to distribute solar and wind-up powered radios in Sub-Saharan Africa. Kristine had seen large numbers of children in Rwanda who had been orphaned either by the genocide or due to the AIDS epidemic; sometimes young teens were the heads of households of several siblings and they had no money to attend school or access to vital health information. Kristine and her team realized they could leverage radio and the renewable energy technologies of solar and wind-up, to offer a connection. When we presented the award, Kristine was overwhelmed with emotion; the prize money would help her organization connect many more children to resources that could save their lives. Since then many millions of people have accessed life-saving information and resources thanks to the radios, lights, and other products her organization, Lifeline Energy, has invented and distributed.

The Tech Awards have now provided well over $4 million in cash prizes to nearly 300 technologists working on all kinds of different projects in fields like economic development, education, health, and the environment. I was honored when The Tech Awards Committee set up the Global Humanitarian Award in my name in 2004, and subsequent winners have included Kristine Pearson, Bill Gates, Jeff Skoll, Gordon Moore, Dean Kamen, Mohammad Yunus, Queen Rania Al Abdullah of Jordan, and former Vice President Al Gore.

In 2014, we introduced the "Laureate Impact" award, given to a previous winner who had made great strides in his or her goals since initially being recognized. What a moving experience it was when Salman Khan of Khan Academy took the stage. He talked about how he was on the fence in 2009 about whether he should quit his job to fully develop Khan Academy, or whether he should continue to do it as a sort of hobby. He told the audience that the day the letter arrived informing him he had been chosen as a 2009 Laureate, he "took it as a sign" that he needed to go all in.

Talk about scaling up impact: In 2009, roughly 100,000 people per month were accessing Khan's free online courses in math and other subjects. In his 2014 speech, he estimated 100,000 million people had viewed the non-profit's 3600 videos on every subject from the French Revolution to advanced calculus, and in 2015 the company estimated nearly 600 million lessons had been delivered. And now he is broadening the vision further to globalize and localize the instruction, with translations into 36 different languages underway. Mexican philanthropist Carlos Slim, for example, has funded the translation of Khan videos into Spanish and projects to extend the concept's reach and improve access for the world's poorest people. In one of those necessary paradoxes I talked about earlier, Sal Khan is figuring out how to be both global and local.

In 2015, Becky and I were happy and pleased to attend the celebration where our dear friends John and Tashia Morgridge received the Global Humanitarian Award at The Tech Awards dinner. You'd be hard-pressed to find more generous and determined philanthropists than John and Tashia, who have made important contributions to improving education around the world. But one of their great gifts is conveying how much fun and enjoyment they get out of their philanthropy. They both have a ready twinkle in their eyes, a capacity for hard work, and a great devotion to the causes they believe in and to one another.

In a business like high tech there is very little looking back; few of us have either the time or personalities content to keep rehashing the good old days. But The Tech Awards have become a very satisfying experience in honoring and rewarding people who are technically creative and also have the grit, determination, and seriousness of the Valley's pioneers. Without those pioneers, we would not have the fundamental network and equipment that makes today's innovations in both the private sector and in development and philanthropic arenas, possible.

As President Ford said, "Clocks and calendars may mark the passage of time, but they reveal very little about the aging process. True youthfulness is the vigor of imagination, and impatience with limits, and the embrace of possibility...that's why Silicon Valley will always be the most youthful of places. You reject complacency, an intellectual narcotic...you honor the risk-takers who create jobs and set our standards." He made a point of noting that Silicon Valley's entrepreneurs and innovators speak many languages, hail from many countries, observe many different religions, but "they have this much in common: Even in times of difficulty they look at problems and see possibility. They do not fear change, they court it as a natural ally."

One of the neat elements of bringing the award winners together is how excited they are to network with one another. Fostering collaboration between smart, driven, problem-solving people was exactly what we wanted this award model to do, and what the founders of the Valley who inspired the successes that made The Tech possible were all about. "If this evening is about anything," as President Ford said during some dark days for our country when optimism was in short supply, "it is about hope."

MORGANISM

Financial independence and success are important motivations in life. But you can do well and pursue a larger goal of doing good — whether by creating powerful new tools and products, helping drive a healthy economy, protecting natural resources for everyone's benefit, or by giving a hand up to those less fortunate. Hope and optimism are humanity's driving forces.

Applied Materials' innovative products set high standards in the semiconductor equipment industry.

Clockwise from top left: the AME 7800 Epitaxial Reactor (1978); the revolutionary AME 8100 Batch Etcher series originally introduced in 1981; the Smithsonian Institution recognized our team for producing the P5000 Single Wafer CVD reactor; (bottom) the Endura High-Throughput Physical Vapor Deposition (PVD) machine (1990).

Clockwise from top left: Our team opened the Applied Materials Japan Technology Center in Narita, Japan, 1983; The 1991 book my son, Jeff, and I co-wrote, *Cracking the Japanese Market; Strategies for Success in the New Global Economy*; In 2002, *Business Week* included me among ethical CEOs who provided strong financial returns and "built enduring companies without bending the rules"; In 1996, President Bill Clinton presented me with the National Medal of Technology and Innovation.

Top: Vice President George H.W. Bush visited Applied Materials in 1988; *Bottom:* Our management team at the first NASDAQ public opening in Times Square, 2001 including EVP Sass Somekh, EVP; EVP and CFO Joe Bronson; President Dan Maydan; me; and EVP David Wang.

Clockwise from top left: In 1997, I traveled with Applied's diverse Asia-Pacific team representing managers from China, Japan, Taiwan, Korea, Singapore, and the U.S., down the Yangtze River to China's Three Gorges Dam; With China's President Jiang Zemin. I first forged a friendly relationship with him when he was the country's Vice Minister of Electronics; In the 1980s as "Quality Man" I kicked off a zero-defects campaign at Applied.

Clockwise from top left: In 1999 our board dedicated a statue of Albert Einstein in Israel just a few weeks before Einstein was named the "Man of the Century;" Dr. Glen Toney, Applied Material's group vice president of human resources, embodied our corporate "conscience"; Former President Gerald R. Ford at the first Tech Awards in 2001, flanked here by Becky and me, and (l-r) Santa Clara University President Paul Locatelli and my friend, high-tech marketing expert Regis McKenna.

Top: When I joined Applied Materials in 1976, our management team had its work cut out for it but we soon were focused and ready. Standing behind me from left to right: VP Corporate Development Chuck Sutcliffe; VP and General Manager of Semiconductor Systems Herb Henderson; Controller Steve Pursell; VP Marketing Bob Graham; VP of Technology Walt Benzing.

Bottom: I retired from Applied Materials as CEO in 2003, and I left the board as Chairman Emeritus in 2009. This photo is from my last board meeting. From top left, standing: Stephen Forrest, VP for Research at the University of Michigan; Aart de Geus, Chairman and CEO of Synopsys, Inc.; Willem Roelandts, Chairman of Xilinx, Inc.; Philip Gerdine, Retired Executive Director (Overseas Acquisitions) of Siemens AG; Charles Liu, Senior Managing Partner of Hao Capital China Fund; Dennis Powell, Executive VP and CFO, Cisco Systems, Inc.;

Seated, left to right: Gerhard Parker, Retired Executive Vice President, New Business Group of Intel Corporation: Alexander Karsner, Former Assistant Secretary for Energy Efficiency and Renewable Energy at the U.S. Department of Energy; me; Michael Splinter, President & CEO; Thomas Iannotti, Senior VP and Managing Director, Technology Solutions Group, Americas for Hewlett-Packard Company; Deborah Coleman, General Partner of SmartForest Ventures LLC.

Satellite image of the northern Sierra snowpack (NASA)

The complexity of all systems is increasing.

Philanthropy

(And why good management always matters, even beyond business)

Leading an organization demands desire, perseverance, listening, being alert to change, and the willingness to make decisions and manage the consequences. When you have those attributes, you are going to develop court sense. However, it's a fair question to ask, what about life beyond the business court? Do the skills and management tips we've discussed apply in life more broadly? I believe they do.

One reason I wrote this book to share what I have learned in business, is that since I left Applied Materials I have devoted a significant amount of time to philanthropy, especially to conservation organizations. I have been impressed with so many people I've met in these organizations who have taken on difficult and worthwhile challenges. And I've offered some coaching to non-profit managers who are brimming with intelligence, passion, and energy, but sometimes have limited management experience.

I want to be careful how I talk about management challenges at non-profits. It's unfortunate that sometimes impatient business people get involved with non-profits (in the same way they do with politics) and immediately bark out a list of ways non-profits need to be "run more like a business." I have too much respect for the complexity of what these organizations are trying to accomplish to think in those simple terms. What's more, I also know plenty of executives who have amassed large fortunes and then wasted small fortunes trying to "reinvent" philanthropy or start their own non-profits from scratch. Convinced they have fresh approaches to old problems, they don't do basic research and due diligence, including having frank conversations with folks working in the area and reviewing case studies of why previous approaches haven't worked.

Both sides, in other words, can learn from each other. In fact, the issue is not so much that we need to transfer the tools of business to non-profits, it's that I can promise you that if you take the issues most start-up companies have and list them next to the management challenges many non-profits have, you would not be able to identify which is which. All organizations benefit from certain very basic management principles, particularly organizations that are interested in growing. All of us, whatever missions we give ourselves, can be more effective in reaching our goals if we are alert to opportunities and disciplined in listening for signs of trouble and fixing problems before they escalate.

When I coach non-profit managers, I tend to repeat some of my most fundamental management tips and processes. You now have an understanding of where and when I first learned many of them and how they have worked at different organizations from the cannery, to the military, to start-ups, to major global corporations. I have focused on tips that work regardless of the size or domain of the organization.

As we move into a new section of the book that looks at my career in philanthropy and working with non-profits I want to summarize some of the management ideas that have consistently delivered the best results over the course of my career. I hope you have recognized other suggestions that are useful to you as you have read this book, but I am emphasizing some that have most consistently been helpful to me. The first five are basic ways of doing business that I learned in the cannery; the second five apply to managing organizations that are striving for significant growth. I hope that gathering them in one place and drawing a few connections to more examples will be a useful exercise and a simple reference. Then, I am going to go into some detail from the most recent phase of my involvement with different organizations, both as a philanthropist funding projects, but also as a board member and a coach trying to help the organizations optimize their resources and talent.

CHAPTER 18

10 key Morganisms that work for any organization

Respect and trust your people. Without those values, you will never be a successful manager. A key element of respect is modeling every behavior you expect in your organization and encouraging personal discipline and healthy habits so your teams have the stamina and energy to enjoy long term success.

As a leader, the character of your organization will never exceed your own. Make sure you exhibit every trait and quality you want your people to exhibit. A culture of trust and respect is vital. If you don't trust and respect an employee, that person should not be working for you. That is your responsibility. If you set an example of taking responsibility for your own decisions instead of scapegoating, your people will do the same.

Likewise, take care of your personal health and fitness and pay attention to physical dimensions of the workspace, such as safety and general morale. Encourage people to wear comfortable shoes to work so they can get up and take a walk during the day. Moving around during the day keeps the mind sharp and the body more relaxed. I've often scheduled "walking meetings" with people I need to speak with one on one. The importance of respect is consistent with the ideas of Abraham Maslow and his pyramid of basic needs, which has parallels in managing employees effectively. Only after employees' very basic needs are met first — physiological, safety, and a sense of love and belonging — will they have the self-esteem, comfort, and confidence to advance to self-actualization, or going beyond minimum expectations to develop and use higher level skills.

Finally, always model and reinforce the importance of planning. Organizational success is a marathon, not a sprint. Today, many individuals and organizations run at an unsustainable pace that is reactive but not strategic. I always urged my teams to spend 5 to 10 percent of their time planning and to start each day reassessing and reaffirming their priorities. You must plan to succeed. And you must plan...to succeed.

TWO

Value collaboration. Treat your partner, customer, or supplier's success as equivalent to your own.

Most organizations must develop the ability to collaborate internally among teams and also with outside partners. When you are engaged in any effort that demands collaboration, you must treat your partner's issues as paramount and do everything you can to resolve friction and help your partner succeed. This is the spirit of Mike Travaglio at our family's cannery; it is the essence of a committed service organization.

When you build this kind of relationship with a partner, it has been my experience that it can pay off for you both in ways that have little to do with the original collaboration parameters or other contractual obligations. For example, in the early 1980s, Applied was facing a quarterly loss that violated the covenants of a long-term loan we had in place. General Electric had been an early venture capital investor in the company and we had a good relationship. I got a call from GE's controller asking me if the company could increase its ownership of Applied to 20 percent so that GE could include Applied's earnings in GE's earnings going forward. We worked out a deal where GE bought $10 million worth of stock at a premium and it also extended a long-term loan of $10 million to us at a favorable interest rate, and we agreed to work together to optimize some technology. This rebalanced our debt to equity ratios and our original loan was back in compliance. GE benefited, and we benefited.

Not much later, I called Jack Welch and I explained that I was working to improve the management talent inside Applied; I asked if he might recommend some "high pots," which stands for "high potential" management talent from within GE who might consider joining Applied. It might sound like a strange request: Why should GE give up a high pot to help Applied? The answer is, because we were partners. Jack sent over about ten resumes, and from that batch we hired an outstanding GE executive named Dana Ditmore. Thanks in part to Dana's GE experience, he set up a focused global service organization for us that was unique in our industry. Service wasn't just a function for us, it was a separate business.

Dana embraced and enhanced our attitude about service, which was: we are not just selling a service, we are partnering to maximize our customer's success and we will commit to doing whatever that reasonably takes. You cannot build a healthy and productive partnership when you ignore your partner's issues, or your partner perceives a constant threat of you unfairly exploiting the relationship. This is true in business, marriage, friendship, non-profits, grocery stores, softball teams, international treaties, and neighborhood associations. GE was consistently the most helpful investor we had and gave us invaluable access to its management training and development programs; we also worked on useful collaborations with the GE medical systems groups, which also produced highly complex systems. If you convey that you appreciate and want to help your partner succeed, my experience is you will receive the same support in return when you need it.

My sense is that collaboration within an organization has become increasingly difficult to manage. I have been reading lately about a backlash that is developing because companies have over-emphasized the mechanics and tools of collaboration while missing the point of it: Messaging apps, open office set-ups, and forcing employees to interact more during the day have become the New Thing. But the idea that to free up the power of teams you just tear down the walls and force them to communicate more can be counter-productive.

To produce the very hard work of engineering, design, invention, and other knowledge work, employees need time to concentrate without interruption. When I make "value collaboration" a pillar of my fundamental management advice, I don't mean "schedule a lot of meetings." In fact, the "concrete" C in the "C to the 6th" presentation I mentioned in Chapter 15 is the linchpin: A manager needs to make clear a concrete purpose and, ideally, the decision he or she wants to make before scheduling any meeting. Managers should also pay attention to the work style of employees and avoid interrupting their concentration with low-value informational catch-ups, check-ins, team-building sessions, and other activities that can masquerade as collaboration but actually amount to distractions. This is where a situational management approach can be helpful in calibrating how much interaction and oversight a given employee requires to be successful.

THREE **Always listen for and even seek out signs of trouble. Bad news is good news if you do something about it.**

"Good news is no news, no news is bad news, and bad news is good news — if you do something about it." Create a culture that looks for and identifies problems as they occur and rewards quick response. As a manager "porpoise" into your organization periodically and talk to everyone at every level about what's going on, particularly if there is a problem. If you are listening, you will "hear" problems before you get confirmation of them through official channels. You will hear hints of concern, or discontent, or frustration. Or, where you once heard voices sounding optimistic, energetic, or excited you suddenly might not hear those qualities. Don't be like the person who gets in the car and hopes that odd engine noise will just go away. It won't.

In the previous example about our relationship with GE, before GE ever called me, I was hearing concerns from our controller. He warned that there could be serious consequences to our balance sheet, and therefore to our loan covenants, if orders did not materialize and the slowdown in semiconductors continued. Because I was aware of that, I immediately acted on GE's interest in increasing its ownership. Facing a problem squarely instead of going into a defensive or denial posture means you're giving yourself more time to solve it before the consequences escalate.

FOUR | Develop court sense and align with driving forces around you to create momentum.

In making decisions about the future direction of an organization, it's critical to assess the driving forces. Driving forces can be macroeconomic factors, technology innovations, industry directions, and global trends. Moore's Law was a driving force that helped us at Applied Materials, for example. Other driving forces today include a global interest in reducing reliance on fossil fuels, or the aging of the "Baby Boom" cohort. Micro driving forces can be unique, possibly fleeting opportunities such as a competitor's strategic shift or stumble, or tax incentives or other government supports that may expire.

It's a good exercise to periodically look at the driving forces related to whatever you are doing. Assess whether you are positioning yourself to take advantage of the changes. Look at the demographic you think represents your most important customers or funding sources and seek to understand what new ideas or cultural themes matter to them. Realize that this is a "best guess" domain but when you make a decision, keep recalibrating and adjusting.

I made a best guess when I first joined Applied: I made epitaxy and CVD the centerpiece of our product focus. As time went on, that business developed for us and became profitable. The true potential for epitaxy was in adapting it for use in creating memory chips, but that was a very difficult technical challenge. As the years went on and we developed other technologies addressing big markets, several of our CFOs recommended that we sell the epitaxy business because they thought we could get a better return on capital elsewhere.

I considered their recommendations, but did not follow them. Every time I spoke with customers I could see that they wanted this technology and they were assigning smart engineers in their organizations to help us in trying to make it work. This porpoising with customers revealed their commitment to be a powerful driving force:

We eventually did make it work, and today that business brings in more than half a billion dollars annually to Applied Materials.

I've always liked that song *The Gambler* by Kenny Rogers and the refrain: "You've got to know when to hold 'em, know when to fold 'em, know when to walk away, and know when to run." Business strategy is always a risk, but court sense and assessing driving forces will shape your instincts for what is likely to work.

FIVE

Stress the importance of making decisions and managing the consequences. Do not wait for perfect information before you decide: Implementation is 90 percent of the job.

Cost of Perfect Information

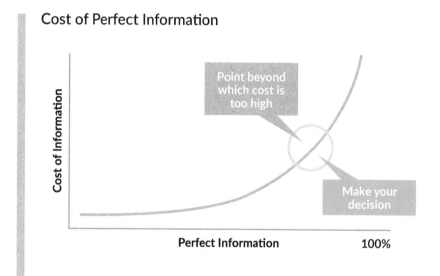

Voltaire said, "Don't let the perfect be the enemy of the good." That's good advice. Time is wasted and opportunities are lost when people become fixated on having perfect information rather than trusting their instincts, making decisions, and then managing the consequences. Organizations in motion can alter course much faster than they can go from zero to 60. Decisions create momentum.

You can streamline decisions by identifying the key driving forces. In the early 1990s, we needed to expand Applied's manufacturing operations. We were struggling with the cost of real estate, labor, and taxes in Silicon Valley. States were competing for business and reaching out to attract our investment. We could have analyzed the opportunities indefinitely, but in my mind the driving force was people — we needed engineering talent. Austin, Texas was near universities that were training a lot of talented engineers and many wanted to stay in Texas. The city of Austin was considered a plus when we were recruiting new talent from other cities and even Silicon Valley. We prepared a detailed analysis to implement the decision to go to Austin, but access to talent made the decision to go relatively easy.

In the story about Cissy Leung's perseverance with the P5000, another important element of the story was that I had a difficult decision to make whether to make or buy CVD product capability. At the time Bob Graham, a senior member of my executive team at Applied, felt strongly we should not risk developing our own system and instead should buy a competing company called Novellus. Novellus had a product called the Concept One. It was not going to match the uniformity we had targeted for the P5000 or have single wafer processing, but it was thought Concept One was almost ready for introduction, and it was considerably cheaper.

This was a real dilemma. There were different ways to look at the driving forces and experienced managers who did not agree. I had more faith in our internal development team than Bob did, and I had a feeling Concept One was not as ready for prime time as many thought. I did believe it was promising and could eventually complement a product like the P5000. It would have stretched us too thin to try to introduce the two products at the same time. When Bob indicated that he was going to join Novellus as CEO if we didn't buy the company, I wished him well and was sorry to lose him. Bob joined Novellus and did a good job marketing and selling Concept One and he built Novellus into a strong competitor. However, after I made the decision to support our internal team, we managed the consequences: I increased Dan Maydan's budget to help him speed up the development process. I warned Wall Street we'd have some quarterly losses until it was ready. I porpoised to visit Cissy and the teams developing the vital robotics and P5000 system regularly. It all paid off: We achieved an enormous technical innovation with the P5000 and created one of the industry's most successful series of new products for years to come.

Always stay on top of whether your original assumptions and execution are panning out and don't be afraid to have a Plan B at the ready. One of my favorite Plan B stories occurred when my team from Applied went to Japan and observed all the elements of "just in time" inventory systems. We were impressed by how radical a change it represented from U.S. manufacturing systems that included keeping large inventories of parts on hand. However, parked outside the plant at Honda were two helicopters. If the JIT system broke down somehow and a part could not arrive using the normal shipping system, the helicopters could be sent to get the critical parts to keep the line moving. The resources saved by not warehousing large backlogs of parts could easily pay for an occasional Plan B helicopter run. Honda's leadership anticipated the possible, occasional downside of a decision to use JIT and put an emergency plan in place to prevent an expensive loss of production if a snag occurred.

Build teams deliberately; look for both competence and complementary skills and character.

In building an organization it is essential to hire people who are fundamentally competent in whatever it is that they do, be it finance, technical writing, engineering, or service. Not only should you be looking for competence for the job at hand, but for a person whose skills can grow into the next level of the job. In addition to the usual measures such as academic record, job experience, and recommendations, do not stop calling references and former employers of a candidate until you come across at least two negatives that you can live with. That takes asking better questions and thinking more deeply about the job you're hiring for and the picture of the employee the reference is painting.

For example, if you're hiring a product designer who gets high technical marks and hits project deadlines, but who is known for being chronically late to work and sometimes being short-tempered, those negatives may be tolerable shortcomings. If you're hiring a customer service manager who is chronically late and short-tempered, that is a no-go.

Now, realize that competence is essential but not sufficient for success in teams. This is true at any scale, including a start-up company or a global non-profit or the executive suite of a major corporation. Certain qualities are always valued, such as intelligence and energy. However, other traits that tend to be about personality, such as the need to get credit, or introversion, or communication weaknesses, need to be balanced or at least addressed or the team can become dysfunctional. At Applied Materials, we grew so quickly that we used assessment tools like the Winslow Profiles to help us understand the dynamics of our people so we could assemble teams with complementary skills and therefore have a higher chance of success. In any organization, you must think about group dynamics and balance them for the good of the project.

SEVEN Understand and commit to doing the "whole job."

Most organizations are like airplanes. An airplane has distinct systems that work together to deliver the optimal result. Some help the plane take off, some keep it flying in a stable path, some monitor passenger safety and comfort, some create back-up resources for emergencies. All key functions must work, or the airplane won't fly; if only some work, the airplane may reach altitude but eventually will crash.

An organization may sell a product or a service, but it needs other functions and processes that support the mission: it needs a system to spend and control cash; it needs facilities and equipment; it needs human resources and a hiring process; it needs a quality process; it will have regulations to follow and reporting requirements. Without many of these in place, the organization won't even get off the ground. Over time, without all of these functioning, the organization will crash.

It's a paradox of management that you must set priorities and focus, but you must also create a plan to understand, monitor, and optimize every critical function. You must, as George Farnsworth reminded us so often at Applied, do "the whole job." Remember the "plate-spinner" running up and down a line of plates to keep them all going, revving up each plate as it starts to wobble. Make sure you assess and understand the basic functions your organization must execute for you to move forward in a predictable away, and then commit to a regular porpoising process for checking in and making sure you know which plates are wobbling.

EIGHT

Reinforce individual ownership of problems by always asking, "Who owns the monkey?" Create an accountable culture, and do not tolerate the victim mindset. A manager ideally is "first assistant" to his or her direct reports.

Effective organizations communicate well and empower people to make decentralized decisions. Ultimately, when you lead a growing organization, it's useful to think of yourself as "first assistant to" your direct reports. You want people at every level to understand the organization's goals and objectives and make decisions that align with those goals. This will never happen if you adopt an authoritarian posture or overturn decisions in a very public way to let everybody know who's boss. Concepts like Ken Blanchard's Situational Leadership Management matrix can be helpful in guiding how closely you monitor and help a given person in a given situation. It's been said that the difference between a good leader and a great leader is that a good leader wants to be highly thought of, while a great leader wants his or her people to think highly of themselves.

There are two aspects to accountability that are important to understand. First, an accountable attitude is the opposite of a victim mindset. In an accountable culture, employees are comfortable acknowledging reality, warts and all. Individuals do not just wait and hope things get better or spend their time crafting excuses or pointing fingers at others for mistakes, they take responsibility for finding solutions and improvements.

This posture is related to a corollary management concept, what I call "owning the monkey." You don't just buy a monkey, you have to take care of it, adjust to its behavior and consequences, and, in short, take responsibility. When you empower employees to make decisions, you also empower them to solve problems that arise from those decisions.

Say one of your reports shows up in your office one day with a problem — the monkey — on his or her shoulder. As a manager you want to acknowledge that you see the monkey, you care about the monkey, you may even pet the monkey for a few minutes. But you can't let that employee leave the monkey behind for you to take care of. You want to be sure that when your employee walks out the door of your office, the monkey goes, too. Owning the monkey means the responsible person cannot pass the buck; the individual must think through the consequences of decisions, and it helps train partners and customers that their point of contact will solve the problem. There is no need to escalate to the CEO's office at the first sign of trouble.

NINE
Proactively prepare for the next major shift and always "face the elevator door." All organizations grapple with cycles.

At the cannery and at Applied Materials, I ran businesses that were fundamentally cyclical. However, at some level all organizations, including non-profits, grapple with cycles. Early at Applied we developed the idea that we could best manage through cycles by reminding ourselves to "face the elevator door."

It's human nature to aim for a goal and then assume when you get there life will be easier. In business, people have a tendency to think that if they just hit some magic size or hit a particular milestone, they not only will achieve success but it will become easier to be successful. This is not true in business or in much of life, for that matter. Variables are always shifting. The macroeconomic context changes, new technologies and other dynamics disrupt existing patterns and strategies, wars break out, a competitor stumbles, disasters affect commodity prices — all kinds of things happen that can help you or hurt you. There are very few industries where managers can push the "autopilot" button and lean back and take a nap.

As a leader of an organization trying to grow and be successful, you are always going to be riding in an economic elevator that is moving, either going up or down. In inherently cyclical industries, this becomes a potentially high-reward, always high-risk ride and the penalty for misjudging the direction at any one moment can be severe.

Facing the elevator door means being ready to capitalize on opportunity (the elevator door opening) regardless of where you are in a cycle. Pursuing an opportunity usually takes capital, so you prepare yourself squirreling away cash when business is good, and raising it when capital markets are receptive. In general, many companies get into trouble by overly optimistic revenue projections that they use to justify over-spending when business is good and demand is high. At Applied we were always careful to save when business was good. Then, as our competitors struggled to deal with a business contraction, we had the money to increase R&D and roll out products to supply the next wave of demand.

Non-profits also live in a cyclical environment. Their fortunes often are pegged to business growth and strong stock markets, which put cash in their donors' pockets. By collecting and saving resources during strong financial cycles, during weaker cycles they, too, can be opportunistic in obtaining facilities or assets at a discount or preparing new campaigns to launch when the giving climate improves.

At Applied, we even faced the elevator door in our corporate giving and planning: We contributed 1percent of our pretax profits to community affairs, but established a constant level of funding by that department. In good times, we put amounts above that funding level in a foundation. That meant the foundation could maintain a consistent level of giving to our communities even when we experienced short-term financial pressures (and odds were the community was, too, so our support was even more important).

TEN   Since modern life is filled with paradoxes, help your teams understand and work within those tensions.

Today's most effective organizations must be global and local; product development must be fast and also low-defect; companies must attain critical mass but interact with customers in a personal, human way (this is sometimes called being both big and small). Non-profits face their own set of paradoxes: They need to be efficient and develop repeatable processes, but they need to be flexible to deal with individual human beings with unique challenges and capacities.

Paradoxes create tension. A common mistake is to ignore the tension and just keep adding more responsibilities to people already working very hard. When you give orders that ignore an underlying tension, employees become insecure, in themselves and in your leadership. They worry: "Am I the only person who is having difficulty trying to do two opposite things at once?" They become paralyzed, gun-shy. It's a little like the new football mentality to address concussions, where coaches are told to tell players, "Hit as hard as you can, but don't hurt anybody."

We all must cope with paradoxes. There is a term in professional auto-racing called "shake speed" that conveys a paradox I often felt as a CEO. Shake speed is the point where the vehicle is going too fast to control and may crash. To compete, Applied Materials needed to develop products and capitalize on opportunities as fast as possbile — without losing our ability to maintain quality and provide excellent service to customers. I thought of running Applied as driving with my right foot on the gas, my left hovering above the brake in case I heard the sound of trouble. We had to run near but not at shake speed. Go too slow, your competitors beat you; go too fast, you beat yourself.

You can actually make paradoxes work for you by first, understanding and acknowledging that they exist, and secondly, reassuring your people that they have the skills to keep making good decisions. Remind them that their experience has developed their instincts: Make a decision, manage the consequences.

I recently heard four-star General Stanley McCrystal of the U.S. Army talking about the importance of empathy in leadership; he said even in war, the ability to convey that you understand how a given person feels in a situation that may be confusing, stressful, or complicated gives a leader an advantage in winning the individual's trust and confidence. Paradoxes may force certain choices about priorities up the chain, but that is where your job is to manage near but not beyond shake speed.

CHAPTER 19

New horizons

By my early 60s, I had spent most of my career at Applied Materials. I never had any desire to leave my job as CEO to run any other company or serve in government. Many executives talk about how it's important to keep taking on new challenges and not get stale at the CEO spot, but I never felt that was an issue for me. In more traditional companies, I would say ten years is a reasonable assignment for a CEO. In that period, you've made some good moves, you've made some mistakes, and you've fixed the mistakes. The trouble is, it is human nature as time goes on to spend more and more time defending what you've done rather than positioning the company for its next leap forward. At Applied, on the other hand, our "extreme sport" demanded so much flexibility, change, and challenge from year to year there was never time to check the rearview mirror to see who was second-guessing me. The market and our products were changing constantly. I can't say I ever took seriously the opportunity to interview for another position. Internally, the board and I had discussed that my 65th birthday in 2003 was probably a good target for my retirement. That would mark over 25 years leading the company.

In 1988, Harvard Business School Professor Jeffrey Sonnenfeld wrote a book called *The Hero's Farewell*. He interviewed 50 former CEOs of major corporations and spent years analyzing their departures. Some were smooth, easy transitions; others fought leaving until a bitter end. Sonnenfeld claimed there were four kinds of CEOs: Monarchs, Generals, Ambassadors, and Governors. There are many nuances to his book-long analysis, but basically Monarchs and Generals tend to identify very closely with the heroic leader role and a sense of mission. They feel uncomfortable leaving their positions because their egos are heavily tied up with their status. They often hang around too long. Ambassadors and Governors tend to finish up their tenures with a greater sense of accomplishment and satisfaction. Governors tend to jump immediately into another demanding job. The Ambassador group probably is closest to my CEO personality type. Ambassadors don't tend to prolong their goodbyes and they also don't feel a need to replicate their experience in a new place, although they enjoy sharing hard-won insights.

When it is time for a CEO to leave, succession issues become pervasive in a company. This can create a distraction. Executives tend to handicap the internal horses and align with the contender they think will get the job. As the various scenarios play out, lower level managers hold back making decisions based on whether they think the odds-on favorite will like or not like what they want to do next.

The idea of promoting from within is always an attractive idea. You like to think that in addition to developing the executive team to do a better job for the company, you have helped individuals personally develop and take their skills to a new level. If a single internal candidate distinguishes her or himself, has a vision for the future the board thinks makes sense, and has the respect of employees, the transition when the CEO is ready or has to step aside theoretically can be very smooth. That appeared to be what happened at Apple when Tim Cook stepped up to the CEO job after Steve Jobs, and also when John Chambers succeeded John Morgridge at Cisco. An internal candidate is intimately familiar with the company's business, its challenges, its strategic goals, and its capabilities. In fact, when you are the leading company in a given industry sector, like Applied was as I neared retirement, it is difficult to find a good candidate from outside your company who adds value.

On the other hand, it's not easy for a single executive from a good team to distinguish him or herself above all others. The process of grooming possible successors can be divisive. Good CEOs build a complementary team, as I have described. Those on the team who thrive tend to be very good at their key domain deliverable — marketing, manufacturing, product development, sales, finance, government relations, and so on. Or executives may have a reputation for a certain kind of skill that's not tied to a formal function, such as deal negotiators or "fire fighters" who are good at handling crises or fixing dysfunctional processes. The issue is that if these types have aspirations to someday be CEO, will they understand their weaknesses and invest in working on those? And realistically, will they have time to do that? Or, being highly competitive individuals, will they focus on getting credit and sometimes even sabotaging others?

Just to make things even more complicated, in a technology company the company lives and dies on new product development. For the senior technology and R&D executives, managing a group operating at the state of the art leaves little time for rounding out your skills in marketing or finance. Yet when that next level opening appears, a board is going to be concerned that an R&D leader doesn't have a broad enough skill set to keep the entire company on course. That is one reason why it is much more common for technical executives to go off and start a company rather than get promoted into their existing company's CEO spot. At the new company, they can build a new team that has strengths that they personally lack and investors will bet on their technical capacity and drive to make the new venture work.

There was a period in Applied Materials' life when our Dr. Dan Maydan was directly running projects and earned a higher bonus than I did as the CEO. I had fellow CEOs and investors remark about the discrepancy to me as if it was shocking. That kind of thinking results if you let your ego trump common sense. The more successful Dan was in meeting the tough development targets that fueled his bonus, the higher our stock rose, and the more valuable everyone's stock in Applied was. He deserved every nickel; he drove our product development so successfully we achieved and held a leadership position in our industry for years. Everybody at Applied Materials benefited from Dan focusing on technical product development; and we compensated him for the vital role he played in keeping us ahead of the pack. As the years went by he grew as an executive and he eventually became President of Applied Materials until he retired as President Emeritus.

As the 21st century dawned, Applied Materials had several executives who also were excellent in their areas of expertise and responsibility. Our consultant Adizes was helpful in maximizing their potential. Dan, Adizes, and I worked very hard together to help them become better managers. The executives grew and learned how to get decisions made in a complex global corporation. In fact, they made up a highly complementary team, but over the years they had developed some issues with one another and there was friction. Dan and I had managed to get them to work together pretty well, but we doubted they could find a way to work together if we were not there. I had some frank conversations with each of them about this, but none of them emerged as the clear leader. This was frustrating to me. Unfortunately, it was pretty clear to me and the board the promotion of any one of them was going to mean the others would leave. The board finally decided we should look outside the company for a suitable candidate.

The rule of three

One of the tips we always preached at Applied Materials was what I called the "Rule of Three." That meant two things: first, always have, know, and focus on three priorities. Most of us do many more than three things per day, per week, per year, but I always took time every morning to make sure I knew exactly what my top three priorities were so that as I budgeted my time and added or subtracted from my calendar every day, those priorities were reflected.

I encourage people to have list of priorities for a week, a month, three months, and finally a year. Checking these periodically helps you to prepare for a priority out further in time. You may need to gather information, hire talent, get permissions, etc. The right way to review this list is to make sure all your activities every day are moving you past short-term priorities and toward long-term goals. Don't let the urgent constantly rob time needed for important long-term priorities. Another common mistake is to put off aligning every day's activities with a long-term goal, as if the long-term goal is what you plan to "get to" in a year.

MORGANISM

Remember two 'rules of three': First, always understand your top three priorities and make sure your short-term activities support your long-term priorities. Second, always keep in mind three people who would be good additions to your company or organization.

The other rule of three was related to one of the elements that I felt should be a priority for every employee: always develop and keep a personal list of at least three people who would be a good fit to work at Applied. Being reminded to do that made people more alert when they were in meetings or even social situations around Silicon Valley or when on the road.

For many years, one name on my personal list of three good candidates to join Applied was an Intel executive named Michael Splinter. Mike had started his career at North American Aviation. Then, he spent about 20 years rising through the ranks at Intel, as a global technical and manufacturing executive and more recently in sales and marketing. Intel was a key customer of Applied's. I knew Mike well; also I knew how highly his colleagues thought of him.

Ordinarily you would not try to recruit a top executive from a customer's company. However, my thinking was it was good to check in periodically with prospects working for customers, because if the person was looking to leave their company anyway, it was better for Applied Materials and for our customer if they joined us. It happened that for a number of years every time we had a possible opening at Applied, Mike had just received another promotion at Intel, so the timing didn't work. But as the board and I thought about what a good candidate would look like, the dynamics kept leading back to Mike. The industry was changing and therefore a key global customer's perspective offered significant value. Also, Mike had operated at scale, and he understood our industry very well.

At Intel, Mike had been considered a strong internal candidate to succeed Craig Barrett as CEO. However in 2003, I learned that another candidate, Paul Otellini, had been named President. That indicated that Paul had the inside track. I realized that meant Mike might be tempted to look elsewhere for a comparable CEO spot. I scheduled our periodic lunch.

With Mike such a valuable executive, I was very straightforward with him: I had an excellent relationship with Intel and had known its executives for many years. I did not want to get into a bidding war for Mike. If he personally and professionally felt the time was right for him to leave Intel, I asked him to commit to that. I felt certain our board was willing to make a fair and attractive compensation offer once he made a decision that he would be leaving Intel. I immediately made plans for Becky and me to go up to his home in Granite Bay that weekend and have dinner with Mike and his wife. The dinner went very well, and I asked him to decide by Monday if he was ready to "walk the plank." On Monday he called and agreed to take the job.

My next chapter

CEOs tend to be high-energy people. In terms of what comes next there are some standard options: taking on another full-time position; joining a corporate board; working as a business consultant; "angel investing" or using private money to support start-ups as an individual rather than as part of a venture capital fund. Others pursue politics or appointed positions in government such as ambassadorships or special councils or trade groups.

I had plenty of time to prepare for my departure. As I prepared to leave Applied, I felt that I had spent enough time in corporate boardrooms. And for reasons I have already spelled out, investing a lot of energy in Washington politics at a time when the insights of business leaders were not being considered in a serious way did not appeal to me. But Becky and I had always shared an interest in public service and philanthropy. Over time I realized that philanthropy was the main activity I wanted to focus on for my next phase of life. Fortunately, I knew and had worked with some outstanding business leaders who became philanthropists. People like Dave Packard, Gordon Moore, and John Morgridge were all friends of mine and they were excellent models.

In 1993, well before I left Applied, Becky and I had started our own family foundation. I wanted us to go slowly in this process. Many business people charge into philanthropy with good intentions and blazing guns, only to quickly become discouraged and even give up. Executives are used to being in control, giving orders, demanding metrics on their return on investment. I'll get into more about that shortly, but neither politics nor philanthropy responds well to that aggressive command and control mentality. Philanthropy is often aimed at complicated, intractable challenges; if solving certain problems were easy, somebody would already have done it. In business, you can buy the talent and tools to accomplish many things; in philanthropy, you have to develop capacity in a much smaller pool of people and resources.

So, initially, the Morgan Family Foundation made gifts to our local Community Foundation. That approach enabled our family to separate the tax benefits from our gifting and it allowed us to work with an organization that understood local needs and was set up to effectively distribute funds. They could do the work of vetting organizations and making sure funds were used according to our wishes.

We wanted the family foundation to both serve as a giving structure for us, but also as a way to teach our children and grandchildren about both investing and giving. We learned a lot and the foundation quickly became a way for all of us to pursue some of our personal interests and passions in a way that helped organizations trying to make the world better. It was rewarding to see how some of the experiences Becky and I had given Jeff and Mary as children, especially in the outdoors, had developed in some very interesting and satisfying ways. I believe they contributed to both Jeff and Mary becoming what I would call "systems thinkers." They appreciate the need for multi-dimensional solutions to complex problems.

The Santa Claus model doesn't scale

We also learned a few hard lessons ourselves. Several of my friends and I once got the idea to cut through the bureaucracy of giving and just award "hero" grants to individuals we read about in the newspaper or saw on television. There had been a couple of very dramatic acts of courage by young people that inspired us to want to reward courage in our community. We gave the funds to a Community Foundation to distribute.

Frankly, it was a mess. Good intentions not withstanding, this is not a model that produces effective results. Sometimes we couldn't find or keep track of the winners. Or the winners were wary of getting lured into some kind of scam and didn't collect the money. Another friend of ours personally proposed to underwrite the rehabilitation of an area of Central California that had become very run down. The neighbors could not agree on what improvements they wanted so he eventually cancelled the offer! These experiences proved to us the value of operating less like Santa Claus and more like investors in strong programs and people who have a long-term view. It's more bureaucratic but ultimately it is more effective.

As time went on, Becky and I realized we each had areas of particular interest. I have had a lifelong interest in conservation and establishing a sustainable planet, for example. Becky was instrumental in getting the regional stewardship effort for local regions to involve business, government, and academics to work together to improve the business climate, education, and various government services. She also feels a deep affinity for young women's challenges, particularly teen mothers. There also were domains like education and youth projects that were equally important to us both, and our whole family was excited about our family foundation providing assistance to our son, Jeff, after he first raised funding to launch the Global Heritage Fund (to do that he secured the help of Bill Draper, a pioneer venture capitalist, and a few other start-up supporters). Global Heritage Fund seeks to protect and restore endangered cultural heritage sites in the developing world.

Our family foundation organized its giving into these key areas. We encouraged Jeff and Mary to identify their personal areas of interest and each member of our family board had discretionary funds they could mark for distribution to projects they wanted to support.

Just to clarify a few basics about philanthropy, a foundation is primarily a funding organization that provides financial support to non-profit groups that have programs and projects in a particular area of need (on a global basis, non-profit organizations tend to be referred to as "NGOs" which stands for "non-governmental organizations"). We were not interested in starting or running these organizations, just identifying good ones and supporting their work. As we paid more attention to the nonprofit sector, Becky and I saw differences in how organizations managed their resources. We developed preferences about how we wanted our funds to be put to use. We were more inclined to work more directly with organizations involved in the spaces where we wanted to make a difference, and we became more active and involved givers — like investors. We realized that we wanted to provide more than just dollars. Soon, we would find ourselves deeply involved in several projects that occupy much of our time to this day.

CHAPTER 20

Nature for people

By the late 1990s when I still was CEO of Applied Materials, the challenge of creating a sustainable planet was looming larger and larger for me. By this time, I had traveled to many countries where there was very little support for conservation concerns and I saw firsthand that conditions were degrading fast.

One of the most striking experiences I had in my travels came in 1997. After the annual SEMI Trade Show in Taiwan, the Applied Materials Asian management team organized a sightseeing trip down the Yangtze River from Chongqing to Wuxi. The Three Rivers Gorge Dam was under construction. We motored down river on a large cruiser holding about 100 people. The river cuts through steep, towering gorges that twist in serpentine patterns as the river flows. Many parts of the journey are dramatic and stunningly beautiful.

But the extent of environmental degradation in the area was sobering. The Yangtze is the world's third largest river system, behind only the Nile and the Amazon River; it begins in the mountains of Tibet and flows into the East China Sea. The size of the forests along its banks was cut in half in the last century. During Mao's Great Leap Forward in the late 1950s, vast sections of forest along its banks were leveled to supply firewood to fuel the "backyard furnace" foundries peasants were encouraged to build and run in order to make steel out of scrap metal. In such a heavily sloped area, removing the trees meant that after every rain huge amounts of topsoil washed into the Yangtze. When we visited, the river was an opaque chocolate milk color. The deforested land was converted to agricultural use, but the topsoil washing down the slopes also carried fertilizer that created conditions in the river that killed many fish and aquatic plants.

Construction on the Three Gorges Dam began in 1994 and was finished in 2012, long after we visited. It is the world's largest power station. It also was designed to help control the floods that have killed many people along the path of the river through the centuries. Unfortunately, the consequences of the dam on the health of the river ecosystem have been substantial: The dam itself has created a reservoir for sediment and organic and industrial waste that no longer continues downstream, destroying water quality. Also, the project displaced over 1 million people and flooded 13 cities and dozens of towns and villages where no efforts to remove toxins from foundries and other activities were conducted prior to the flooding.[3] As I looked at the murky river, the deforested slopes, and the many villages black from decades of burning coal and wood, I was convinced that I had to do my part to help the world begin to repair damage from large-scale projects and haphazard development.

Santa Cruz Island

Witnessing environmental damage on this large scale made a deep impact on me. But the event that launched a more committed phase of my conservation work actually occurred much closer to home. In 1998, to celebrate my 60th birthday, Becky arranged for our family and some friends to take a trip to Santa Cruz Island off the coast of Santa Barbara. This is a unique and special ecosystem. Santa Cruz is the largest of California's eight "Channel Islands." It has 77 miles of coastline and more than 1000 species of plants and animals. There are twelve species on Santa Cruz Island found nowhere else on Earth.

In the early 19th century the island had been owned by a family that grazed pigs, sheep, and cattle there. The sheep and pigs had gone feral

---

[3] TNC (The Nature Conservancy) would later work with the Chinese to help them improve their water management and dam-building strategies. This is very important since the Chinese will build most of the dams worldwide in the next 20 years. A "Three Rivers Partnership" was formed around the Yangtze, the Mississippi, and the Pantanal in South America. That, plus consulting projects have produced improvements in dam building, and freshwater river strategies both in China and the U.S.

and depleted the vegetation. By the late 1970s, it was an ecosystem in crisis. Bald eagles that ate fish had been native to the island, but DDT spraying decades earlier had wiped them out. That opened the door to golden eagles from the mainland. Unlike bald eagles eating only fish, golden eagles prey on small mammals such as the Santa Cruz Island Fox, which nearly went extinct.

In 1978, The Nature Conservancy stepped in and purchased the island. TNC was launched in the 1950s, and by this point had grown to have local affiliates in every state; it had done impressive work rescuing small important properties and ecosystems in many areas of the U.S. On Santa Cruz Island, careful management led to the rebounding of the native fox population and the return of bald eagles. Non-native golden eagles were moved to the Rockies; and the bald eagles introduced from pairs raised at the San Francisco Zoo began repopulating the island. The executive director of the California Chapter of The Nature Conservancy at the time, Steve McCormick, hosted our trip. He and I spoke at some length.

Nature *for* people

I had heard good things about TNC. One reason I looked forward to speaking with Steve was that Becky had been impressed with the role the organization took on to reduce the environmental damage that rice straw burning was causing around Sacramento. Each fall after harvest, rice fields contain a high volume of dry straw debris, which rice farmers traditionally burn. However, rice farmers were coming under intense pressure from the local community and others angry at the smoke and particulate the practice created. TNC helped negotiate a creative alternative: Since the Sacramento Valley wetlands are a primary stopping point for migrating ducks, TNC convinced rice farmers to actually flood the fields after harvest, dramatically expanding the wetlands. That created an opportunity to create private duck hunting clubs on the land, which helped compensate the farmers for the higher expenses they incurred to deal with the rice straw when they couldn't burn it. The increase in use of the wetlands by ducks has steadily expanded the duck population (more than compensating for the tiny fraction lost to hunting), and created a more vibrant ecosystem.

If they could not have reached that agreement, the farmers eventually would have lost the right to burn the debris and might have gone out of business. Instead, they became partners in conservation, which the communities appreciated. It fit the Silicon Valley leadership model Becky pushed as CEO of Joint Venture Silicon Valley — bring the public and private sectors together to make things happen.

The conservation world has some factions that would prefer to rope off wild areas so most humans never enter them again. From what I've seen that achieves little except creating enemies. TNC was one of the first major conservation organizations to realize that conservation needs to be about saving nature *for* people, not saving nature *from* people. It also is focused on scientific analysis and careful evaluation and assessment of lands. Setting aside important watersheds, forests, and wildlife corridors also demands responsible use and enjoyment of resources. Farmers and ranchers can be tremendous partners in conservation, with a deep respect for the land and a long-term view. Similarly, boaters, hikers, backpackers, hunters, fishermen, and casual visitors have shown they can enjoy ecosystems while having minimal negative impact. What's more, when they appreciate the value of biodiversity and preserving species, they become allies and advocates for ecosystems in other arenas.

As Steve reinforced during our conversation, TNC was using eco-regional strategies: within a region, the organization formed partnerships, recognizing that land trusts and other community-based organizations provided the local knowledge, experience, and network that were critical to achieving TNC's long-term conservation goals. I respected TNC for collaborating from a posture that represents one of my management principles: all partners need to benefit from a deal and each partner should treat the others' needs as paramount. The next year, I joined TNC's California Board of Trustees.

Because of our special interest in the northern Sierra, where our family had skied and vacationed for many years, I made a point to learn more about the issues facing that region. Becky and I spent time with Jim Gaither, Jr., TNC's lead eco-regional ecologist for the Sierra. I was impressed by Jim's knowledge of the habitat and ecosystems and by TNC's potential to provide leadership across the region. In addition to supporting his research as a board member, in 2002 the Morgan Family Foundation gave a 4-year gift of $1 million to TNC's Northern Sierra Project.

Again, management is often about dealing with paradoxes. Just as a modern global corporation has to be both global and local in how it does business, so does global conservation find itself grappling with opposing tensions. A common one is related to the phrase "Not In My Backyard," or NIMBY. In concept people the world over agree that environmental issues are important. On the global level we ask: Are we properly evaluating the impact of human activities on clean air, water, and soil quality? Are we on course to sustain a planet with just over seven billion people today that will grow to nine billion by 2050? It's not difficult to find agreement that the answer to those questions is probably no, as a planet we could do a much better job of conserving and protecting many key resources. We should decrease pollution and clean up toxic waste, invent cleaner new technologies, limit development in fragile wild areas.

Ok, all in agreement. Good, now where do we start? Who goes first? Who should be in charge? And when we clean up that toxic waste from a wild area, where do we put it? Suddenly, we telescope down to the local situation and backs go up. That's when governments balk and say, "Why are you focused on what we're doing when our neighbor X is a much bigger offender?" That's when industry sectors lobby for regulators or governments in general to prioritize the Other Guy's issue — for example, cleaning up a watershed from agricultural run-off instead of forcing farmers to reduce waste.

To affect change we must apply the larger goal location by location by location. International coalitions, nations, regions, states, counties, municipalities, and private property owners are just a few of the stakeholders with something to say about any given plan. Layers of law, history, culture, social trends, unique biological systems and species — the list goes on and on — shape the solutions as well.

Beyond 'bucks and acres'

Everything begins with a realistic assessment. Just taking the northern Sierra region, for example, what I soon learned was that some of the northern Sierra's challenges were an artifact of a plan going back to President Abraham Lincoln. When work began on the transcontinental railroad in 1863, the federal government granted railroad companies ownership 20 miles each side of the roadbed to every other square mile of land, keeping the squares in between. The grant allowed railroads to pay for construction by using or selling their sections without giving them complete control of a huge region. In the mountains, railroads held on to their private sections, while many public sections became part of the national forests. Timber companies eventually acquired close to 75 percent of the private land, creating a checkerboard pattern of alternating private and public land across the central Sierra region. This checkerboard ownership pattern that persists today presents significant conservation and land management challenges. Dealing with the checkerboard was one of a number of projects in which we felt a connection and urgency to help, and it would lead to a much more significant initiative I'll talk about in the next chapter.

In 2003, the same year I retired as CEO but was still chairman of the board of Applied Materials, Hank Paulson, the CEO of Goldman Sachs, asked me to join the TNC Asia Pacific Council of business leaders. He and Lee Kuan Yew, the Prime Minister of Singapore, had created the council to advise the TNC management in Asia. The council did a trip to Hong Kong with a preliminary meeting in Palau. We discussed how TNC had the opportunity to work with the Chinese on a plan to protect large wilderness areas and improve the environment.

This initiative was going to be different than most TNC projects because what TNC typically did was buy land or establish easements to put in preserves. In China the government owned all the land. The organization's efforts there would need to be focused on communication, marketing, and knowledge transfer. To be successful in conservation, China would have to educate its own people about the value of wild lands and biodiversity. It had to come up with incentives to motivate local communities and government structures to clean up and/or protect ecosystems.

I had an important and experienced ally on the AP Council and later the TNC Global Board in supporting TNC's work in China. Shirley Young had previously been a General Motors vice president who lived and worked in China. Shirley is Chinese and she had keen insights to the culture and strategies that were most likely to be effective. At every meeting, we found ourselves in a kind of "tag team" discussion where we reinforced and supported what the other person had said about the importance of building a core capability of communication, marketing, education, and organized knowledge transfer.

Shirley and I saw an opportunity to create a brand image for TNC that stood for objective use of science and thoughtful, rational, often creative solutions. As that developed, it would reinforce our efforts at fund-raising in Asia and help get political leaders and influential people on board. Within TNC, we needed to sharpen our knowledge-transfer capabilities; we needed to look at our projects, which had been fine-tuned for particular environments, and see the larger ideas and approaches that might transfer to other regions facing similar challenges.

I gave Hank the best advice I could offer on TNC strategy in Asia. A few months afterwards, Hank became the Chairman of TNC's then board of governors. Next, Steve and Hank asked me to join TNC's board, which met in the Washington, DC area, but I resisted. I had traveled so much for so long I did not want to take on any regular commitments east of the Sierra.

Fate had other plans, so let me provide a little background on the nature of the challenge Hank and Steve were trying to take on. The national organization had actually gone through a pretty tumultuous decade. In 1990, the TNC board realized the organization needed an overhaul. It had grown top-heavy and slow to respond and its fund-raising had stalled. TNC brought in a CEO named John Sawhill who had had an impressive career at McKinsey. He shaped up the organization on a number of fronts and had attracted a large number of well-known figures and business leaders to the board. Fundraising improved, and the scope and number of projects TNC took on increased.

However, Sawhill died unexpectedly in 2000, and TNC lacked experienced leadership ready to step in. Worse, at the point when Hank was recruiting me, it was in some public relations turmoil. It had ended up on the wrong side of a highly critical story in *The Washington Post* inferring that TNC was doing transactions that benefited various board members and cronies. The article was unfairly negative in my opinion, in part because TNC was trying to think for the long term, and it was trying new approaches to protect ecosystems that sometimes provided near-term use for private parties but eventually transitioned into permanent conservation areas.

Another case where bad news is good news if you do something about it. The article and some of the critical voices in it were like an ominous sound in the canning line. Whether they deserved the *Post's* harsh criticism or not, clearly something was out of kilter at TNC. The attention made clear that the organization had grown quickly and its leadership was not able to develop a strategy and manage all the different activities that local affiliates were getting involved in. Plenty of local chapters were doing excellent work in their regions. But as the challenges became bigger, crossed state lines, required national fund-raising campaigns, and involved federal tax laws and lands and international issues as well, TNC needed to rethink the parent organization's structure, mission, and strategy and shore up talent and resources.

In most challenging situations facing communities, the best way to achieve a sustainable solution is to get all stakeholders, public and private, engaged early. Avoid the temptation to invite others "on board" late in the process, when they will feel marginalized. Beware of creating a board or committee with too many observers; each stakeholder should have a role, deliverables, and a responsibility to make and manage the consequences of decisions.

One of the most critical strategic concerns was that the TNC board was divided on whether it should remain focused on U.S. conservation or expand to a more global organization. Based on my travels and my perception of the various ecological crises developing around the world, I thought TNC should definitely aim to be a global force in conservation.

I didn't see any other organization effectively filling that role on the global stage and thought it was an important opportunity for TNC and a critical need. The challenge was that existing management had experience in land deals — buying parcels and establishing easements. Internally they called their strengths "bucks and acres." Going global would require broader strategic thinking, better management skills, and experience and understanding about operating globally.

I finally told Hank and Steve McCormick (who had been chosen to succeed John Sawhill as CEO) that I would serve on the board for a year to try to help them through this crisis. I ended up chairing the board's nominating and governance committee, and we added human resources oversight to the committee's responsibilities. Hank was experienced at dealing with Congress, which was looking into TNC's activities. I was focused on helping create a more effective board and helping Steve with the multitude of TNC's internal issues. I agreed with an independent committee report that we needed a smaller but more engaged board that met more often. We reduced the number of director slots from 41 to 21, and we increased meetings from three times per year to four and expected attendance. We defined three advisory councils: trustee, science, and conservation. Pete Correll, a seasoned board member, stayed a couple of years beyond his term to lead the audit committee. The Nominating Committee quickly prepared a table of preferred talents and began to search for someone to eventually become head of the Audit Committee which led to the excellent choice of Teresa Beck, a Utah chapter trustee, who had risen through controller and financial jobs to become President of American Stores. Luckily, from the Illinois chapter, trustee Muneer Satter, an experienced global investor was added to the finance committee chaired by Gordy Crawford of Capital Research fame. The Global board had about 21 people with the breadth and depth of experience — scientists, global executives, state trustees, and government — all willing to prioritize TNC in their schedule.

In taking on the CEO's job, Steve had walked into a difficult situation and one for which he was not fully prepared. He had been the respected California state director and was hired to pursue a global expansion, but the board and trustees were split on whether TNC should even go global. Steve did not have the global management experience needed to sort this out, and he resigned.

Global efforts require that executives have flexibility and openness to different ways of operating, and a willingness to travel a lot of "seat miles" to gain firsthand knowledge. In my opinion, leading a global organization like TNC requires not only the outstanding management and leadership skills to run a complex organization but also actual extensive international experience. As the board initiated a search for a new CEO, I emailed the board that if we were going global, we needed its full support. And candidates for TNC president must have the international travel scars required for developing high-level relationships overseas with partners, government officials, and businesses.

Teresa Beck chaired the search effort. A few leading candidates emerged including a former Goldman Sachs executive named Mark Tercek who had experience in Europe and Asia. Teresa made sure the committee had done its homework. In line with my beliefs about recruiting, she had the positives and more importantly the negatives clearly researched. Mark had been recommended by several different sources from the conservation community to a member of the search committee, Frank Loy, a former Under Secretary for Democracy and Global Affairs. That was a good sign. I also felt that we would be well-served by a leader who had come from either the management consulting world or investment banking; in both those fields, individuals have to parachute into complicated, often high-pressure situations and use an orderly process to analyze what is going on and discern what the options are. That pretty much defined what the next TNC President was going to have to do around the world.

Mark came to California toward the end of the selection process and stopped by to visit with me. As I often do, I invited him to take a walk. During the couple of hours we covered many subjects as I tried to assess the potential of long-term success and to understand what the positive characteristics as well as the negative might portend. Just as in the for-profit world, you would like to develop good candidates internally. However, the stars often don't align that way, especially when an organization needs to enter a new strategic or growth phase. I thought Mark would do a good job taking TNC where we should go.

The final step was board approval. Interestingly, this illustrates the importance of settings for good decision-making. The TNC board made its first global trip to a preserve in the mountains outside Quito, Ecuador. We had an opportunity to support the first of what became an important global priority for TNC: creating funds to preserve watersheds that provide fresh water downstream to local people. Visiting the preserve highlighted the opportunity in front of us. Water is one of the most valuable natural resources in a world with a growing population. It drove home the powerful needs that we could help fill in an environmentally responsible way.

During that meeting the board unanimously agreed to support a Global Strategy and to hire Mark as president. And that, in turn was a "watershed" moment for TNC and I think we were all surprised as we gathered our global capability how strong it really was. Creating a sustainable world is an enormous challenge; however, the excellent global capability from trustees, management, scientists, other staff, and the support from TNC's extensive relationships around the world give me great hope.

CHAPTER 21

Not just reports, progress

My intent to serve for one or two years on the TNC Global Board turned into three terms for a total of nine years. When I look back on the experience today, I think one reason I stayed as long as I did was because the situation felt so similar to Applied Materials in the 1980s. TNC had strategic and personnel challenges and it needed to create systems and better processes, but it had huge potential. Once Hank, the board, and the management team cleaned out the obvious problems and tamped down major fires, you could see great opportunities. TNC had talent, base capability, and people who are like Applied people — they're smart, committed, they'll go anywhere and do anything to be successful collectively. And they do things for the right reasons.

Another element of what made working with TNC fun for me was that I had spent most of my career running a company that made big, complicated pieces of equipment that ultimately manufactured technology that operated at nanoscale — the big machines that make the little chips. What Applied did made possible innovations ranging from the Internet to smartphones, but it was always a challenge to explain advances in semiconductor technology, let alone our contribution on the equipment end. To get investors up to speed and excited about a new strategic direction or innovation, we sometimes had to walk them through technology primers involving physics, materials science, and chemistry, in addition to electrical engineering. And then we'd get to the business implications and global competitive landscape.

The conservation goals of The Nature Conservancy on the other hand, were as obvious as a mountain range, as clear as a Sierra stream, as inspiring as a fresh ocean breeze. The underlying ecological systems were no less and possibly even more complex than semiconductor manufacturing equipment, but it was fun to work on projects where you eventually could walk on, float or sail across, smell, touch, and see the results of success. Neither organization was ever about doing "easy" things, but TNC's objectives were a lot easier to explain.

One of my personal key priorities was to convey to our TNC teams that environmental expertise and developing creative solutions to preserve ecosystem may be Job One, but without developing excellence in management, knowledge transfer, marketing, and collaboration, you have not done "the whole job." The outward-looking element is missing in many NGOs. Their people may be well trained and have a keen understanding of what's going on locally or in a region, but it's important to have a mandate to share and leverage that knowledge. It is not enough to write it all up in a report or visit an area once or twice. It is important to set goals and take action alone and with partners.

An example of knowledge transfer that made a real difference came several years ago when the government of Mongolia asked TNC to help it establish an ecologically sensitive economic development plan. Mongolia has undergone a big transition in recent decades. Extraction industries are transforming the country's economy, but traditionally a huge share of its population depended on herding livestock across its vast grasslands. Several new issues are challenging: Traditionally, herders had grazed equal numbers of sheep and cashmere goats; as demand for more valuable cashmere has risen on world markets, they began grazing more goats. The problem is that goats eat not just the leaves but also the roots of the grasses, which kills the plants. Add periodic droughts and once-lush grassland can become a desert. Also, vast regions of Mongolia were leased out for mining which was impacting habitats, and combined with extensive poaching, several native animal species such as gazelles, were threatened.

Our Asia Pacific Council took a trip to Mongolia before our scheduled Council Meeting in Beijing. We flew about two hours east of Ulaanbaatar in a large Russian helicopter and spent three days in the remote Eastern Steppe, which is a vast, beautiful, remote region that represents the largest remaining intact temperate grasslands on Earth. Standing on these plains and looking out at the gently rolling hills, we realized that it was probably very similar to how Montana and the Dakotas looked centuries ago. We realized that we had TNC experts who understood grassland ecosystems and their dynamics from studying these regions of the U.S. Therefore the project was an opportunity for TNC experts and state trustees to work with the TNC team in Mongolia to exchange knowledge and experiences.

That was a fascinating trip for me. Mongolia has wonderful friendly, ecologically caring people wanting to move intelligently into the modern world. On one outing we drove to a herder's traditional mobile summer home. These are called *gers* (Westerners sometimes call these tents made of a wooden frame covered with wool "yurts"). The basic design dates back to the days of Genghis Khan. As we approached, we saw a portable windmill and as we got closer there was a solar panel on the ground. Next to the panel was a car battery. Inside the *ger* there was a satellite phone charging, and across the room there was an active matrix color TV.

TNC helped the government design a plan for protected areas designed to help gazelle populations rebound and support other species and grassland plants. TNC also raised funds to support more rangers in this vast region to cut down on poaching.

Another situation at TNC illustrated two of my fundamental management principles: first, don't overthink a decision, but aggressively manage the consequences of the decision; secondly, value collaboration and partnership. Between the southern tip of Asia and northern Australia, thousands of miles of coral reef connect and surround six island nations: Indonesia, the Philippines, Malaysia, East Timor, Papua New Guinea, and the Solomon Islands. The reefs of what is known as the "Coral Triangle" are nurseries, feeding grounds and home for nearly 40 percent of the world's reef fish species, plus whales, sharks, dolphins, manta rays, and other marine animals. The reefs also provide livelihoods and feed millions of people around the world. They lure tourism dollars, generate export revenue, and buffer coastal communities from the onslaught of tropical storms.

Unfortunately, the reefs face a number of assaults. Overfishing, and particularly destructive fishing techniques such as commercial trawling as well as explosive and cyanide fishing, have depleted fish stocks. Rising water temperatures, sea levels, and ocean acidity also have taken a toll, and some scientists estimate that we could lose up to 70 percent of our planet's coral reefs over the next 50 years.

In March 2007, our TNC Asia Pacific Council met in Sydney, Australia. We had a discussion about the threats to the Coral Triangle, and we all agreed this was a significant global threat that demanded our attention. A point of urgency was that the upcoming meeting of the Asia-Pacific Economic Cooperation Forum (a meeting of the leaders of the 21 countries bordering the Pacific, which was started by President Clinton in 1989) was scheduled for Australia in September, just six months out.

The Australian Environmental Minister was at our meeting, and there was a discussion; the TNC team said it could get a plan together over the next "couple of months." This is a common time frame you hear in the non-profit world; organizations see themselves as operating on very lean staffs and the idea of adding a significant project seems like it might break the camel's back. But when I heard that timeframe, I thought our team was over-analyzing a decision it had the experience and instincts to make. I asked the management of Asia Pacific Region to prepare a one-page strategy *by the next morning*.

They did. We began implementing that plan on the spot. Members of the AP Council, and the Asian management team, and TNC Global Board immediately contacted the President's Offices and Ministries of the key countries. September came, we were ready, and Indonesia, the Philippines, Australia, and the U.S. agreed that this unique ecosystem deserved a comprehensive plan to protect it, including regulations and enforcement capacity. They agreed to fund the effort. It was a great collaboration success. Later, the U.S. Ambassador to APEC stopped by my office in California to commit her continued support.

I initially was an Asia Pacific Council member, then later Co-Chair with Moses Tsang, a Hong Kong executive. Moses is one of the most passionate conservationists and effective fundraisers I know. That was important because funding for TNC in Asian countries came mostly from the U.S. To stimulate Asian giving to TNC, Jeff and Mary had an excellent idea: They suggested our family foundation give a challenge grant to match new Asian donors up to $25,000 each. Bob Wilson, a major donor to TNC, also had a challenge match to get TNC donors to donate outside their state. By combining the Asian donors' $25,000, our $25,000 equaled $50,000 which Wilson then matched. That was a compelling proposition that we could get $100,000 for each $25,000 Asian donor. That small start and hard work by all involved has resulted in TNC China becoming self-funding. One of the most satisfying elements of this evolution was when the China TNC organization made a commitment to raise funds for its own projects, but also committed that, once those targets were met, it would raise an amount equal to 30 percent of that budget to be used by TNC outside China. Now the focus is to get Indonesia and other Asian countries to generate their own funds.

I feel very lucky that Hank Paulson thought of me for the Asia Pacific Council. I brought the experience I had gained doing business in the region to the new challenges of trying to help with conservation issues. From my first trip to Japan in the 1970s, my travels in Asia and my education in the different cultures of its many countries have proven to be one of the most interesting and rewarding aspects of my career at Applied Materials. By operating with an open mind and respect for others, we repeatedly disproved the popular wisdom that U.S. companies couldn't succeed in Asia. It reinforced for me that diversity is an exciting and enriching dynamic in life, and I saw that play out every day in the many cultures that pulled together at Applied Materials. My experiences on the Asia Pacific Council for TNC gave me an entirely new and important perspective on conservation and environmental issues in Asia, and it allowed me to stay engaged in the rising importance of the region.

MORGANISM

As any kind of organization expands, fear of making decisions creeps in. A leader must make clear the value of making a decision, moving forward, and then managing the consequences. Most experienced people instinctively know the right course.

CHAPTER 22

Non-profits face similar issues as start-ups

With the governance, global strategy, and Asia Pacific Council functioning, my focus in TNC turned to management development and best practices and processes. I tried to adopt the role of a coach to the management teams.

In the last chapter, we talked about a few issues from my list of ten key management principles that I perceived were applicable early on at TNC. For example, the Coral Initiative, the effort by the nations in Southeast Asia and the U.S. to protect the fisheries and coral, was one where they might have justified studying the possibilities to death and yet ended up with exactly the same recommendations they came up within 24 hours. Instead, they formulated a solid starting plan from the overnight recommendations and the Asia-Pacific Council and the TNC World Office endorsed it. That created momentum. The strategy was successful and the Coral Triangle Initiative came out of the APEC Leaders meeting that fall.

But on the broader scale, the organization had been thinking about and debating whether to go seriously global for several years. That was a strain on everybody. You need to do the due diligence; but it's the kind of situation that prolongs friction between managers, board members, and trustees who disagree, and staff people may posture and position for whose strategy they think is going to prevail. It's a distraction. When a decision like that looms, an organization needs to study hard, make the decision, and move forward. I became somewhat famous in TNC for using the phrase "Book it and ship it." In the manufacturing business, that simply means, "We're finished building this. Let's move on." But I used it at TNC as a way of saying, "No more dithering. We've done our best here, now let's put the decision in motion and see what happens." If problems develop you manage them or you may change your mind, but kicking the can down the road over and over saps energy.

Mark Burget, managing director of North America and executive vice president of TNC, put it this way: "TNC's biggest shortcoming may be our disproportionate focus on planning, internal discussion, etc. In "book it and ship it" I hear a plea to get on to execution. This is a challenge for any organization, but especially for a mission-driven organization facing very large, complex challenges. We could easily spend the rest of our lives talking about environmental problems and feeling pretty good about how smart we are. Jim reminds us to get to work on making change happen in the world. Make the purchase, get the easement, attract the funding, hire the person, close the opportunity. As William Blake said, 'Execution is the chariot of genius.'"

With the smaller board and with experienced, engaged members on the committees, TNC was soon able to move on to deciding whether to accelerate globalization of the organization. Hank and the subsequent board chairs, John Morgridge, Roger Milliken, co-chairs Steve Denning and Teresa Beck, and Craig McCaw all understood and have supported a global mission. I have been pleased with the progress TNC is making as an effective global conservation organization. Decisions are based on science and project-based experience. It has impressive depth and breadth of knowledge and capability developed in the U.S. and other parts of the globe. Its strategy is well integrated at different scales, and managers have become more and more skilled as managers.

These experiences at TNC prompted me to reflect on some of the similarities between start-ups and non-profits. At the highest level I think they tend to fall into three general issues.

ONE

Like small, growing companies, non-profits typically have limited resources and need to prioritize and then focus.

At Applied, some of our businesses were losing money when I arrived; that made it easy for me to clear those off the table and focus on the one that had market traction. But in non-profits, unlike business start-ups, the opportunities they choose between are not potential markets where customer acceptance or rejection helps focus the company's efforts, rather they tend to be the causes or regions that funding sources want to impact. Donors feel an urgency to act in a specific place and often in a specific way, rather than having a realistic sense of the ability of a given organization to impact the problem.

As Mark Burget puts it, "We think about customers differently. It's hard enough to understand what ecological integrity means in any given place. Most ecological systems are more complex than we can understand. And then you have political, social, economic systems involved. Here success in a situation tends to be based on different measures, including demonstrating a basic humanity and respecting that of others." Nonetheless, non-profit organizations must align their capabilities and the agendas of their funding supporters if they actually want to do good. And then they must prioritize and focus.

TWO

Non-profits that emerge from a small group of people united around a cause tend to develop a dysfunctional hub and spoke structure, just as start-up companies do.

Often people join non-profits because of a deep commitment to a mission. However, when the staff exceeds a handful, if everybody in the organization is reporting to the executive director, dysfunction is inevitable. A good leader needs to be able to communicate that in a growing organization, hierarchy is a good thing. It actually speeds up decision-making. Effective boards could be a great resource in helping with this, but even very skilled business people just don't seem to invest much time in structural issues at non-profits. These non-profit boards can end up filled with observer types, busy business people or regional representatives who like the idea of supporting the work, but who are not as engaged as a board member should be.

As a non-profit shifts to a more hierarchical system during a growth phase, leaders need to create processes and a decentralized structure so that people can efficiently make decisions and get information to do their jobs. Consider a simple example from a small business. Let's say you have a pop-up food truck and next you want to open a restaurant. It's no longer you and your best friend driving the truck, shopping, cooking the food, selling the food out the window, and counting the money at night. If you want to build a successful restaurant, you need a larger facility, but also a properly designed kitchen and a new cadre of employees doing different tasks. You don't just assemble those things and push "start." You must manage them all. You have to decide which tasks you will handle and which your best friend will run. You don't want every person you hire to call you every time they are debating whether the market tomatoes look fresh enough to feature that night, or whether the problem with a sink is serious enough to call a plumber. You want the people on the front line of activity to feel empowered to make good decisions.

In a hub-and-spokes structure, the people on the end of spokes aren't sure who is in charge of what or who has authority to do what, and they often don't have the latest information on what's going on along the other spokes. Remember the chart about leadership versus management: Both roles are essential in the effective transition of a business to the next level. The leader inspires everyone to work hard to create the best restaurant in town with the happiest customers. The leader raises the money to make it all happen, and hires the best possible people. But creating an organizational structure and functional processes is the job of management. A manager tunes the structure and process to fit the work and the people, then urges employees to make and take responsibility for decisions. They will make mistakes, but you must make sure they own the monkey. If you step in and fix situations for them, or punish them for reporting a problem, they will not make decisions.

THREE

In non-profits, as in any for-profit company, the biggest day-to-day challenge is to create and nurture a culture with a strong capacity to implement.

Implementation partly is about an attitude: Just do it. It's when strategy meets a bias toward action and thoughtful completion. People tend to get comfortable with process and reports. The great value of decentralized management is that you write a different kind of report when you know you have to make a decision or are handing it to the final reviewer or decision-maker, not just to a chain of people who keep passing it up the ladder. And so if you push wise, accountable decision-making power deep into your organization, you energize everybody to be more efficient and do a better job. You develop a psychology of making decisions and managing the consequences. Remember the one-page strategy we developed overnight that sent a significant international initiative in motion in the Coral Triangle. I believe that only 10 percent of success is strategy; the other 90 percent is implementation.

CHAPTER 23

Collaboration in the northern Sierra

There is one more common challenge in traditional business that also is so important in the non-profit space that I feel it deserves its own chapter. In fact, it is something that inspired Becky and me to launch a new model for conservation.

If you want to grow an organization and build significant value, you must develop the ability to collaborate. Some of our biggest successes at Applied, such as our ability to penetrate the Japanese market at a time when so many other U.S. companies said it couldn't be done, had their roots in collaboration. A lot of companies talk about collaboration, but it's just lip service. Collaboration is not about scheduling a lot of meetings or forcing people to physically interact more. As I've explained, to be a successful collaborator, there are several guiding principles that you must embrace, including that you need to be willing to put your partners' needs ahead of your own so that you can both succeed.

But if that attitude is somewhat rare in business, as Becky and I became more involved in philanthropic projects, we could see that it was almost entirely absent in the non-profit sector. In fact, non-profits can be ruthlessly competitive and wary of one another. The reason is that non-profits are constantly fund-raising, and all the organizations in a given space tend to target the same donors or same kind of donors. In theory, this should create a market check on organizations and winnow out the ones who are not using their resources effectively. It should force organizations to focus on their strengths instead of diluting their resources.

In practice, the opposite occurs. Organizations pick projects on the basis of what they think offers the most compelling fund-raising story, rather than ones that reflect their true capabilities or the most important needs. They may not be forthcoming about their challenges because "competitors" may exploit that information to gain an edge with donors. They don't like to admit weaknesses (nobody does), but therefore it's hard for them to seek partners to complement their strengths. These are not necessarily personal failings of the non-profits' leaders, but these patterns limit the effectiveness of their organizations. Becky and I thought there was an opportunity to develop a more extensive project in the Sierra Nevada.

The Sierra Nevada is the longest, unbroken mountain range in North America, a 400 mile-long expanse of granite peaks, deep forests, and sparkling lakes that inspired John Muir to call it the "Range of Light." From this extraordinary expanse of wildness flows the one resource our modern society cannot live without — water. A full 60 percent of the water that supports life in California and also all of Northern Nevada begins as rain and snow falling on the Sierra. The Sierra also supports the greatest diversity of plant and animal communities in California, from Sierra big horn sheep to the spectacular birds of Sierra Valley. Finally, the Sierra plays a more intimate role for many people as a treasured place we go to hike, ski, and explore with our families. The region we wanted to focus on begins just south of Lake Tahoe and encompasses 5 million acres.

We brought together five partners that were all respected, competent, and had worked together in pairs. It's called the Northern Sierra Partnership (NSP). And now, eight years into what is a path-breaking model of collaboration for non-profits, we have the evidence that it can be done. Collaborations are never easy. There always are egos on the line, personalities that clash, complexities from within and without that must be overcome. But we brought together partners willing to use the management principles I've stressed and the rules of collaboration that worked so well for us at Applied.

The NSP partners prioritized the most environmentally significant acres in the 5 million-acre region. To date, we've raised $142 million in public and private funds and conserved over 50,000 target acres of key properties in perpetuity, and we have a strategy to preserve as much as three times as many. Those numbers suggest that you really can achieve synergy among non-profit partners. I hope someday other organizations, both in conservation and in domains like education, can use our experience to set up their own collaborations and partnerships.

A small check goes a long way

The first investment Becky and I made in the northern Sierra was a $500 check she wrote to the Truckee Donner Land Trust (TDLT) in 2000. The organization is led by a man named Perry Norris, who spent much of his career involved with education and the Outward Bound programs. Perry has an intense passion for conservation and deeply understands the issues of the Truckee region.

At nearly 6000 feet elevation, Truckee, California, is where the famous Donner Party was stalled when it tried to find a more direct route to California than the Oregon Trail. Many members of the party died of exposure during the exceptionally bad weather of 1846. Today, Truckee is within 30 minutes of half a dozen popular ski resorts including Squaw Valley, Alpine Meadows, Northstar, and Sugar Bowl. Bay Area residents and others who love to ski and enjoy the outdoors have flocked to new developments in the area with all-season homes and amenities like golf courses and spa resorts. As a consequence, the region is in danger of aggressive development ruining the natural beauty and wildlife habitats.

Our first investment was not large, but our relationship with Perry developed. Within two years, we saw an opportunity to make a larger grant for an important conservation acquisition. Developers were eyeing Schallenberger Ridge above Donner Lake for its beautiful views. The problem is that development would encroach on an important watershed, and it threatened to dramatically alter the look and atmosphere of the lake and Donner Lake Memorial State Park.

We liked the idea of our family foundation acting as a stimulator for other investment so that an organization with an opportunity could make a rapid, critical move in a particular time window. We gave Perry and the TDLT $50,000 to seed the acquisition of Schallenberger Ridge. TDLT had good relationships within the community and an understanding of local issues. We also felt that the deal would help Perry with other potential donors if he could point to a high-profile success saving this iconic ridge.

Last but not least, TDLT had done that rare thing: collaborated with another non-profit. Perry had struck up a partnership with Dave Sutton of The Trust for Public Land (TPL) and that gave him supplementary skill sets, experience, and capacity for the Schallenberger deal. This was the kind of collaboration that seemed vital if we were going to make a real difference in this region.

The two organizations had complementary values and motivations, but they had different areas of expertise and access to resources. TPL is a national organization that works with federal, state, and local agencies to obtain funding for conservation-related purchases, acquire properties, and then transfer the properties to the U.S. Forest Service, other government agencies, or non-profit land trusts to manage as conserved areas. In the northern Sierra, TPL had created a multi-year initiative to address the consequences of President Abraham Lincoln's 19th century land ownership plan throughout the Sierra — the checkerboard sections of railroad and federal lands I talked about in Chapter 20.

The Sierra Checkerboard Initiative is a plan to consolidate and protect the remnants of environmentally strategic lands across the checkerboard. With such fragmented ownership, trying to set aside lands large enough to conserve wildlife and preserve watershed dynamics is very difficult and tedious work. The logistics alone are complex; layer on creating a new pattern of ownership that meets the human, economic, and ecological needs of the Sierra Nevada that have evolved for more than 150 years. When the two groups successfully purchased and conserved Schallenberger Ridge, both teams achieved an important victory for their organizations and for the public.

Pairing up for progress

Soon, we realized that several other organizations in this region were having success working in pairs as well. We were optimistic that with the right support and leadership, we could build an even bigger partnership in the northern Sierra — and ideally we could inspire non-profit organizations to work together to achieve goals they could not achieve independently.

For example, TNC's Jim Gaither and his colleagues Henry Little and Greg Low, understood the value of having local partners. As a national organization, they realized that local knowledge and relationships were absolutely critical when working with folks like multi-generational ranchers and landowners. Families have complex connections to their land; there is not a "cookie cutter" approach to doing conservation easements or other transactions that works in every situation. Around 2004, TNC reached out to a man named Paul Hardy who at the time was forming the Feather River Land Trust (FRLT) in a region that he and his family had long called home. Paul, a trained research biologist, had worked at UC-Davis and for the U.S. Forest Service. He served first as a consultant to TNC. He was hired to help with their final stage of the Sierra Nevada Eco-Regional Plan, which later became TNC's Northern Sierra Project.

Jim Gaither believed that the formation of the Feather River Land Trust would be critical to successful conservation in the region. Gaither introduced Paul to us and Paul led us on a tour of the Feather River watershed, including Sierra Valley, Clover Valley, and Genessee Valley. We learned there were 230 or more species of birds in the area during the year; there was good potential for preservation and that would create possibilities for a birding center as well as economic opportunities for tourism. We liked the way Paul talked about the community and how to work with it. Later that year I asked our daughter, Mary, to join me on a canoe trip Paul had set up to tour the Maddalena property, newly acquired by FRLT. There were extensive wetlands on this working ranch. The Feather River region, once intensely exploited for its timber, is an exceptional habitat for birds thanks to its extensive wetlands and meadow systems. It also offers significant economic value for working ranches. I always gained useful information by porpoising into the different levels of Applied, but it turned out to be a lot more fun porpoising with a canoe paddle in my hand to see for myself the incredible beauty and conservation potential of an area like Sierra Valley. We made a three-year capacity grant of $111,250 to FRLT in 2006. Those resources helped Paul hire the organization's first development director and begin building a strong base of support.

In 2004, to better understand the needs and the opportunities, we paid for the preparation of a report on Environmental Conservation Opportunities in the Northern Sierra Nevada. It confirmed for us that there was an opportunity for a large-scale ecological effort. At the Morgan Family Foundation we were putting the pieces in place to make a bigger move, and a key element in 2006 was hiring as director of Environment & Stewardship Programs for our Foundation, a woman named Carol Olson, a smart executive who had been CEO of the Mountain View Chamber of Commerce.

Becky and I sat with Carol and discussed issues and values that we felt were critical if we were going to be involved in the northern Sierra:

Broad impact. We wanted to seed projects then leverage other funding. We were not looking for personal control and credit, we were looking for high impact; collaborating with other foundations and organizations was the way to achieve that.

Strong leadership. Partners needed to appreciate the importance of timing and driving forces in creating opportunities.

Long time horizon. We wanted to take positions that encourage the long-term stewardship of landscapes. We wanted attention to preserving biodiversity, particularly around vulnerable riparian corridors. It wasn't enough for us to just conserve the land and move on; we wanted a viable plan for how the land would be restored and maintained well into the future.

Unique role. We wanted to work in the void and fund areas that other funders might reject. In the non-profit world certain capacities are critical but it can be hard to raise funds for more abstract activities. People like the idea that their gift goes to buying a piece of land, for example, but they may not be as excited about funding a study that helps an organization make better land-use decisions in general.

Good plan, good people. Becky and I stressed our mutual conviction that good decisions are based on both strong concepts and people capable of executing on the plan. Neither works alone.

With this guidance, Carol visited the Morgan Family Foundation grantees in the northern Sierra in September, 2006. She reported back that while the region had outstanding organizations and smart, visionary leaders, there were some serious challenges as well. There was a lack of local capacity for large-scale impact, a lack of resources, and no coordinated approach to attracting new funding opportunities. Carol's analysis was essential; she welcomed and leaned in to the bad news so we made sure we were going in with our eyes open to the challenges. We discussed those, as well as the larger driving forces related to the undertaking. We weren't put off by the idea of hard work, and after much thought and analysis were motivated to move by these driving forces:

1) Development pressure would only increase. The population of the Sierra Nevada region had tripled in 30 years. Truckee and Reno were increasingly putting pressure on the surrounding areas for more development. Unlike the southern Sierra where 90 percent of the land was in public ownership, 50 percent of the northern Sierra land was in private ownership and therefore susceptible to irresponsible development. Neither the partners nor the foundation were anti-growth, but we wanted to see the region embrace "smart growth" approaches that concentrated new development in existing communities. The problem was that developers were opting for sprawling resort and second-home development on the outskirts of communities. They were building golf courses, which raise water use and chemical run-off issues, and wanted to convert wild areas and key wildlife corridors to scenic but environmentally-costly resorts and vacation home neighborhoods.

2) All moves had to consider changing natural phenomena such as climate and wildfire threats. Due to a history of poor management practices in northern Sierra forests, the region was susceptible to catastrophic wildfire. For millennia, forest fires shaped ecosystems like the northern Sierra by periodically burning the underbrush and stimulating the growth of large, healthy trees. For the past 100 years, however, the practice of extinguishing virtually all wildfires has led to an unnatural buildup of brush and small trees, making Sierra forests a tinderbox waiting to ignite. Climate change was also influencing the interval and severity of wildfires and the impact of those fires on local economies and watersheds. The forests of the northern Sierra have the potential to be among the largest and most productive carbon sinks on the planet but new approaches would be needed to address the increased risks of stand-destroying wildfire. Smarter forest management would have benefits for not only flora and fauna but also for people and communities so it had to be part of our conservation thinking.

3) Water quantity and quality will be critical issues in California for the foreseeable future. The northern Sierra furnishes water to more than 60 percent of California's population and supports the Nevada cities of Reno and Sparks. It needs to be an integral part of the solution to California's water problems. Unfortunately, there was a lack of clarity and focus on this region as part of the solution. It was crucial to position our conservation efforts as not just about the animals, plants, and recreation, but as the smart way to protect wild areas providing what may be the world's single most precious resource: clean water.

Communication and public education were essential to tie all these larger forces into the explanation of our agenda and ideas. In line with TNC's approach that conservation needs to be about saving nature for people, not saving nature from people, we needed to focus on the value of ecosystems, not fixate on preserving one species at great cost to people or other systems.

There also was a dynamic we needed to face realistically: the communities most likely to benefit directly were not a good source of financial support. Because of the relatively sparse population of the region and the nature of the economy, philanthropy in the northern Sierra was minimal. A study done by Sierra Business Council in 2006 showed that philanthropic dollars were disproportionately expended across the state: $600 per capita in the Bay Area, $200 per capita in the Los Angeles region, $80 per capita in the Central Valley, and $10 per capita in the Sierra Nevada. There seemed to be considerable philanthropic funding for conservation in the Bay Area, along the Coast, and throughout Southern California. But while many Californians spend time in the

Sierra Nevada region and get their water from it, they don't realize the importance of the region to the health of the entire state — or appreciate the threats it faces. On the positive side, our likely funders were sophisticated when it came to analyzing return on investment. Our dollars could not only go further in the northern Sierra due to lower cost of lands there compared to the Bay Area, but seeding projects within these organizations would have a big leveraged impact.

We had no desire to create yet another stand-alone organization. Non-profit organizations tend to take on certain functions and activities that are mainly about prolonging the life of the organization. We had a different goal, as I mentioned earlier: that of stimulator. We wanted to spark activity in a specific place and time, achieve a specific set of goals, and then eventually go away. We wanted to make an impact, and leave the partners in healthier financial shape, with stronger reputations, more donors, and enhanced capacity than when we started. We wanted the group to come together and appreciate the value and meaning of working together. In return, each partner needed to offer its strength and capacity to the effort.

In February 2007 the Morgan Family Foundation board of directors approved a $1 million pool of funds to be awarded to The Nature Conservancy, with the idea that it would lay the groundwork to orchestrate a coordinated approach to conservation across the greater landscape in the region. We also made a $500,000 investment in an effort by Truckee Donner Land Trust and the Trust for Public Land to purchase Waddle Ranch. The acquisition of this 1,462-acre property in the heart of Martis Valley was one of the Sierra Nevada's largest and most complicated conservation efforts in recent history. It was also a model for partnership between two organizations that joined forces on negotiating and fundraising.

Adapting the model

The original structure empowered TNC to efficiently administer our funds to worthwhile projects implemented through partners. The work in Martis Valley was very good, but we immediately sensed that the structure we had set up might not be the most efficient and effective at pouncing on good opportunities as they arose. We wanted to inspire enthusiasm and a sense of urgency to identify and go after key properties. We met others who felt the same way. Around this time period, Becky and I would frequently talk about the larger possibilities.

Over a cup of coffee together in our kitchen one morning, Becky and I discussed that instead of having TNC oversee the distribution of grants to these organizations, we needed to find a structure where they actively worked together as partners. The vision emerged from the work of Jim Gaither at TNC that identified the most environmentally and strategically important land in the northern Sierra, and Dave Sutton's efforts with the Checkerboard Initiative for TPL. We determined that under one supporting organizational umbrella, we could provide a booster rocket for a time to cover more regions and types of conservation projects. We knew they had different strengths. The question was could we get them to work together?

Like most challenges worth taking on, it wasn't easy. We created a unique approach to collaborative conservation with five organizations that we have yet to see copied anywhere, despite powerful evidence that a partnership among organizations with different roles and domains can work. We had to make course corrections. We have had to spend considerable time and energy on interpersonal communication and negotiation between the partners, as we asked them to do things that non-profits rarely do.

Let's focus on the elements that might be most helpful for others attempting to think about a social or environmental problem for which collaboration can be helpful.

First, make sure you have a balanced team. Early on we identified five entities we wanted to work with: The Trust for Public Land, The Truckee Donner Land Trust, the Feather River Land Trust, The Sierra Business Council, and The Nature Conservancy. Four were conservation organizations, but the Sierra Business Council lead by Steve Frisch was made up of over thirty towns in the Sierra to assure the economic interests of the region were represented. We also reached out to Michael Mantell at the Resources Legacy Fund, an organization that had been instrumental in the development and administration of many statewide conservation initiatives, and he agreed with us that more could be accomplished through collaboration. We convened the five organizations in a "Northern Sierra Funding Summit."

Collaborations work best when each partner brings a high level of competency but also complementary strengths. In business, those strengths may be qualities like additional products, new markets, strategic thinking, operational experience, or excellent sales skills. Organizations have different kinds of resources, executives have followed different experience paths that may be valuable, and then you want to make sure the personalities can work together. Among the five partners was a global organization with extensive resources in all 50 states and several countries (The Nature Conservancy); a national organization skilled in working with federal and state agencies (Trust for Public Land); two regional land trusts with knowledge and sensitivities to issues and opportunities in the northern Sierra (Truckee Donner Land Trust and Feather River Land Trust); and finally, the Sierra Business Council, which represented the interests of communities throughout the Sierra Nevada.

Second, use your analysis of driving forces to galvanize decisions and build momentum. Agreeing to collaborate "in theory" and hoping to find work to do together is not sufficient to get people focused. At the April 2007 summit, we tried to focus the potential partners' attention and urgency by discussing driving forces and other factors that augured for immediate action. Establishing a plan to conserve, restore, and enjoy the fantastic northern Sierra was clearly an effort at the right time, at the right place, and with the right capability. At a tactical level, we had some clear opportunities: The Governor had created a new agency to support the region called the Sierra Nevada Conservancy (SNC). The Governor and the California State Legislature were supportive, bonds had been passed, and grant programs would soon be available. Groups that could present a collaborative strategy would be the most likely to receive this support. Clearly, regions that organized quickly to submit funding proposals would be in the best position to obtain support from the state.

Secondly (and, in retrospect, ironically) in 2007, the economy was going strong. After the "dot com bomb" several years prior, technology had recovered and other elements of the economy were enjoying the cost-savings of innovation. On a state basis, there was a tremendous level of individual wealth in Silicon Valley and the rest of the state. Foundations were doing well and looking for new opportunities for impact.

The environment was a rising issue, particularly in regard to climate change, catastrophic fires, water, and habitat destruction. The media and others were moving beyond the doomsday talk of global warming and were now focused on sustainability and a green economy. I felt that people were actively looking for ways to support a sustainable planet but feeling a little overwhelmed by the options. The northern Sierra offered a familiar and frankly beloved option; it could become a laboratory to test sustainability ideas and large-scale conservation's impact on climate change adaptation. It could also help scientists study strategies to enhance carbon sequestration, optimize water availability to the state, and improve other ecosystem services.

Another key message was that land costs in the region were so much more affordable than those in the Bay Area, where many donors were likely to come from. We needed to communicate the urgency to potential donors that there was an opportunity to move quickly to protect a lot of land, but that situation was not going to go on indefinitely. Lands in Sierra Valley, about 25 miles from Truckee and Reno, were clearly in the path of the next phase of regional development. Some properties were in a generational transition. Many had been homesteaded in the 1800s and now many of the descendants wanted cash. Properties were coming on the market for the first time in years and we had to be facing the elevator door and be ready to act.

Later, as an example, one of our major successes was the work we did to preserve Webber Lake, owned by a family that was only the fourth official owner beginning with the U.S. Government in 1850. With the Truckee Donner Land Trust in the lead, we enabled the landowner's goal of preserving the lake and meadow for public use, and we saved the upper reaches of the Little Truckee Watershed. That watershed provides much of the water for Reno and Sparks in Nevada; it merges with the main Truckee river out of Lake Tahoe. It also has a diversion below Webber Falls that sends some water north to Sierra Valley, adding to the wetlands that feed the Wild and Scenic Middle Fork of the Feather River. The Feather River, in turn, drains to the Oroville Dam in California. This opportunity would not last much longer: Once land transitioned from long-time owners, property values were bound to shoot up and speculators and developers would move in. We first focused on getting a solid preliminary plan for the region. Our foundation made a grant to Resources Legacy Fund for planning support in the amount of $25,000. Michael Mantell was a true partner with us and Resources Legacy Fund (RLF) matched the amount and the Northern Sierra Partnership was in the works. An additional $100,000 was given by the two organizations several months later based on the scale of the effort and the potential impact being envisioned.

This was an exciting time. In fact, then-Governor Arnold Schwarzenegger made a visit to Donner Lake to support NSP's work and it seemed like even Mother Nature lent her endorsement: In the middle of his speech, a bald eagle made a swooping dive to skim the surface of Donner Lake and grab a trout.

But we had serious and difficult details to work out going forward. Most importantly, we had to get the partners collaborating on fund-raising instead of competing with one another. The partners decided that a Campaign Committee needed to be formed — a group of individuals who could attract top donors to the effort. Later renamed the Governing Council, the members of this body would serve as advisors, offer their own networks to increase the fundraising capacity of the partnership and fulfill other non-profit board-like duties. RLF, as fiscal sponsor, would provide the fiduciary responsibility.

Becky and I agreed to co-chair the Campaign Committee and in December 2007 the Morgan Family Foundation board of directors pledged $10 million to the Northern Sierra Partnership. To motivate the Committee and the partners, the pledge was a challenge: the gift would be accessible when NSP raised an additional $50 million in private fundraising. We structured it in this way because we were trying to build a partner capability that could have a significant impact. To meet the goals, the organizations would need to collaborate and expand conservation fundraising for the northern Sierra.

The elevator reverses direction

Each of the partners brought a unique strength to NSP, and all had other sources of funding outside of NSP. But the differences in their missions and their own self-protective instincts made them nervous about sharing donor lists. We hired an executive director who we borrowed from TNC. Then, we hit our first speed bumps. The subprime mortgage crisis in late 2007 had triggered a landslide of bad news throughout the financial services industry that spread to the economy as a whole. The country was headed into a period of recession, and fund-raising outlooks that had seemed so promising the previous year were now grim.

On the positive side, we'd secured a $10 million commitment from the David and Lucile Packard Foundation and enlisted the help of Mike Sweeney, executive director of TNC California. Mike got involved in early strategy and organization, and he facilitated a $2 million grant from TNC. We also received two individual gifts of $100,000 each. On the negative side, some donors Becky and I had been confident would join us in the northern Sierra, did not. As an economy pulls back, the list of what philanthropists consider their most critical investments contracts as well. We found that some foundations that had been active in conservation did not want to get involved in land purchases; they wanted to work on changing policies and on projects overseas. We could see the challenge for private and public fundraising was going to intensify. So much for retiring from an industry with dramatic cycles!

It was a beautiful late spring day in 2008 when 100 guests of the Northern Sierra Partnership toured the Sierra Valley region and enjoyed a BBQ at Lucy Blake's ranch. Becky had known Lucy, who was the founder of the Sierra Business Council (SBC), for some time. When Becky ran Joint Venture Silicon Valley, she met with regional stewardship organizations forming across the state, including SBC. Lucy had pioneered innovative approaches and solutions that fostered community vitality, environmental quality, economic prosperity, and social fairness in the Sierra Nevada. SBC was serving a critical role in Sierra Valley by introducing local ranchers to conservation easements and other tools for retaining their properties as working ranches. Lucy had left SBC and moved on to several other important projects in environmental advocacy and policy, but she was a passionate supporter of what we were trying to do. She shared our belief that collaboration not only among organizations, but also between organizations and communities, is critical.

Unfortunately, the weather and company were a lot more inspiring that day at Lucy's ranch than the economy. What's more, we could see that the partners were struggling to work together. During a very difficult economic period for the country, raising funds to keep themselves afloat in addition to advancing the partnership was tough. One point of light was that as our interactions with Lucy Blake continued, Becky and I were more and more impressed with her energy, local knowledge, and capacity. Over time, we urged her to replace us as Chair of the Governing Council, and eventually in June 2011, she became president of the partnership.

Lucy's first priority as president was to work with the partners and the Governing Council to complete a detailed strategic plan and marketing tools for NSP. To learn from best practices nationwide, she hired a fundraising firm to advise us on how to staff and execute a coordinated campaign. Our foundation supported this step and provided additional funding for it, realizing that the level of collaboration we were hoping for was something altogether new. We also supported a philanthropy position at TNC focused on the northern Sierra that was filled by Elliott Wright. Through Elliott and Lucy's leadership, and the focused efforts of all the partners and the Governing Council, the partners have been able to protect some incredibly important conservation lands they would not have been able to preserve alone, such as the Little Truckee watershed. We have healthy, intense debates about project priorities, with different partners advancing their view of the most important opportunities. The good news is that NSP's efforts began with a grounding in science. We have a plan. The measures of our success are not only the total acreage conserved, but the key points of leverage and connection that a given property may represent. We make strategic moves to connect important watersheds and wildlife corridors and protect natural areas that provide society with important ecosystem services like fresh water filtration and carbon storage.

Every piece of land has a story, a social history, and an environmental role in the region. Those interested can find in depth stories and details about the keystone projects NSP has conserved at *northernsierra partnership.org*. But one particularly satisfying project involved the protection of one of the northern Sierra's real gems: Independence Lake.

Independence Lake

Independence Lake is a key resource in the Little Truckee Watershed; it is a 2.4 mile-long lake 15 miles north of Truckee and resembles Donner Lake as it was a century ago. The setting at the base of some steep cliffs dotted with evergreens and aspen is spectacularly beautiful. The lake also is a unique refuge for the Lahontan cutthroat trout — a fish that has been lost from 99 percent of its historic range. The surrounding forest is home to black bear, mountain lion, and the Truckee-Loyalton deer herd. Bald eagles and osprey hunt fish in the shallows. What's more, the lake is part of a vital watershed that provides water to large communities in Nevada, especially during drought periods. The lake feeds the Truckee River, which crosses the border to the communities of Reno and Sparks.

At one point in the 1970s, the Disney Corporation considered buying the property and building a family-oriented ski "village" in the area; much later, Steve Jobs of Apple wanted to buy the area around the lake and set up a private conference retreat. What was always an issue, however, was the lake's role in supplying fresh water to the region. Jobs' plan stalled, for example, when the state water authorities refused to give him the right to control the water in the lake (by law, private landowners in California cannot own a dynamic water resource, they can only obtain rights to utilize or draw from water on their property).

TNC's Nevada team had been trying to come up with a plan to buy and conserve Independence Lake for years, and NSP became a participant in that effort. TNC finally acquired the land around the lake in 2010. TNC's ability to work with then Senate Majority Leader Harry Reid from Nevada was critical to achieving this purchase, and it's an excellent example of how TNC, as a national organization, had resources and relationships that complemented those of NSP.

But the NSP team brought vital contributions as well, including our commitment to public access. Out of concern for the Lahontan trout, TNC originally planned to prohibit fishing in the lake. But there are other fish species in the lake and TDLT knew local people and visitors would enjoy hiking, boating, and fishing. The result was that we came up with a plan to prevent the introduction of aquatic invasive plants and animals by providing watercraft for free that was never used anywhere else; we implemented forest management strategies to decrease the risk of wildfire; and we allowed visitors to enjoy the property and lake in ways that are compatible with the conservation of this precious resource, such as by requiring that fishermen follow catch and release for the Lahontan species.

NSP held a July 4 weekend celebration at Independence Lake in 2015, and it was satisfying to see the friends and family of NSP get together to celebrate conservation with a picnic and boating on the lake — and even a little fishing.

Independence Lake and many other successes were made possible by the foundational planning, trust building, and shared vision of NSP. I will never forget a celebration at Royal Gorge after we secured about 3500 acres of what is the largest cross-country ski area in North America. A woman who lived nearby came to me and said she was so excited about our work that she had taken out a $25,000 mortgage on her home so that she could make a contribution to the fund-raising campaign we had run. As you recall, one challenge Carol Olson had identified was that it was going to be difficult to raise funds in the actual region being impacted. This woman's excitement gave me hope that continued efforts by NSP that were sensitive to local communities and scientifically supported in terms of our priorities, could ignite local pride and support for our efforts that would be a positive factor for many years to come.

This has proved to be true. The strategic plan is guiding our work, the leadership is strong, and the procedural infrastructure is in place. With the Partnership's support, the partners are operating at a faster pace and bigger scale. NSP, and TNC's David Edelson even partnered with a non-NSP organization called American Rivers Conservancy to preserve 10,000 acres of checkerboard to consolidate the land at the headwaters of the North and Middle Forks of the American River. Each success tends to build on the one before, attracting new support from private donors and public agencies in a virtuous cycle that enables the Partnership to get more done.

The Partnership is now entering the long home stretch of our campaign, a three to four year period in which we hope to conserve another 100,000 acres of high priority lands across the northern Sierra with a new emphasis on acquiring conservation easements on private land. This is an appropriate strategy when the goal is to protect the natural resource values without having to provide for public access.

A major focus of NSP's work, with TNC and Feather River Land Trust in the lead, is the 120,000-acre Sierra Valley, which rivals Lake Tahoe in size and beauty, but remains one of California's best-kept secrets. Sierra Valley's wetlands support the greatest diversity and concentration of waterfowl, shorebirds, raptors, and other birds in the northern Sierra, and are a key stopover on the Pacific Flyway. This region is a birder's paradise. It is also the largest agricultural landscape in the Sierra Nevada, one that was settled in the mid-late 19th century by Swiss Italian families.

In Sierra Valley, the primary focus of NSP's work will be to partner with local ranching families to conserve ranches with easements and ensure they are managed for sustainable agriculture and wildlife. We will also look for opportunities to acquire a limited number of properties to enhance public access and create new opportunities for education and low-impact recreation, while preserving the unique character and culture of this historically rich ranching community.

Through the work in Sierra Valley, NSP is continuing to engage new government partners like the California Department of Conservation and the USDA Natural Resources Conservation Service that recently decided to invest $9.97 million in our Sierra Valley project. The agencies, just like private donors, are interested in opportunities to leverage their resources, and working with groups like ours that can bring additional state and private funds to the job.

As this book goes to print, the Northern Sierra Partnership is still a work in progress. While much work lies ahead, our family can see that the time, energy, and funds we've invested have had a real impact on the ecological, economic and human prospects of the northern Sierra. As we hoped, what began as a modest plan to enhance the level of collaboration among groups we supported has evolved into a fully functional partnership that is attracting the kind of investment needed to get the work done. Collaboration is never easy, but the partners are seeing the many practical benefits of working together to achieve their ambitious vision.

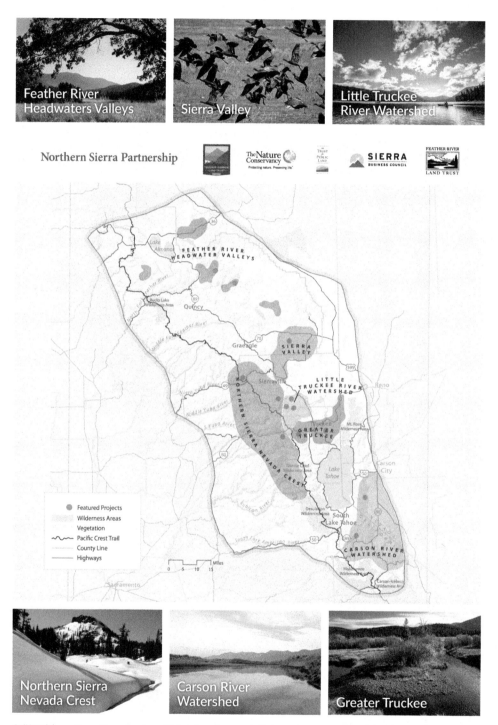

California's northern Sierra is a beautiful and environmentally important ecosystem that supplies fresh water to California and northern Nevada. Becky and I have been pleased to help protect and support this region through the Northern Sierra Partnership.

Clockwise from top left: My first meeting with The Nature Conservancy's Asia Pacific Council (APC) Hong Kong 2002; APC visit to Mongolian Steppes before a Beijing meeting 2009; The 'checkerboard' that NSP and other conservation groups have struggled for decades to reconnect to create wildlife corridors and other protected regions; Becky and me at Independence Lake; Birding by canoe in Sierra Valley; Mark Tercek presenting me the Oak Leaf award for conservation leadership; Northern Sierra children enjoying the Feather River Land Trust's excellent environmental 'learning landscapes' program.

CHAPTER 24

Final thoughts

There is a concept that has interested me since long before I joined Applied Materials. I call it systems thinking.

"System" is a word you hear all the time in high-tech. Sometimes it refers to activities that at least on the surface are specific and discrete. The computer on your desk, for example, has an "operating system," a set of instructions that tells the microprocessors how to run the computer. The jobs under its control may include booting up, keeping track of date and time, and other tasks that the computer must perform so that an application can help you do something meaningful.

At Applied Materials, we designed and built hardware systems that performed complex tasks like applying gases to the surface of silicon or moving a wafer from one vacuum chamber to another at high speed. Our use of the word systems referred to all the different pieces of hardware equipment we sold, but also to a basic underlying concept or logic of design — both software and hardware — that controlled not only how the individual pieces of equipment worked, but also how components worked together, and how they all worked within the manufacturing schemes and systems of our customers.

As the Internet exploded in the late 1990s, I was struck by how the world was experiencing orders of magnitude leaps in systems complexity. By developing the capacity to connect every computer and every individual user in a way that the user perceived as simple, the Internet allowed ordinary people to join a worldwide system where anyone could generate, retrieve, store, analyze, combine, and communicate information.

As it was happening, it was hard to imagine how this miracle would unfold. Young people today may laugh at the term miracle, but when you grow up on a rural farm and you realize you have watched the basic building blocks of all this appear one by one — the stringing of power and telephone lines to rural areas; the laying of fiber optical cables under the sea; the launching of satellites; the invention of solid state transistors — it is very impactful. In the course of my lifetime, I saw the blinking, hot lights of the dinosaur-sized ENIAC computer sputtering to solve simple math problems transform into a pocket device that lets me sit down with a cup of coffee at my kitchen table and interact with real-time images of my grandkids on an adventure halfway around the world. To me, it is a miracle!

Systems innovation and complexity have created dilemmas for managers. For one thing, they drive power more deeply into organizations. We forget that just the invention of email alone disrupted many existing systems. Early on, companies asked themselves, can we safely allow employees to interact with customers or partners over email? Would it enable the easy selling of trade secrets? What if a low-level employee emailed information that was used to make investment decisions — would the company be implicated in insider trading? Some companies had invested heavily in specific customer-handling pathways that prevented outsiders with questions from interacting with anyone but "authorized" representatives. Today, most companies embrace the improved transparency and customer interactions the Internet has enabled, but that did not happen overnight. It required thoughtful management to do it well.

In 2003, I was named the 24th Robert S. Hatfield Fellow in Economic Education at Cornell University and to commemorate that honor, I gave a speech at Cornell titled "The Networked, High-Tech Economy: New Systems Require New Thinking." I talked about some of the incredible new opportunities of the networked global economy, and I pointed out that almost all had their roots in Moore's Law. While the Internet was impacting our lives more and more, I noted, it was just the most visible example of systems increasingly controlling and influencing us.

That very summer, a minor transmission error in the East Coast power grid had created a massive blackout. It was a good reminder that at the same time systems are incredibly powerful, they also can be fragile. All industries participate in global market systems where a new advance in Seoul can spell life or death for a small technology company in San Francisco, and where manufacturing jobs no longer need to be anywhere near a company's headquarters. More ominously, I told the group, "More and more the world is posing threats in the form of systems. Terror networks like al-Quaeda are systems." From international trade to humanitarian aid, I continued, we operate as a nation in complex, global political and economic systems — and those systems are blending, adding to the complexity.

I pointed out that this increase in the importance of systems thinking would require Cornell University's colleges and departments to collaborate extensively to educate their graduates of the future. As an aside, Becky's and my giving to Cornell has been mostly targeted at cross-departmental and cross-college projects in order to further systems thinking.

Now, more than a decade later, I look back on that speech and I am struck by the fact that while I talked a lot about new developments, between the lines I salted in the same advice and tips that I have reinforced in this book. Those tips are about systems that are fairly complex but also consistent. I'm talking about human systems.

The details change, the motivating forces may cycle, the tools that we as managers give to our employees may get dramatic upgrades. But the basic recommendations of this book are about the management of human systems. In my experience, the advice works in a cannery and it works in a massively networked world. The recommendations cut through complexity and even fear. If you hire high-caliber people and trust them, switching to email will not suddenly trigger unethical and inappropriate behavior. If you force people to "own the monkey," it doesn't matter how many transistors the monkey has, the point is to make employees take responsibility, and learn to identify the key issue and solve it. The details of most challenges are less important than the attitude of an organization in moving toward its goals.

Court sense off the court

To thrive and succeed in a complex world, you can't just slog forward every day checking off boxes in a linear fashion. You have to anticipate problems, process new variables, and adjust your strategy. This is systems thinking.

And systems thinking requires court sense. Our family did quite a bit of river rafting when Jeff and Mary were growing up and Mary became a weekend guide on some of the northern California rivers. Recently I had a great conversation with her where she shared that she thought time she spent working as a river guide had been good preparation for her eventual career as a surgeon. As she explained what she meant, I realized Mary had developed her own version of court sense. Mine came from basketball and hers came from rafting. As a guide you have to have skill but you also have to pay attention to the larger factor like the skill of your guests, the current, the weather, hazards like rocks or a log that can appear suddenly. You have a plan but you also have to paddle down river with your head up and your eyes open. You have to develop the confidence to make an adjustment very quickly when conditions change. You can't ignore a sign of danger or a problem that might sink the raft. She said that looking ahead and being able to quickly formulate a backup plan in an emergency was part of being a good surgeon; most of the time things go as planned but when they don't, you have to be prepared by knowing the patient's medical history, the availability and risks of certain options, and then you must quickly adjust. As the surgeon you lead the care team, and the better your court sense the better the outcome.

Jeff graduated from college with a degree in regional planning which is all about understanding the way traffic, utilities, commercial zoning, and other elements of a city system must work together for optimal results for its residents. Much later, he launched the Global Heritage Fund as he realized that cultural heritage sites were being lost or damaged because of what could be called compounding system failures — overpopulation, lack of sustainable employment, plundering, even terrorist activities such as the demolition of the Bamyan Buddhas in Afghanistan. The NGO world has a lot of projects designed to save a particular site or species. The trouble is, narrow, short-term projects tend to have limited, short-term impact. Jeff launched an organization that took a comprehensive, long-term, systems thinking approach to preserving cultural sites and artifacts. Making a cultural site the centerpiece of eco or cultural tourism offered an opportunity to inspire local people to treasure and protect their own heritage, provide jobs, and benefit the community economically from the tourism. The whole system is considered.

Becky and I have always tried to encourage our children and now our grandchildren to spend time in nature and to think deeply about ecosystems and their interrelated components. One of my best memories ever is a trip our entire family took to Botswana in 2013 for a photo safari. In this rich, beautiful environment, we all had our eyes and minds opened to the forces of nature that modern life obscures. We appreciated the power and the roles of the different animals, and we also learned about threats to wild places created by mankind. Going forward, Jeff is looking into technologies that help preserve these places and the animals within them, such as surveillance cameras with satellite transmission capacity. Mary, meanwhile, has helped launch the Donellas Meadows Systems Training Fellowship at her alma mater, Dartmouth. That effort is aimed at modeling complex systems challenges such as climate change and cleaning up the Great Lakes, and then helping business and government prioritize and take action. Jeff and Mary are keenly aware that at the end of the day, success in conservation and environmental protection can only happen within a context of human systems. Politics, culture, and collaboration are all factors.

I was convinced early on at Applied that merging the management of human systems with a complex world is crucial. I challenged the Cornell Dean of Engineering to think about that idea in a more focused way. Dean John E. Hopcroft, who had been head of the Systems Software Department, became Engineering Dean in 1994 and he took an interest in my challenge. I committed funds for him to use however he thought would make progress. One day, he called me and suggested our family foundation support a Professor Raffaello D'Andrea to enter a Cornell team in the International Robo Cup competition pitting university and corporate robotics teams against one another. We liked the idea. That team won against the likes of MIT, Toyota, and many other formidable competitors. The Cornell team had the best and most reliable system approach, and guess what: Cornell Systems Engineering was suddenly popular. They won three times and retired but systems thinking and implementation was well established at Cornell.

It's exciting to see creative people use systems thinking in unique and powerful ways. The Tech Awards recognizes inventors trying to impact a variety of systems from items enhancing basic survival to global information challenges. For example, in 2012, a group won a Tech Award for a "home stove system" that addresses a serious problem in developing countries: respiratory damage from wood smoke created by cooking and heating. The team invented a wood-burning stove that reduces the amount of fuel needed for cooking fires, reduces toxic smoke substantially, and also captures electricity that can be used to power phones or lights through a USB port. Systems thinking again.

At the end of the day no matter how impressive and far-reaching certain systems become, all worthwhile enterprises seeking success are human systems that will require leadership and management. The basic demands and challenges of management have not changed since my cannery days. Ultimately, the simple tips I've tried to convey about trust, integrity, fairness, and respect lead to ethical and positive businesses and innovation that help humanity move forward.

I've written this book to leave a more formal legacy of my thoughts and tips for anyone who may have the impression that leaders are anomalies, special people born with the skills and talents that evade the grasp of the rest of us. Not everyone is as fortunate as I was to have a dad and a granddad who talked to me like they did, taught me the reasons for things we were doing, and set a good example of how to be ethical, effective business leaders. Most important was that they didn't try to make it all seem overly complicated or suggest that it required brilliance or special talents to learn to manage. I hope I have done the same here in trying to carry on their legacy.

Whatever kind of organization you may lead — a global corporation, a department, a family business, a start-up, a non-profit, a neighborhood watch group, a photography club — think deeply about the role and power of good management and encourage your team to learn the principles, too. Anyone can be a better decision-maker, leader, and manager. Anyone can come to appreciate a quote I once heard at Cornell: "There they go. I must hasten, for I am their leader." That paradox echoes the irony but also the goal of good management. Empowering others to go forward with confidence and to succeed with less and less guidance from you is how your organization will accomplish what no one can do alone. I have found that unlocking and encouraging excellence in others has been the most satisfying aspect of my career.

To your success.

Acknowledgments

In this book I mention many people I have encountered along the path of a long and satisfying career, as well as some who made the journey with me. The support of my wife and friend Becky for more than half a century has been an essential part of my story, and I've benefited from the loyal friendship of many others.

Because it is not a detailed history, however, I also find myself frustrated that many people who were important to me on both a professional and personal level do not appear. I want to say to past and present employees of Applied Materials all over the world that it was your competence, commitment, personal growth, and willingness to collaborate globally that made this story possible. I have spoken with many of you in recent years and I always appreciate it when someone says how lucky and special it was for us to work together. I agree.

There also are many people at The Nature Conservancy, the Northern Sierra Partnership, the Applied Materials board, the Semiconductor Equipment and Materials International board as well as other boards and advisory councils on which I served, from whom I learned much and hope I helped. It was the learning and advice of my friends in the Young Presidents' Organization (YPO), World Presidents' Organization (WPO), and our various ski groups and friends that helped me maintain perspective over the years. I have been fortunate to be involved with Linda Verhulp and the outstanding individuals at the Morgan Family Foundation who have helped many youth, education, environment, and stewardship organizations.

There also are a group of people who helped me put this book together and whose help in fact-checking and reading drafts was invaluable. Vice President of Applied Materials Joe Pon read several drafts and helped me keep the historical and factual commentary on track. I appreciated Dan Hutcheson's feedback and insights about the context of the times and the technology. Becky's cousin Ethan Hawkes offered important perspectives as a young executive and entrepreneur — one of my most important target audiences. My longtime executive assistant Betty Moyles brought her usual intelligence, attention to detail, and wisdom to the manuscript. Bill Davidow; Chuck Holloway; Dan Martin; Alex Martin; Jeff Morgan; Manfred Kerschbaum; Randhir Thakur; Mark Burget; Allan Marty; Lucy Blake; and Dennis Hunter also contributed their insights.

I want to especially thank Joan O'C. Hamilton whose career as a journalist and editor enabled an engineer to communicate a complex story about managing human systems in a very technical world. The talented team at AKA–Ahmann Kadlec Associates provided the creative and effective book design.

Jim Morgan
November 2016

Making semiconductors

Why the "heartbeat of the modern world" was a driving force in the semiconductor industry and in the fortunes of Applied Materials

In the 1960s my friend Gordon Moore made a prediction that later came to be known as "Moore's Law." It began as a technical observation that the number of transistors the industry would be able to place on a computer chip would likely double every couple of years. Eventually, it came to represent an innovation force that was called the "heartbeat of the modern world." That's a poetic summary by Michael Malone, but I agree with the characterization. It has become the guiding principle for the industry to deliver ever-more-powerful semiconductor chips at proportionate decreases in cost. Without the dynamic Moore's Law refers to, there would be no smartphones, no Internet, no digital medical imaging, no Instagram or Skype, no LED lights, no self-driving cars, nor literally hundreds of thousands of other inventions that depend on relatively inexpensive small form factor but powerful computer processing.

Nobody debates the significance of semiconductors. On the other hand, explaining the basics of semiconductor technology is not the simplest of tasks and does not exactly invoke poetry. I didn't want to turn my book of management tips into a science and technology seminar. But for those with questions about this technology who would like a little more explanation, what follows here is a primer on the technologies and processes that both drove Applied Materials' success — and that represent the incredible reach of what Applied Materials, itself, made possible in the modern world.

The basics of semiconductors

Electrically speaking, there are conductors (general metals, such as copper or aluminum) that efficiently transport electrical current, and there are "insulators" (such as ceramics or rubber) that stop a current in its tracks. But there also is a third category in between, literally called "semiconductors" made from pure elements such as silicon or germanium, or compounds such as gallium arsenide. The special aspect of semiconductors is that they can be chemically altered or "doped" in a process that dials the material's conductivity up or down depending on what you're trying to do. Think of it this way: An electrical signal is like a runner; a conductor is a smooth, open running path; insulators are like walls; semiconductors are gates that might be wide and open, or narrow and more complicated to navigate, depending on how fast and in what direction you want that runner to travel.

The early electronic devices, such as radios, televisions, and the first computers like the ENIAC, were made using vacuum tube technology. Inside vacuum tubes, current was conducted across a wire inside a vacuum. It worked, to a point, but the machines were large, hot, slow and unstable. Early televisions, for example, often were sold with extra "tubes" for when the original set inevitably would burn out.

By the late 1940s, Bell Labs scientists invented the transistor, or solid-state switch that replaced the fragile vacuum tubes and allowed much more power to be packed into a small space. By the late 1950s, Bob Noyce at Fairchild and other scientists began figuring out how to put more and more semiconductor-based transistors on a "chip." Soon, those chips were arranged to create a programmable "microprocessor" that is the essence of a computer.

In 1971, a microprocessor commonly contained about 2300 transistors, using circuits 10 microns wide — one micron was about the cross section of 100 human hairs. Moore's Law was the driving force in the electronics revolution, however, and by 2001, a typical microprocessor had over 40 million transistors on it. Through the years, technologists frequently have predicted the looming demise of Moore's Law, in part because the high clock speeds of the chips generated a lot of counterproductive heat. However, the industry rose to the challenge and figured out new designs that overcame the predicted limits. In 2015, several companies commercially produce chips with more than 5 billion transistors on them.

How semiconductor chips are made

Semiconductors begin as polycrystalline silicon created from a highly purified form of metallurgical grade sand. The chunks of polysilicon are placed in a rotating crucible where they are heated to a molten state. In a process similar to repeatedly dipping a wick in wax to make a candle, a small piece of solid silicon (seed) is dipped in the molten liquid silicon. As the seed is slowly withdrawn (by mechanical means) from the melt, the liquid quickly cools to form a single crystal ingot. The resulting log-shaped ingot of single crystal silicon is more than 99 percent pure.

This ingot is then ground to a uniform diameter. A diamond saw blade slices the ingot into thin wafers. The cut wafers are then processed through a series of machines where they are ground (optically) smooth and then are chemically polished.

Next the wafer, a roughly 15 millimeter thick, round slice of a semi-conductor material varying in size 6 inches to 12 inches in diameter, is sent to a wafer fabrication area in a semiconductor company like Intel. The fab device is in an environmentally controlled "clean" room free of dust or other particulates that could contaminate the process. The fabrication of a semiconductor chip on a silicon wafer is a series of repetitive steps — from 500 to1000 — that takes place over many weeks.

After cleaning, the wafers are super-heated to 1000 C and the first step is that an insulating layer is formed on the surface of the wafer. In the so-called "patterning" step, photolithography is used to project a specific mask pattern on the surface of the insulator, and then the next series of steps imprint that pattern and wash away the unwanted elements so the first layer of circuit is formed. In subsequent steps, "doping" involves putting chemical atoms such as boron or phosphorus onto the area that has been etched away, which creates specific conduction characteristics on the surface.

The wafer will eventually travel through many different pieces of production equipment. Many layers are created and eventually, if you sliced through the wafer and looked at the cross section it would look like a layer cake. Finally, a diamond saw slices the wafer into single "chips" containing millions of transistors; they can vary from 1 X 1 millimeter to 10 X 10 millimeters. Each chip is then assembled into a package appropriate for the end use; contact lead wires are connected to enable its function in a device.

Semiconductors vs. semiconductor equipment

The focus of Applied Materials has always been enabling the manufacturing of semiconductors. It's a challenge that actually involves two different industries, but it's not uncommon to see stories or lists in the press that lump together what actually are critical distinctions.

The semiconductor industry companies, like Intel, Texas Instruments, and Samsung design the circuitry that is used in electronics devices and then they manufacture the chip and incorporate the chips in semiconductors that are sold to device companies. Semiconductor companies use electrical and chemical engineering to create signal-processing pathways that allow the operation and control of many kinds of devices. The essence of Moore's Law is that for 50 years semiconductor companies have figured out how to move electrical signals more efficiently on smaller and smaller footprints. Increased power combined with miniaturization is why today we have the processing power of an ENIAC on a tiny iPod Nano. Semiconductor companies sell the semiconductors to companies like Apple, Hewlett-Packard, Sony, Nikon, and other makers of electronic devices.

However, a separate industry, the semiconductor equipment industry, designs and builds the equipment that is capable of churning out mass quantities of the desired circuitry on those wafers. Applied Materials produces the large machines that produce the tiny chips and is the leading company with the broadest product line in this multi-billion dollar global industry. Semiconductor companies like Intel and Samsung buy highly precise manufacturing equipment from companies such as Applied and ASML, but the semiconductor companies actually produce the semiconductors.

In this book, I have used analogies to the restaurant industry to illuminate the differences but also the linkages in these two industries. Semiconductor companies are like Chipotle or Olive Garden, which actually produce and sell food based on their own recipes. They gather their own "ingredients," in this case silicon and various gases and chemicals, but they purchase the equivalent of industrial ovens and griddles from semiconductor equipment companies like Applied Materials.

There are limits to the restaurant analogy, because an oven is a fairly simple device. In semiconductor manufacturing, the design of the chips is a sophisticated science, but the technology of creating machines to churn out these exquisitely designed chips is itself incredibly complicated. It has to accommodate hundreds of separate steps of chemical and light processing steps and robotics. It's also true that changes in the design of chips often necessitate changes in semiconductor equipment.

Semiconductor companies know what they want from equipment companies in terms of performance, but they don't need to know how to make the machines. However, equipment makers need to thoroughly understand the chip designs and needs of the semiconductor companies in order to create the best possible machine design for manufacturing. That is why our "flying wedge" strategy at Applied was so important. By creating a relationship of trust with our customers through outstanding service, we could gain an early and thorough understanding of where their research was headed and what their needs would be down the road.

The two industries' fortunes are tightly linked. Semiconductor companies are always trying to improve the efficient production of complicated chips; that is critical to their profitability and they are willing to spend a lot of money to buy cutting edge equipment. However, a slowdown in the purchase of semiconductors more broadly or the failure of a major company's chip design to inspire electronic device companies to buy it in large quantities can stop orders for equipment dead. That's what creates the dramatic booms and busts we've seen for both industries over the last few decades.

Sources: Semiconductor Industry Association, industry publications, Applied Materials.

Morganisms worksheet
A checklist for managers

Learning to be a better manager is a lifelong process. Frequent review of basic principles followed by course correction if necessary, is critical. In this self-assessment, I have listed the 10 key Morganisms and questions you might reflect upon in assessing whether your management style aligns with these principles. After each section, give yourself a score between 1 and 5 (1 being rarely, 5 being always) representing your overall alignment with and adherence to the tip. Then check your total score at the end.

1. Respect and trust your people

- Does your "tone at the top" show respect for every employee's strengths, contributions, and personal health, comfort, and safety?

- Are you praising accomplishments publicly but coaching in private?

- Are your managers clear they should avoid heroic interventions and support employee decision-making?

- Do employees have the opportunity to exercise and eat properly?

- Are you asking yourself tough questions, such as: Am I being consistent in my leadership and example? Am I walking the talk?

Rate Yourself

RARELY	OCCASIONALLY	SOMETIMES	USUALLY	ALWAYS
1	2	3	4	5

2. Value collaboration

- Is your team clear on the idea that for your collaborations to succeed both you and your partner must succeed?

- Are you immediately addressing signs of arrogance or sarcasm in employee conversations about customers, colleagues, or competitors?

- Can you easily list the most important customer concerns and project challenges?

- Is your team predictably delivering on commitments and giving adequate warning when there is a problem?

Rate Yourself

RARELY	OCCASIONALLY	SOMETIMES	USUALLY	ALWAYS
1	2	3	4	5

3. Listen for and investigate hints of trouble

- Are you making time to "porpoise" into your organization in a low-key fashion to listen and understand? Do you remind yourself and others daily to listen, learn, and lead?

- If you hear whispers about politics or gossip, are you investigating the causes?

- It's important to celebrate successes…but only up to a point. Are you using meeting time productively to focus on addressing bad news, challenges, or missing data you need to make better decisions, rather than the "easy" subjects and good news? Are you and your managers welcoming early warnings of trouble rather than "shooting the messenger?"

Rate Yourself

RARELY	OCCASIONALLY	SOMETIMES	USUALLY	ALWAYS
1	2	3	4	5

4. Develop court sense and align with driving forces

- Can you readily answer the question: "What is the essence of our business?" Do you revisit this question quarterly?

- Are you routinely scanning for key opportunities and threats on the horizon?

- Do you have a plan to address disruptive technologies, customer perceptions, or emerging competitors?

- Are you proactively addressing internal driving forces such as salary and benefit comparables, personnel changes, structural frictions, and unique leadership opportunities?

- Are you periodically thinking about a wide range of issues: strategic and tactical, global and local, the good, the bad, and the ugly?

- Are you identifying activities and efforts you're doing today that can be eliminated or simplified or managed in a better way?

- Is your team acting on customer suggestions?

Rate Yourself

RARELY	OCCASIONALLY	SOMETIMES	USUALLY	ALWAYS
1	2	3	4	5

5. Make decisions and manage the consequences

- Have you made clear to your team that the power of momentum is more important than striving for near-perfect information, in other words, do they have a bias to act?

- Once decisions have been made, is there a clear action plan, identified milestones, and an owner to manage them?

- Are you staying close to team members who appear to either over-reach or dither over decisions? Are you making timely suggestions — or necessary changes?

Rate Yourself

RARELY	OCCASIONALLY	SOMETIMES	USUALLY	ALWAYS
1	2	3	4	5

6. Build complementary teams

- Do you have a clear sense of your own strengths and those of your team? Are you constantly alert to the need to shore up vital skills that may be lacking in both individuals and the organization?

- Are you alert to the need to balance teams in terms of competencies, personalities, cultural perspectives, gender, and other factors?

- Are you making sure your team is hiring not only for the job at hand but for a person who can grow into the next job?

- Do you have a list of three individuals you are trying to develop or hire? Are you taking the long view and keeping in touch with them?

- Have you determined two negatives you can live with before making an offer to a potential candidate?

Rate Yourself

RARELY	OCCASIONALLY	SOMETIMES	USUALLY	ALWAYS
1	2	3	4	5

7. Commit to doing the whole job

- Do you periodically review more than bottom line numbers and product development? Are you also scrutinizing quality and organizational development, as well as customers, projects, and production?

- Are there effective audits of objectives and results?

- Are you alert to signs of a "victim" culture and making clear you value accountability?

- Are employees reporting issues and concerns both inside and outside their area of responsibility?

- Do your people appreciate the need to fight tunnel vision on challenges? Do they understand the need to step back and assess the whole job?

Rate Yourself

RARELY	OCCASIONALLY	SOMETIMES	USUALLY	ALWAYS
1	2	3	4	5

8. Reinforce individual ownership of problems

- Does your team pursue an understanding of what created a given problem or roadblock and how to prevent it going forward?

- Do employees understand the concept of "owning the monkey," i.e., that every issue and challenge must be assigned a problem-solver who is close to the customer or partner or business objective, and who will see it to completion?

- Are you careful to support and assist your reports in solving problems without dramatic public gestures or interventions?

Rate Yourself

RARELY	OCCASIONALLY	SOMETIMES	USUALLY	ALWAYS
1	2	3	4	5

9. Proactively prepare for the next major shift

- Do you review trends in all aspects of the organization and adjacent areas periodically?

- Do you have a working forecast of imminent shifts in the economy or business momentum?

- Are you saving during the good times and looking for pre-emptive investments to make during difficult financial downturns?

- Are you putting aside 5–10 percent of your time to think about long-term strategy and anticipating long-term trends by making smart investments now?

Rate Yourself

RARELY	OCCASIONALLY	SOMETIMES	USUALLY	ALWAYS
1	2	3	4	5

10. Understand and manage paradoxes

- Do you have a clear sense of the important paradoxes your organization faces? (for example, the tensions between being global and acting local; operating at a rapid pace but with attention to quality; managing teams that must collaborate but also have focused, quiet work time)

- Are you making clear that you understand the conflicting tensions, but reassuring your team that they have the skills and judgment to navigate them effectively?

- Are you reinforcing that it is possible, in fact essential, to create a stable, predictable work environment even in a period of rapid change?

Rate Yourself

RARELY	OCCASIONALLY	SOMETIMES	USUALLY	ALWAYS
1	2	3	4	5

Total score across the 10 Tips: ___

45-50 = Congratulations, it looks like you're a high performer. Keep it up.
40-45 = You're well on your way. Reinforce strengths and work on consistency.
30-40 = Keep focused and ask for feedback as you strengthen your skill set.
10-30 = Take a step back and assess your management style. Develop an improvement plan.

Additional resources

Business tools

http://www.wmbridges.com

William Bridges' model of change is one I found exceptionally useful in running a fast-moving company in a cyclical industry. Many managers fail to appreciate the impact and consequences of change on the psychology of employees. I often used this chart to reinforce that we understood the stress change causes, but that it creates opportunities that benefit everyone.

Bridges Model

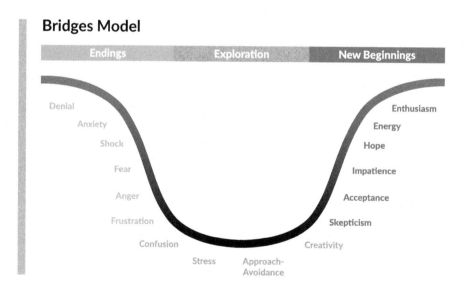

http://www.kenblanchard.com/Products-Services/Leadership-Fundamentals

Ken Blanchard's model is enormously helpful in avoiding the pitfall of using a management style that fits the personality of the manager rather than one designed to best manage the strengths and weaknesses of individual employees.

http://winslowresearch.com

Winslow assessments provided me a powerful tool in balancing work teams in the early years of Applied Materials.

http://www.adizes.com

Ichak Adizes' analysis and programs for organizational development played a role in empowering many Applied Materials' executives to take on greater challenges, bringing success to the company in the process.

http://www.appliedmaterials.com

More information on the business and technology of semiconductor equipment manufacturing is available at **Applied Materials Inc.**

Philanthropy

http://www.morganfamilyfoundation.org/about.htm

This link provides more information on the projects **The Morgan Family Foundation**, which supports in youth programs, education, natural resources, and regional stewardship. One of our family values is: "Generosity is contagious and should be encouraged in others."

http://northernsierrapartnership.org

The Northern Sierra Partnership is a regional conservation partnership Becky and I helped launch. It is a unique example of the power of collaboration among non-profits: We have raised $142 million in private and public funds and conserved 50,000 target acres of ecosystems that play a vital role in providing clean water, protecting diverse species, and retaining the region's natural beauty and environmental integrity. It's our hope it could be a model for other non-profits in other domains.

http://www.nature.org

I respect **The Nature Conservancy's** model of nature for people, rather than fencing off nature from people. They are innovators and have achieved impressive successes on a global basis.

About the authors

James C. Morgan ran Applied Materials Inc. for nearly three decades — one of the longest tenures of any Fortune 500 CEO. The company was near bankruptcy when he joined; when he retired as CEO in 2003, Applied was a multi-billion dollar global leader with more than 15,000 employees. Quite an achievement for a former Cayuga, Indiana farm boy who grew up herding cows, harvesting corn, and working in his family's vegetable cannery. Along the way, Jim collected and tested his management principles in such realms as the military, the diversified conglomerate Textron, in venture capital, on corporate boards and government commissions, and in the non-profit arena. He has served as both a California and a global director, and co-chair of the Asia Pacific Council of The Nature Conservancy (TNC). Recently he and his wife, Becky, have founded the Northern Sierra Partnership, which fosters collaboration among conservation organizations in order to preserve and restore one of the world's great mountain ranges.

Jim also served as Vice Chair of President George W. Bush's President's Export Council and as an adviser to President Bill Clinton and Congress on U.S.-Pacific trade and investment policy. He was an active member of the Young Presidents' Organization (YPO). He holds an undergraduate degree in engineering and an MBA from Cornell, and he co-authored the 1991 book, *Cracking the Japanese Market: Strategies for Success in the New Global Economy*. Among Jim's many recognitions are the Semiconductor Industries Award, the IEEE Robert N. Noyce Medal; the Silicon Valley Leadership Group Lifetime Achievement; the Global Humanitarian Award; the National Fish and Wildlife Foundation Award; and TNC's Oak Leaf Award. In 1996, he was presented with the National Medal of Technology and Innovation by President Bill Clinton.

Joan O'C. Hamilton is a Silicon Valley-based writer and former technology correspondent for *Business Week* magazine.

CPSIA information can be obtained
at www.ICGtesting.com
Printed in the USA
FSOW04n0241090217
30590FS